RAILROADS
AND THE
GRANGER LAWS

RAILROADS AND THE GRANGER LAWS

GEORGE H. MILLER

THE UNIVERSITY OF WISCONSIN PRESS

MADISON, MILWAUKEE, AND LONDON

Published 1971
The University of Wisconsin Press
Box 1379, Madison, Wisconsin 53701

The University of Wisconsin Press, Ltd.
27–29 Whitfield Street, London, W.1

First printing

Printed in the United States of America
Pantagraph Printing, Bloomington, Ill.

ISBN 0-299-05870-0; LC 75-138059

TO THE MEMORY OF
MY MOTHER AND FATHER

CONTENTS

vii

MAPS

PREFACE

R OBERT MCCLOSKEY, in his study of *American Conservatism in the Age of Enterprise* (Cambridge, Mass., 1951,
p. 79), refers to the "Janus-like character" of the Supreme Court's
decision in the important Granger cases of 1877. In upholding
the power of the state legislatures to regulate railroad and warehouse rates, the Court looked back to an earlier period of government regulation while at the same time laying the groundwork
for a new era of public control. It is within this general context
that I have sought to explain the origins of the Granger laws
and to determine their relationship to earlier principles and procedures of rate regulation, as well as to modern methods of control.

The laws under review in the Granger cases were passed by
the four states of the upper Mississippi Valley in the early 1870s,
and they have generally been attributed to agrarian influences
associated with the farmers' movement of the late nineteenth
century. In this light they appear to be populistic, radical, and
quite out of harmony with the laissez-faire assumptions of the day.
When set against the background of previous rate law and policy,
however, the laws appear far less radical and in no sense agrarian.
I have tried, therefore, to reevaluate their place in the history of
American public-service law and to place them in what appears

to be a more appropriate historical framework. It is as much a matter of perspective as it is of reinterpretation.

I have placed my emphasis on railroad regulation, specifically on the powers of the states to control fares and freights. Other aspects of the railroad problem and the closely related subject of warehouse regulation have been treated only insofar as they bear upon this central theme.

Because parallel legislation in four neighboring states is involved, a certain amount of repetition in the treatment of political events has been inevitable. I have tried to keep this to a minimum by focusing on different aspects of rate control in each state. The chapter dealing with Illinois puts its stress on the evolution of basic principles of rate control; the chapter on Iowa concerns itself primarily with economic conflicts and their impact on the law. In dealing with Minnesota I have emphasized the problem of balancing the state's promotional and regulatory aims and have used the city of Rochester as a case study in public protest. In the chapter on Wisconsin I have relied largely on the great number of secondary works dealing with the subject and have stressed the importance of politics in the shaping of regulatory policy.

After tracing the full history of the legislative struggle over public regulation, the story of the Granger cases seems anticlimactic. It is clear that the Supreme Court was merely reaffirming an established principle when it upheld the restraining power of the state legislatures with regard to railroad and warehouse charges. The significance of the Court's ruling appears to lie in the fact that it would allow statutory regulations only in the case of businesses it considered quasi-public; purely private enterprise would be beyond the reach of the police power. Through its assumptions about the sanctity of private business, the Court introduced points of law not present in the legislative struggle. There is less continuity than one would expect, therefore, between the struggle over state control in the legislatures and that which followed in the courts. For this reason I have placed the review of federal litigation after the summary chapter on the Granger laws; it seems more appropriate to use it as an epilogue.

Permission to use the Burlington and Illinois Central Archives in the Newberry Library and the Cunningham-Overton Collection of Charles E. Perkins Papers in the custody of Richard C. Overton is gratefully acknowledged. Part of my research was facilitated by a grant from the Fund for the Advancement of Education of the Ford Foundation. Chapter five appeared in slightly modified form in the *Mississippi Valley Historical Review* (March 1954).

In preparing this study I have benefited from the counsel and criticism of many teachers, colleagues, and friends. Professors Frederick Merk, Verner W. Crane, I. L. Sharfman, William R. Leslie, and Richard Overton have been particularly helpful. Mrs. Dorothy Foster typed and frequently corrected the final manuscript. I am especially indebted to Professor Sidney Fine of the University of Michigan for encouragement and assistance at every stage in the development of the manuscript. I am grateful for his generosity and his patience.

G. H. M.

Ripon College
May 1970

RAILROADS
AND THE
GRANGER LAWS

one THE RAILROAD
PROBLEM IN THE
UPPER MISSISSIPPI
VALLEY

THE RAILROAD PROBLEM confronting the states in the late nineteenth century was inherent in the unique characteristics and unusual size of the industry. The nation's first big business did not conform to accepted principles of economics or to traditional standards of public law. Because railroad transportation was relatively cheap—much cheaper than any other form of land transportation yet devised—it turned trade out of older channels and disrupted established mercantile interests. At the same time, railroads found themselves compelled by state policy to compete with one another for traffic, and this, plus the fact that railroading was an industry of unprecedented high fixed costs, pushed road managers into business practices that defied the norms of behavior identified with common carriers. Depending on the location of alternative means of water and rail service, the benefits of competition fell unevenly on the community at large and created gross inequalities in the price of transportation for some customers and communities. Cheapness and competition, so desirable in principle, proved to be a mixed blessing when associated with a railroad.

All the states made attempts to deal with the railroad problem at some time during the latter half of the nineteenth century. Illinois, Iowa, Minnesota, and Wisconsin, the four states of the

3

upper Mississippi Valley, came to grips with the problem in the ten-year period following the Civil War. None of them solved it, to be sure, but one of them, Illinois, succeeded in devising a set of principles and procedures for public control of rates that forms the basis of our modern system of regulation, and the four states together succeeded in provoking a major constitutional crisis over the rights of the states to interfere with any form of private enterprise. Their legislation, the Granger laws, thrust the conflict between the railroads and the states into national prominence and brought into focus the many economic, political, and constitutional issues involved.

The complexity of the railroad problem in the upper Mississippi Valley can be traced to the overlapping and conflicting patterns of trade that formed during the period of settlement. Illinois, Iowa, Wisconsin, and Minnesota were occupied by two distinct waves of westward movement. The earliest settlers had come into the area from the south, principally from the Ohio Valley, in the years following the War of 1812. Fanning out through the valleys of the great river and its tributaries, they had reached the head of navigation at the Falls of St. Anthony during the 1830s. They were sufficiently numerous to bring statehood to Illinois in 1818, and they laid the political and economic foundations for state government in Iowa (1846), Wisconsin (1848), and Minnesota (1857). Meanwhile, a second wave had rolled in from the east following the line of the Great Lakes. Settlers had pushed cautiously into the area along the shores of Lake Michigan in the 1830s, and their numbers had reached flood proportions during the 1850s. By 1870 they had swept across the Mississippi Valley and on to the Missouri River and Red River of the North. The two frontiers merged and intermingled their peoples; nevertheless, they retained their separate identities. The clash of interests between the two was to enliven the politics of the region for many years to come.[1]

Although many of the early settlers were drawn to the area by the rich deposits of lead ore in northwestern Illinois and southwestern Wisconsin, the principle attraction for both the southern and eastern pioneers was land. The thick prairie soils of Illinois and Iowa were particularly suited to corn, while spring wheat flourished in a broad band on either side of the borders between Illinois and Wisconsin and between Iowa and Minnesota. With winter wheat, oats, and barley serving as secondary crops over much of the area, the upper Mississippi basin became one of the richest grain producing regions of the world.[2]

Each of the two groups of settlers was supported by marketing systems that supplied its needs and disposed of its surplus products. The pioneers from the Ohio Valley looked to southern markets which in turn gave access to larger national and world markets through New Orleans; the settlers coming by way of the Great Lakes were tied to eastern markets which provided entry into the world market through New York City and other Atlantic coast ports. A highly profitable trade in grain and grain products developed in each case, and when the two waves of settlement overlapped, a brisk competition ensued. Farm products might move either to the South or East, depending on prices and the cost of service, but each system had its own special characteristics and its own claim to the loyalties of the region.[3]

Commerce on the Mississippi River and its tributaries followed patterns established in Ohio and Kentucky. The products of farm, mill, packing plant, and distillery were placed in bags and barrels and loaded aboard flatboats, keelboats, or paddlewheelers. Trade began at virtually any point along a navigable waterway and proceeded downstream toward the cotton and sugar producing regions of the Southwest.[4] Although opportunities were somewhat restricted, grain and pork products could be sold at several points along the lower Mississippi or taken through to the larger market at New Orleans. Such trade by its very nature was decentralized and small in scale, if not in volume. Merchants who made it their business to know the trade—where to sell and when to ship— gave it some measure of organization at the outset and gradually assumed control of most of it, but the trade never became highly structured. It remained open to large and small operators alike.[5]

By 1840 St. Louis had emerged as the focal point of commerce in the upper valley. Most of the produce destined for southern markets was first collected at her wharves for reshipment in larger vessels. The city had become the largest flour milling center in the West, was an important wholesale and retail market for eastern and foreign merchandise, and was a major banking center. Its commanding position along the natural lines of trade in the West made it one of the leading entrepots of the country.[6]

In spite of its many advantages, however, the river trade was beset by numerous difficulties. There were rapids at Keokuk and Rock Island which necessitated costly transshipment during much of the year, and alternating periods of flooding and low water made the river unsafe for extended periods of time. These dangers were reflected in high insurance rates. The unreliable character of the waterways, moreover, meant that produce tended to arrive at major centers all at once, and neither St. Louis nor New Orleans had adequate storage facilities. In both cities the public warehouses were a considerable distance from the wharves. If shippers used them, they paid heavy drayage charges in addition to storage fees; if they did not use them, they ran the risk of spoilage. Credit facilities were more or less adequate, but New Orleans was not sufficiently interested in the western grain trade to give it aggressive financial leadership. The Crescent City was committed first and foremost to the cotton and sugar trades, and they absorbed most of her limited credit resources. She was not prepared to give St. Louis the kind of financial backing needed to assure continued growth.[7]

The commerce of the upper Mississippi River, in other words, was not closely identified with the mercantile interests of the Southwest, and this was a serious handicap. The entire river was badly in need of improvement, but nothing was done because of the lack of support by the politicians of the lower valley. New Orleans, furthermore, was not a satisfactory export depot for western produce, and apparently was not interested in becoming one. She lacked the facilities for handling large quantities of grain and grain products, and did not begin to build them until after the Civil War. Inevitably her attitude infected the valley as a whole. The commercial establishment of the river, for all its accomplishments, tended to be conservative and complacent. Its merchants— even those of St. Louis—were content to let trade follow its natural course. They were persuaded that it would always conform to a north-south pattern regardless of man's efforts to direct it. The magnificent artery that formed the basis of their trade dominated their thinking to such an extent that they paid little attention to new forms of transportation and new business techniques. As a consequence, both St. Louis and New Orleans were slow to supplement the rivers with railway service. At best the railroad was seen as a feeder for river traffic.[8]

In spite of its shortcomings, however, the valley marketing system claimed the loyalty of western merchants and producers because it was western-owned and operated. Its service to western interests, even though frequently inadequate and always sluggish, was undeniable. In many ways the steamboat was a perfect symbol of western commercial life on the Mississippi. It ran whenever and wherever the rivers would let it; it carried substantial quantities of foodstuffs, but not very efficiently; it rarely kept to any kind of schedule; and it was almost always a one-owner (or one set of owners), one-boat business. Its owners were rivermen—merchants and captains—who served their own and other western mercantile interests.[9]

The second wave of settlement to enter the states of the upper Mississippi Valley swept along the southern shores of the Great Lakes following the opening of the Erie Canal, and by 1830 its advance guard had reached Wisconsin and Illinois. Chicago, located at the further end of navigation on Lake Michigan, was organized as a city in 1833, fifteen years after Illinois achieved statehood. The tide of migration slowed during the hard times that followed the panic of 1837, but it resumed during the 1840s. Throughout the decades of the fifties and sixties tens of thousands of settlers poured into the region each year.[10]

The geographical limits of the Great Lakes basin are surprisingly narrow along its western edge. At points the watershed which separates it from the Mississippi Valley is less than ten miles from the lake shores. Few streams that are navigable for any distance inland flow into the lakes, the Fox River of Wisconsin being the only important exception. The natural lines of trade for the states bordering Lakes Michigan and Superior flow away from the lakes rather than toward them. Geography, therefore, imposed a number of barriers to commerce on the lakes, and these barriers necessitated an order of trade and transportation markedly different from that of the river.

To enlarge the markets of the lake ports it was necessary to build artificial avenues of transportation, either canals or railways, both of which called for heavy, long-term investment. The opportunities for the development of suitable terminals were limited, and at the western end of the lakes, only Chicago, Milwaukee, and Duluth emerged as major centers. Ambitious rivals like Racine, Wisconsin, showed early promise but fell behind when the railroad builders chose to concentrate on Milwaukee and Chicago.[11] From the outset, the lake trade called for a high degree of economic organization and concentration.

The challenge of a restricted hinterland was met first by a canal and then by a network of railroads. The Illinois and Michigan Canal was opened to traffic in 1848. It joined the Illinois River with a branch of the Chicago River and provided the settlers of the Illinois Valley with access to the lakes. In the same year the Galena and Chicago Union Railroad pushed its tracks ten miles west of Chicago and began bringing carloads of grain back to the lake front. In the following decade other trunk line railroads were built from Chicago: the Chicago and Rock Island, the Chicago, Burlington, and Quincy, the Chicago, Alton, and St. Louis, and the Illinois Central. By 1860 Illinois had 2,790 miles of railroad,[12] most of which contributed to the Lake City's trade.

Wisconsin was served by fewer roads, but their concentration in the wheat country of Wisconsin and northern Illinois made Milwaukee an important terminal which until 1865 rivaled Chicago as a center of the western wheat trade. The many separate lines that served Milwaukee were ultimately merged into two major systems, the Chicago and North Western and the Chicago, Milwaukee, and St. Paul, but in 1860 Wisconsin possessed a meager 905 miles of road.[13]

Minnesota was completely without railroad service in 1860, and the development of Duluth had to await the building of a railway from St. Paul. With the completion of this line in 1871, however, Duluth became an important outlet for Minnesota wheat.[14]

The first railroad from the East reached the Mississippi River in 1854. In the years that followed, trunk lines serving the lake ports were constructed as far as the river, and they established running connections with railroads on the other side. By 1860 Iowa had 655 miles of railroad, most of them tributary to Chicago or Milwaukee.[15] By that year also, a new system of transportation had been imposed upon the upper Mississippi Valley. The river system with its southern orientation had been challenged by a railroad-canal system with an eastern orientation.

The eastern market complex was more highly organized and much more aggressive than its river counterpart, although problems arose which were comparable to those of the river. The lakes were closed by ice for three or four months each year, low water on the St. Clair Flats near Detroit could stop passage at other times, and storms took their toll. But there was less risk and a considerably longer shipping season than on the Mississippi. Great fleets of sailing vessels and steam driven propellers, built to carry grains in bulk with a minimum of spoilage, plied the lakes. After 1870 each of the larger boats carried between 100,000 and 120,000 bushels of grain.[16]

The need for transshipment at either end of the lakes called forth ingenious methods for loading, unloading, and storing bulk grains. Mechanical grain elevators were introduced in the 1840s, making possible rapid loading and unloading of rail cars, canal barges, and lake boats. The grain was stored within the elevator buildings themselves, and many of these towering warehouses were capable of holding hundreds of thousands of bushels. Two elevators built by the Illinois Central Railroad in Chicago in 1858 more than matched the entire storage capacity for grain in the city of St. Louis.[17] Used originally for transfer and storage at terminal markets, the elevator was soon adopted for use in local markets throughout the West. It became the distinguishing feature of hundreds of small railside collecting points.

Grain elevators stored every man's grain together rather than in sacks that retained the seller's identification. This made necessary the development of a uniform system of inspection, grading, and marketing, and warehouse receipts representing so much grain of a specified grade became the instruments of trade. Such a system greatly facilitated marketing procedures and at the same time opened the door for the buying and selling of futures. The regularity of the trade in bulk grains flowing through the elevators of the

West made possible enormous speculative profits, but it also narrowed the spread between the price paid to local farmers and the price for which grain sold in the world market.[18]

With less chance of spoilage enroute and less chance of delay, trade moved smoothly to and from the East Coast. Telegraph lines connected local markets and made possible the daily quotation of eastern grain prices in all the primary markets of the West. Money and credit flowed westward to stimulate the operations of the eastern market. At the eastern end of the line New York City, with its unrivaled port facilities, was the nation's leading export depot for grain. The great eastern metropolis was fully committed to the western grain trade and gave aggressive financial support to the commercial outposts on the lakes. Milwaukee, Chicago, and Duluth, in turn, were able to extend credit to merchants and growers well ahead of harvest time.[19]

The farmer of the upper Mississippi Valley who traded in the eastern market was at the beginning of a long chain of sale that was marked by increasing specialization and complexity. As a rule he sold his grain to a local dealer at a nearby collecting point. If he was fortunate there was more than one town competing for his harvest and more than one buyer in each town. He bought his provisions where he sold his grain. The price paid the farmer for his grain was the prevailing Chicago, Milwaukee, or Duluth price, less freight charges and the dealer's commission. The farmer rarely had any immediate contact with the railroad. He usually preferred to sell to a local grain buyer who arranged for transportation and paid the freight rates; he was sometimes compelled to do so by railroad policy.[20]

The local buyer might be in business for himself, or he might be the agent for a large grain company, a packet line, a railroad, or a flour mill. The dealer in Illinois was generally an independent local buyer; in Minnesota he was more apt to be the permanent or transient representative of some larger company in one of the bigger markets. In any event, the grain was consigned by the dealer to his contact or home office in Chicago, Milwaukee, or Duluth. There the grain went into a warehouse and a receipt for the appropriate grade and quantity of grain was issued. The receipt might pass through the hands of one or more speculators in the lake markets, but eventually it was purchased by a commission agent for an eastern house, and the quantity and grade of grain indicated was reshipped either by boat or by rail.[21]

By 1860 it was clear that Chicago was to be the center of eastern operations in the West. Served by a canal and a growing number of rail lines, it captured more than its share of the market. The energy of the city became world famous as its population grew from 30,000 in 1850 to 300,000 in 1870. The mouth of the Chicago River was lined with elevators designed to handle the transfer of western grains from rail and canal to lake. Its stockyards were the largest in the world, and great quantities of lumber from Michigan and Wisconsin and merchandise from the East moved across its docks on the way to the interior. New, westward-bound settlers poured through the city in ever increasing numbers. Its position of primacy was secure.

The eastern commercial complex, however, was highly competitive. Milwaukee buyers were ready to purchase the grain of northern Illinois and southern Wisconsin if the Chicago price dropped, and Duluth played a similar role in the seventies.[22] Railroads could take trade around and through Chicago as well as to it. The main line of commerce ran down the lakes to Buffalo and through the Erie Canal to New York City, but the path of commerce broadened with each year. Improvements in the Welland Canal let larger ships through to Oswego, Ogdensburg, and Canadian ports; railroads in New York State established rivals to Buffalo at Dunkirk and Suspension Bridge. By 1852 there were railroads paralleling the lake route over its full length, for in that year both the Michigan Central and the Michigan Southern completed their connections with Chicago. Through rail service to the Atlantic seaboard—still complicated by gauge differentials—was now a possibility. Although bulk grain shipments continued to use the lakes, higher priced items including flour could bear the cost of rail freight all the way to the East Coast.[23] There was little room for complacency or conservatism in the eastern market.

That the eastern marketing system was superior to that of the river both technically and economically was beyond question. It was truly one of the marvels of the age, and its contribution to the life and welfare of western communities was incalculable. Its very

efficiency, however, was sometimes a source of alarm and dissatisfaction. In much the same way that the riverboat symbolized the
trade of the valley frontier, the grain elevator typified the workings of the eastern market. The elevator was a great mechanical
contrivance—huge, efficient, and completely impersonal. It was an
indispensable part of an integrated system responding to orders
issued in New York, Boston, and London. Its operations were
continually being refined and rationalized for the benefit of a
world market; but refinement and rationalization almost always
meant loss of local control. The elevators belonged to the railroads
or to companies working in close alliance with them, and by 1870
most of the railroads in the upper Mississippi Valley were controlled by eastern capitalists.[24] Western farmers and businessmen,
including those of the lake ports, felt more and more that they
were dealing with an alien system whose interests were only incidentally identified with their own.

      Railroads did not immediately funnel all of the trade
of the upper Mississippi Valley into eastern channels. St. Louis
remained an important terminal market which continued to ship
large quantities of western produce down river. Until 1861 when
the Civil War closed the lower river, she more than held her own
in absolute terms, since her losses to the lake ports were offset
by increased receipts of grain from southern Illinois and from
newly settled areas west of the river. Furthermore, New Orleans
under favorable conditions, as in 1856–57, was still able to compete successfully for western grain and grain products. The dominance of the eastern market was never complete, and the difference
in prices between the two markets, largely a matter of insurance
rates and costs stemming from delays, was never very great.[25]
      The huge increase in trade at the lake ports during the 1850s
was primarily the result of new business created by the influx of
settlers from the east; only a part of it resulted from the diversion
of river trade.[26] The significant point for purposes of this study
is that two marketing systems were now competing for the rapidly
expanding business of the upper Mississippi Valley. In spite of a
sharp decline in its relative strength over the area as a whole, the

southern market still exercised a potent influence over the primary markets of the West, and the possibility of diverting trade back to the river was always present.[27]

Rivalry among the lake ports must be viewed in the same light. Each port had its own market area resulting from the development of its own hinterland, but the pattern of railroad construction created extensive overlapping. Although each city enjoyed a steady growth in trade, the relative strength of the different markets was constantly changing. Milwaukee was the leading primary wheat market in the world in 1862, but Chicago assumed leadership in the postwar years, and in 1871 Duluth began to claim a share of the trade that might otherwise have gone to one of the Lake Michigan ports.[28] Rivalry among the lake ports, when added to that between the river and the lakes, created a competitive situation of unusual intensity.

The conflict between the river and the lakes found expression in both local and national politics. The settlers from the South tended to be Democratic; those from the East were more apt to be Whig, Free Soil, and later, Republican. In the 1850s the drive for improvements on the Mississippi River was championed by Stephen Douglas, the Democratic senator from Illinois. With other members of the western Democracy, Douglas urged federal support for measures that would help make New Orleans a major export depot for the entire Mississippi Valley. He failed, largely due to opposition within his own party. Whigs, Free Soilers, and Republicans, meanwhile, pushed for federal aid to shipping on the Great Lakes with equal lack of success.[29] This same party alignment was reflected at times in the struggle over railroad regulation.

The hostility of western Democrats toward eastern commercial interests was demonstrated when the Civil War suddenly closed the river and forced virtually all the trade of the upper Mississippi Valley to find an outlet by way of the lakes and the eastern trunk lines. For over a year the east-west avenues of commerce were choked by huge surpluses. Transportation charges rose sharply, and local grain prices fell. Led by Copperhead Democrats who deplored the events that had closed the river, valley interests lashed out at the selfish eastern capitalists who profited from western misfortune. Peace Democrats scored substantial gains in the political contests of the upper valley in 1862, largely because of discontent over high rail rates and low farm prices. The worst of the traffic jam was over by 1863, prices rose, and the Northwest, for the most part, enjoyed great prosperity throughout the remaining war years. As a result, midwestern Copperheadism lost a viable issue, and its strength declined. But sectional antagonism within the valley remained ready to burst forth whenever farm prices sagged.[30]

The problem was not solved by the reopening of the Mississippi, because the river never recovered from the depression imposed by the war. Trade between the upper valley and the South was resumed but never regained its former vitality. The natural course of trade upon which southern commercial men relied refused to assert itself;[31] the river served increasingly as a feeder for the railroads. Although in the immediate postwar years a vigorous new commerce developed on the river north of the rapids at Rock Island, this trade was based almost entirely on traffic between Minnesota and the rail heads at La Crosse, Prairie du Chien, Dunlieth, and Fulton. When railroads closed the gap between Minnesota and the lakes, this trade began to wither. The dominant flow, in any event, remained east-west, and as the production of cereals in the upper valley continued to mount, the railroads and the lake terminals gathered in most of the business.[32]

St. Louis and New Orleans—the latter under Reconstruction rule—made belated attempts to recover some of their lost advantage. In 1866 the Mississippi Valley Transportation Company was organized to carry grain from St. Louis to New Orleans, and grain elevators were finally erected at the two river terminals and at rail heads near the mouth of the Ohio River. The Illinois Central Railroad cooperated with efforts to make Cairo, Illinois, an important shipping point for grain, particularly during the winter months. Barges designed to carry bulk grains were introduced on the river in order to improve the speed and reliability of service. Valley merchants promised extensive improvements on the Mississippi and spoke with renewed enthusiasm of a thriving river trade.[33]

The revival was not without its effect, but every improvement on the river was matched by better service in the eastern market.

During the war the northern railroads had agreed to pull one another's cars wherever gauges permitted, and the peacetime advantages of such service became readily apparent. After the war through freights became more and more available. Special fast freight companies were organized to handle rail traffic between the West and various Atlantic coast ports, and these so-called color lines were able to divert sizeable quantities of bulk grains from the lakes to the railroads. The trend toward consolidation also increased after 1860. Great new systems including the Chicago and North Western and the Chicago, Milwaukee, and St. Paul came into existence under unified management. The Illinois Central, the Rock Island, and the Burlington brought their Iowa connections under closer control. New railway bridges across the Mississippi above St. Louis were constructed at twelve different locations between 1865 and 1874. The rationalization of trade continued, bringing country commercial centers ever closer to the East Coast markets.[34]

Between 1860 and 1873 over ten thousand additional miles of railroad were laid in the four states of the upper valley. By the latter year, three-fourths of all the land in Illinois was within five miles of a railway; only $1\frac{1}{2}$ percent of its land was over fifteen miles distant. Bigger and better equipment enabled the roads to move goods faster and more cheaply. Although the evidence is meager, it confirms the claims of the carriers that average rail rates on western roads were gradually declining.[35] Railroads, grain elevators, and all the attendant paraphernalia of the eastern market system were becoming absolutely indispensable to the prosperity of the West.

This growing dependence on railways spurred a drive among western commercial interests for alternative means of transportation to the eastern seaboard. River merchants north of St. Louis took the lead in a drive to secure new and improved waterways between the river and the lakes. As their primary objectives they advocated the enlargement of the Illinois and Michigan Canal and the development of a new waterway across Wisconsin by way of the Wisconsin and Fox rivers. Chicago mercantile interests, meanwhile, pushed for the opening of a St. Lawrence seaway as a supplement to the New York canal and rail systems. It was assumed that waterways would provide transportation at lower cost, and that they would be less susceptible to eastern domination. The conventions called to consider the construction of new water-ways to the seaboard expressed the mounting resentment in the West over the failure of eastern owned railroads to serve western interests.[36]

By the late 1860s the competition for the trade of the upper Mississippi Valley had become intense. The struggle to maintain and if possible to increase the flow of business through the various marketing systems had produced a welter of conflicting mercantile interests that were extremely sensitive to the slightest variations in transportation charges. Sectional antagonism among the various states and the river and lake ports, and between the West and the East tended to heighten popular feelings toward the carriers and to make the entire problem a volatile political issue. Since the direction of trade was determined by transportation and storage costs, the rates charged by the various railroad companies inevitably became the focal point of western concern. It was becoming increasingly evident that the success or failure of a particular merchant, a commercial center, or an entire marketing system was determined by the structure of railway rates in the whole area west of the Great Lakes terminals. The comparative level of freights for different shippers and different collecting points was the key to a profitable enterprise, and the most cursory examination of rate structures made it abundantly clear that the competitive opportunities in western trade were being radically distorted by arbitrary and discriminatory rate-making practices.

Railroading was still a new industry in the 1860s and 1870s, and most contemporary efforts to explain its operations in terms of economic principles had been quite primitive. Prior to the Civil War most writing on the subject of railroads was concerned either with problems of construction and mechanical engineering or with problems of promotion and finance. Routine business operations, including rate making, were not subjected to careful analysis. As a matter of fact, until more sophisticated techniques of cost accounting were developed, such analysis was hardly possible. The industry was too big and too complicated to be explained in conventional economic terms.[37]

There had been some speculation on the subject of rates and rate theory in the 1840s and 1850s when New England railroad leaders debated the relative merits of high and low rates, but most of the principles governing the fixing of freights and fares were worked out in practice before any attempt was made to rationalize them in theory. Because railroad companies, in most cases, had to construct and maintain their own highways and had to provide elaborate terminal facilities, it was obvious that they were an industry of unusually high fixed costs. This elementary fact of economic life was responsible for most of the early assumptions behind rate-making policies. Since the total cost of operation did not increase in proportion to the amount of traffic, a large volume of business was thought to be desirable, permitting overhead expenses to be distributed over a maximum number of units. This in turn seemed to justify low inducement rates.[38] It was also evident that costs did not increase in proportion to the distance traveled because switching and terminal expenses were the same for short as for long hauls. It seemed practical therefore to seek long-haul traffic at lower rates per mile than were asked for short hauls.[39]

Another consideration was the almost constant existence of unused capacity. Much of the railroads' business was seasonal. At harvest time, for example, there was a heavy demand for rolling stock, but the traffic was largely one way. Should business solicited for the return trip be expected to pay its full cost? Since the train would have to return even if it were empty, would it not be better to accept a low remuneration rather than none at all?[40] Operational considerations of this sort determined most early rate-making policies, and almost from the outset they produced wide departures from a rate structure based simply on distance.

Practical men and theorists alike realized that it was impossible to determine the cost of each individual service performed. Due to the intricacies of the problem, the unit expense per ton mile of any given commodity was simply beyond accurate measurement, and railroad managers were the first to admit it.[41] Cost factors, therefore, were not the ultimate consideration in determining rates.

Charles Ellet, the most influential American railway economist of the period before the Civil War, recommended that charges be fixed "proportional to the ability of the article to sustain them" [42] —in other words, according to what the traffic would bear. Although he arrived at this conclusion by a somewhat different mode of reasoning than that used by a traffic superintendent, he expressed the principle behind most rate schedules of the day.[43] It was the duty of freight agents to originate as much traffic as possible, adjusting the specific charge to the requirements of the local situation and encouraging the longest possible hauls.

The need to adjust rates so as to meet the requirements of the local situation was universally acknowledged by railway managers, and for this reason freight agents were generally authorized to alter rates at will. The printed tariff was merely a guide. Where competition from other lines existed, the agent was permitted to adopt such methods as were necessary to secure the most traffic regardless of the consequences to rate structures. The customary procedure was to deal on an individual basis with each shipper, offering whatever rate was calculated to obtain his trade. Open rate wars were to be avoided if possible, but the frequency of such conflicts attests to the willingness of companies to resort to these tactics when necessary.[44]

In the upper Mississippi Valley during the third quarter of the nineteenth century, the principal concerns of freight agents were the grain and lumber trades. Here as elsewhere the general policy just outlined prevailed, but it was elaborated to include long-term arrangements with other carriers and middlemen who formed the collection and distribution system for these products. Special contracts were made with merchants, feeder lines, boat companies, and warehousemen in order to obtain the largest possible share of the trade. A certain merchant would receive preferential rates along a particular section of track in return for all his business at competing points; an elevator company would get exclusive loading rights at a certain station in return for its valuable services at that point; a line of packets on the Mississippi would be induced to serve one railhead to the exclusion of all others in return for all the railroad's business at that port.[45] In one sense this was all part of the rationalization of trade on behalf of the eastern market; in another sense it was part of the railroads' efforts to stabilize a highly competitive situation.

But competitive forces did not operate with equal intensity over the whole area. Where lines of transportation crossed or converged, these forces had a radical impact on both rates and services, but at other collecting points and distribution centers they were weak and ineffective. The strength of the struggle among local freight agents to increase their business in grain, lumber, and other commodities varied widely from place to place. The results were gross distortions in the rate structures which for many shippers and merchants meant adverse discrimination that could ruin business. The primary source of complaint against the railroads of the upper Mississippi Valley during the 1860s and 1870s, and the principle motive for the enactment of the Granger laws, was the roads' unequal treatment of shippers and localities. "The uprising of the people of the Western States . . . ," wrote A. B. Stickney, a former railroad president, "was not against the aggregated amount of the rates being collected by the railways, but against the discrimination they were practicing in collecting their revenues. This fact should be thoroughly mastered by every mind which desires to comprehend the meaning of the so-called Granger legislation." [46] Other contemporary students of the problem were in agreement.[47]

The discrimination complained of involved both persons and localities. Personal discrimination meant that different charges were being imposed upon different shippers at the same point for the same service. It existed in the form of preferential rates, rebates, drawbacks, underweighing, underclassification, and numerous other devices. Important shippers in competitive markets were able, due to the size of their business, to obtain lower rates than those commonly charged. If they were in business at a number of stations on the same line they might be able to obtain the lower rate at noncompetitive points as well. This result was usually achieved by granting a preferential rate, but in the case of way points it might be reached by raising the common charge above that given to the favored shipper. In any event, the chosen dealer was able to offer a better price to producers and processors than were his rivals. The effects of this form of discrimination were not necessarily passed on to the community as a whole since the price offered by the favored dealers continued to attract business to those points.[48]

Discrimination against localities, on the other hand, might affect the economic well-being of every member of a community. It too was usually the outgrowth of competitive factors, although geographical discrimination was inherent to some extent in railroad economics. As already indicated, the cost per ton per mile of a long haul was considerably less than that for a short haul, and if rates were to be based on cost, points near a given market would be discriminated against in favor of more distant points. Similarly, the cost of handling way freight was greater than that for through freight because of the added expenses of switching and demurrage. But in view of the fact that rates were actually based on what the traffic would bear, the usual discrimination against localities and the more common distortions of rate structure were the result of varying degrees of competition at different points along the right-of-way.

If a community was served by a single railroad the prevailing rate was that which offered the highest net return. The traffic manager had to consider the possibility of encouraging new business through low inducement rates, but normally this was a secondary consideration. His job was "to get the grain out" at the highest possible rate. But wherever two or more lines met or where rail traffic competed with water traffic, the lowest rate to the best market attracted the business, and rates dropped accordingly. Since there was no way of determining just when a rate became unprofitable, it was possible for cut-throat rivalry to reduce rates to the point of absurdity. The result was that long hauls were frequently made at rates considerably below those charged for shorter hauls on the same line in the same direction. In many instances the total expense to shippers of like quantities of goods was greater for short hauls than for long hauls on the same road because of the existence of competition at the more distant point. Way points subjected to this long-and-short-haul form of discrimination were hard put to survive.[49]

Another form of local discrimination, and one that had an important bearing on the particular form of rate regulation adopted by the various Granger states, involved the larger terminal markets. A terminal market is a point of transshipment where goods are unloaded for storage, for wholesale marketing, or for transfer to other forms of transportation. Chicago, Milwaukee, and Duluth were terminal markets, as were St. Louis, Clinton, and Dubuque. Discriminatory rates often tended to divert trade away from or through those markets. For example, goods twenty miles from one terminal might be diverted to another terminal seventy-five miles distant simply because of a more favorable rate to the latter point. Thus trade that might normally go to Milwaukee could be diverted to Chicago. Similarly, traffic was sometimes encouraged by lower rates to pass through one terminal and go on to a more distant center. In this way, Chicago might benefit at the expense of Dubuque in a contest for the trade of central Iowa. The tendency of railroads to encourage long-haul business led them to alter their rate structures in such a way as to promote shipment over the longest possible part of their lines. The ambitious intermediate terminals were likely to be badly treated in the process.[50]

Local discrimination affected the prosperity of merchants as well as grain buyers. Lumber and provision dealers depended on favorable rate structures every bit as much as did the buyer of grain and grain products. Wholesalers at major terminals were always sensitive to competition from markets farther to the east. Wholesale dealers in Clinton, Iowa, for example, might find themselves in direct competition with Chicago merchants for the lumber trade of central and western Iowa. When train loads of lumber rumbled through the river port on the way to the interior without breaking bulk, the lumber dealers of Clinton could place at least part of the blame on unequal railroad rates. After the beginning of fast-freight service on the eastern trunk lines, Chicago mercantile interests were forced to compete with New York in much the same way.[51]

It is obvious that variations in railroad charges tended to benefit the rich at the expense of the poor. The shipper who received a favorable rate was able to enlarge the business that had entitled him to the low rate in the first place, whereas the less fortunate shipper was hard pressed to hold what business he had. Trade centers that attracted more than one railroad grew in importance because competitive rail rates brought new trade and new industry. Capital, population, and enterprise moved toward the competitive centers while the noncompetitive points gained slowly if at all.[52]

Thus the rate-making policies of the railroads together with their systems of alliances restricted and distorted the competitive process and limited equality of opportunity in many businesses. They denied the equal right of small dealers to participate effectively in an open market, and they prevented the independent shipper from choosing his own outlet by dictating the destination of his produce by means of the rate structure. Farmers, millers, and other processors near way stations were unable to compete on equal terms with their counterparts in the neighborhood of rail centers. The trade of a town victimized by discrimination suffered, inducing merchant, banker, and lawyer to move to more promising locations or to stay and complain of the injustice of railroad practices.[53]

The railroad companies, to be sure, were no more content with the results of competitive rate making than were the shippers, merchants, and producers. Since discrimination almost always involved lowering some rate below what was thought to be the level of greatest net return, the companies were diminishing their own revenue, in a sense, whenever they agreed to offer a preferential rate. Furthermore, it was not always to the railroads' advantage to build up the competitive centers at the expense of the way points because this increased the proportionate amount of their competitive, low-rate business. The continuing efforts made by the railroads to people the lands along their rights of way is good evidence of their concern for a healthy local trade.[54] At the height of the Granger agitation in 1873, Robert Harris, the general superintendent of the Burlington, warned that "it behooves the General Managers to mend some of their ways and particularly in the wild, unreasonable and unnecessary cuttings and discriminations that are at the bottom of all this noise." [55] He admitted privately that the furor might have its good effect on railroad operations.[56] Railway interests, in other words, were concerned with the rate problem every bit as much as the general public was. Their frequent resort to pooling arrangements and rate agreements during this period was nothing more than their attempt to solve the problem to their own advantage.[57] The public could hardly be expected to accept these answers to the dilemma, but all parties had a common interest in its solution. The railroads, it will be seen, were not unalterably opposed to all forms of state regulation.

The essential aspect of the railroad problem, then, was rate discrimination in its many different forms. Because of the highly competitive nature of commerce in the upper Mississippi Valley, rate abuses affected that area more acutely than any other. It was clear from the outset that many, if not all, of these acts of discrimination were violations of the basic legal principle associated with common carriers: public transportation companies were obligated to treat all their customers fairly and without favor. When they did not do so the courts were supposed to offer remedies. For protection against unequal treatment, therefore, the people first turned to the courts, expecting to find their rights firmly established in the common law.

two RAILROAD
RATE LAW
1831-71

THE LEVY AND PAYMENT of a transportation charge
involved rights and obligations, supposedly defined by law, for
both shipper and carrier. But railroads did not conform readily
to the body of legal principles that had regulated the use of public
ways and common carriers in the past. The problem was that they
were neither highways nor carriers in the traditional sense, but a
strange combination of the two without precedent in the history
of public transportation. As a result, the aggrieved shipper of the
upper Mississippi Valley found little satisfaction in the courts
when he first complained of the rate abuses outlined in chapter
one.

It is apparent from a superficial examination of railroad mechanics that the peculiarities of railroads preclude traffic upon the
road surface by competing carriers. For this reason, the roadway,
the motive power, and much of the rolling stock came to be owned
and operated by a single, centralized agency. As one contemporary
student of the rate problem observed, when a highway is "no
wider than the wheel of the vehicle which moves upon it," a
monopoly of trade for one organization is almost inevitable.[1] But
the advantage possessed by the owner of a railroad by virtue of
its exclusiveness was offset by an equally important disadvantage.

The road owner was strictly limited to the use of his own roadway and could move only those passengers and goods that were brought to him for delivery at some point along his own right-of-way. If the course of trade shifted, he was unable to follow it without the burdensome task of taking his own roadway with him.

It follows from this brief explanation that the first railroads stood in an unusual relationship to shippers and travelers, and that the circumstances surrounding the fixing of rates were not customary. In any system of transportation the price paid by the user consists of two parts: the toll paid for the use of the roadway and the rate paid for the services of the carrier. In the days before the railroad, the commercial highways of the country were either open waterways, common roads, or improved turnpikes and canals. In any case, tolls were either non-existent or they were fixed under monopolistic conditions, the canal and turnpike policies of the separate states having been purposely designed to protect operators from the competition of rival routes. As a result, tolls were not subject to economic pressures and could remain fixed and equal for all who applied under similar conditions.[2] At the same time, however, carrying charges always tended to be competitive, since any number of persons could operate vehicles on the surface of a highway. In the case of the railroad, the situation was reversed. The carrying charge was set under monopolistic conditions, but the toll was subject to competition since the states refused, almost from the outset, to protect railroad operators from rival routes. A policy of not only permitting, but of actively encouraging, the construction of more than one railroad between two points was adopted, and this introduced an entirely new factor into the economics of transportation. Tolls were no longer non-competitive, but were fixed under market pressures of varying intensity as the owners of independent lines fought to draw their traffic from a common pool.

The old law governing transportation was designed for the non-competitive highway and the competitive carrier; it was not suited to the railway age. Yet until after 1860, the rights and duties of carriers and shippers remained the same as they had been in the days of the wagon and canal boat. The principles of law first applied to railroad rates were a hasty combination of the principles

governing common carriers and public highways, but both separately and together they failed to meet the problems raised by
competitive railroad rate making.

The law of common carriers held that all persons must be
served on reasonable terms and without undue favor. The carrier's
dealings with the public, including the level of its rates, were
subject to the police powers of the legislature and to review by the
courts.[3]

The first forty years of railroad operation in the United States
coincided with basic changes in the economic policies of the several
states. During the middle decades of the nineteenth century the
amount of government interference with the day-to-day operations
of business enterprise was sharply curtailed. The trend toward
economic liberalism, already well advanced in the opening years
of the century, was given dramatic new impetus by the financial
disasters associated with the panics of 1837 and 1839, and from
that time on a much greater reliance was placed upon private
initiative and upon the operation of "natural," competitive market
forces for the promotion and control of business. Still, the amount
of state regulation of business at the time of the introduction of
railroad transportation was extensive.[4]

State law codes, municipal charters, and Supreme Court records
for the early decades of the nineteenth century give an impression
of close legislative supervision over those market activities with
which the public was particularly concerned. Price fixing by
statute or by local administrative order was a relatively common
practice, and as yet, no distinction had been made between public
and private businesses. All businesses—all common callings—were
public by definition, and all came within the jurisdiction of the
lawmakers.[5] The fact that statutory price fixing had become
progressively less prevalent indicated legislative disinclination to
set price levels rather than any constitutional restriction.

The Alabama Supreme Court put the matter succinctly in
1841. When a man named Yuille challenged a statute authorizing
the Mobile city council to fix the price of bread, the court denied
his plea: "There is no motive . . . for the interference on the
part of the legislature with the lawful action of individuals or the
mode in which private property shall be employed, unless such

calling affects the public interest, or private property is enjoyed in a manner which directly affects the body of the people." But the court went on to cite numerous examples of price laws then in force in the state, and it concluded:

The legislature having full power to pass such laws as is deemed necessary for the public good, their acts cannot be impeached on the ground, that they are unwise, or not in accordance with just and enlightened views of political economy, as understood at the present day. The laws against usury, and quarantine, and other sanitary regulations, are by many considered as most vexatious and improper restraints on trade and commerce, but as long as they remain in force, [they] must be enforced by courts of justice; arguments against their policy must be addressed to the legislative department of the government.[6]

As a matter of policy, price fixing had persisted in many callings well into the nineteenth century. Innkeepers, tavern keepers, bakers, millers, and carriers (porters, carters, draymen, coachmen, and so on) were among the employments still subjected to fixed legal limits.[7] The maximum rate for such services was set either by the state assemblies or, more commonly, by local county boards and town councils acting under legislative authority. Such rate regulation, considered to be a normal exercise of the police power, had been going on, in the words of Chief Justice Waite, "from time immemorial."[8] The early laws and charter provisions dealing with railroad rates followed statutory law as it existed in the 1820s and 1830s.

The police power of the legislature over the rates of public carriers was supplemented by judicial supervision. It was established law that all rates must be reasonable and equal for like services, and whenever the law failed to establish maximum charges, the courts were bound to protect shippers and travelers against excessive or discriminatory rates. In the absence of a large number of judicial decisions on this subject, it is impossible to define precisely the law of reasonableness as maintained by the courts in this period. Available evidence, however, indicates that a reasonable rate was a customary rate, unless unusual circumstances could be proven. A difference in rates for similar services was held to be evidence of unjust treatment, but did not constitute discrimination per se. A charge below the usual rate was not unreasonable as long as the same charge was available to others under similar conditions; a rate above the common one was prima facie unjust and put the burden of proof on the carrier. There was no presumption of injustice if the plaintiff's rate was reasonable in itself, even though someone else had paid a lower rate.[9]

The common law definition of unjust discrimination applied only when someone was charged a rate higher than the customary or prevailing rate. It was suited to an era of competitive carriers and non-competitive highways when the public had a choice of carriers, and the carrier had a choice of location. Under such competitive conditions, the tendency was for rates to seek a common level. The threat of unjust treatment from a carrier developed out of conditions of temporary monopoly which permitted that carrier to ask a higher price than usual or to refuse the business of one applicant in order to take the business of a higher bidder. In such cases the courts came to the assistance of the public, since monopoly was no excuse for an unreasonable rate. This was the doctrine that the courts applied to the railroads at first, and it was suitable under certain conditions. But it failed to cover the most prevalent forms of railroad rate discrimination: preferential rates that were lower than the common rate and distortions in the rate structure resulting from arbitrary rate cutting at competitive points. Only the basic principle—that those who do business in a public market and along a public highway must deal fairly and equally with all—was capable of adaptation. The traditional safeguards whereby this principle was implemented were completely inadequate due to the fact that the railroad was a non-competitive carrier on a competitive highway.

Under the common law, the right to collect tolls on a public highway was a power exercised only by the state itself or by another party under a specific franchise granted by the state. If the state chose to delegate its power, it did so under whatever conditions it saw fit to impose. Usually, the state made provisions as to the amount of the toll, and the charters of early American canal, bridge, and turnpike companies almost invariably fixed schedules of charges. A public highway was established for public benefit, and cheapness was one of its intended attributes. The monopolistic character of a turnpike or canal franchise was not to be used to defeat the public purpose.[10]

With few exceptions tolls were levied according to distance, and thus the structure of rates charged between various points of access and egress tended to be uniform throughout the course of the highway. Since it was seldom necessary to offer inducement tolls on a highway that had no rivals, no favor had to be shown to one locality over another or to one customer over another. Preferential rates, rebates, and other forms of discrimination that involved the offering of a rate below the prevailing one rarely appeared. On the forms of personal and local discrimination that became commonplace during the railroad age, the common law was completely silent. Cases involving such abuses had never come before the courts.[11] The hastily combined law of common carriers and public highways failed to protect the public against the practice of rate cutting, and herein lies the source of the railroad problem.

In the eyes of the courts, the early railroad corporations were assumed to be operators of public highways, employing their own common carriers under a government franchise. Both as highways and as carriers, their rates were subject to supervision by the legislature, unless their charters specified otherwise. In any case, they were always subject to review by the courts.[12] In the case of *Beekman v. Saratoga and Schenectady Railroad Co.*, decided by the New York State Court of Chancery in 1831, Chancellor Wentworth summed up the powers of the legislature in this fashion: "The legislature may also from time to time, regulate the use of the franchise, and limit the amount of toll which it shall be lawful to take, in the same manner as it may regulate the amount of tolls to be taken at a ferry, or for grinding at a mill, unless they have deprived themselves of that power by a legislative contract with the owners of a road." [13] The state and federal courts of the United States uniformly maintained this doctrine down to the time of the Granger cases.[14]

The extent of early railroad rate regulation cannot be accurately determined until further studies lay bare the circumstances in each of the separate states. We know only that there was much legislation on the subject and provision for considerably more. It would probably be safe to say that most of the railroad mileage in the United States in the year 1850 was subject to some form of statutory rate restriction.[15] It would be even safer to say that few of the existing limitations had any practical effect.[16]

Following the examples of canal and turnpike legislation, the state assemblies at first concerned themselves almost exclusively with rate levels.[17] In the earliest charters, passenger fares were usually limited to three or four cents per mile, and in view of the fact that passenger traffic was the principal source of income for some of the pioneer roads, this may have been a genuine restriction.[18] Maximum freight rates, on the other hand, varied so widely as to defy explanation. From a low of about two cents per ton per mile they ranged all the way up to forty cents per ton per mile. Rarely did the charters or statutes set rates so low that the companies felt restricted, and rarely were they lower than those resulting from actual boat and wagon competition.[19]

Later charters recognized the futility of trying to impose maximum freight rates, as the complexities of the problem were simply beyond the abilities of an ordinary state assembly.[20] In a large number of cases, therefore, the making of rates was left to the managers of the roads themselves, but a ceiling was put on the annual profits of the company. The power of the legislature to lower rates was reserved for those cases where profits exceeded a certain percentage of the paid-in capital. Ten to fifteen percent was considered a fair return, and the state was not permitted to reduce rates to the extent that the road's net earnings would fall below a specified percentage within this range. Examples of the exercise of this power are probably non-existent, for it was a rare railroad that earned profits of even ten percent in any one year. Those whose earnings were high were able to keep profits within the charter limit by either increasing capital stock or raising rates and reducing traffic.[21]

A third group of charters made no effort to fix maxima either for rates or for profits, but reserved a general power of revision over the franchise which would permit legislative regulation of rates whenever it seemed necessary. Several states maintained their right of regulation by reserving a general power of amendment over all corporate charters. By 1865 fourteen states had written reservation clauses of this nature into their constitutions.[22]

In addition to charter provisions on the subject of rates, there was a considerable amount of general railroad legislation during the prewar years. All of the general acts of incorporation for railroads passed in this period included some form of control over rate levels, the usual practice being to fix maximum passenger fares and to reserve the power to reduce freight rates. Some stipulation on the relation of profits to freight rates was usually included also. It must be borne in mind, however, that such laws applied only to subsequent charters specifically granted under the terms of the general incorporation statute and not to special acts of incorporation which could frequently be obtained through some loophole in the law.[23]

The point to be remembered is that legislative regulation of rates was a normal practice of the early railroad era, even though care was usually taken not to embarrass the owners of the road. When a railroad attorney suggested to a New York assembly committee in 1860 that the management of a railroad corporation was not amenable to public control, the majority report characterized his statement as "novel and dangerous." [24] The power to alter railroad tolls, barring the existence of a legislative contract to the contrary, was taken for granted.

The preoccupation of the state legislatures with the level of rates was due to the traditional nature of this problem. Railroad charters were modeled, in the first instance, after canal and turnpike grants which almost always included some provision as to maximum tolls but which said nothing about toll structure. The general legislation of the period tended to follow the pattern set by these early charters. Since rate structure had not been a problem of the turnpike and canal era, it had not become the subject of litigation or of legislation. As a result, the early railway charters and laws were vague on the subject of discrimination, and they almost never went beyond an undefined provision for equal treatment and uniform rates.[25] The vagueness of these provisions left their application in the hands of judges who inevitably interpreted them in terms of pre-railroad doctrine.[26] The law of competitive carriers and non-competitive highways was applied until it underwent statutory modification. Both American and English courts held that a lower rate at a competitive point was not evidence of unjust discrimination against less favored towns or less favored shippers. As long as the higher rate was reasonable in itself, there was no relief.[27] Discrimination, in the eyes of the law, was still a matter between persons rather than localities and referred only to higher than ordinary rates. The railroad lawyers who took this position during the later struggle had the weight of authority on their side. The common law provided no protection against the practice of rate cutting.

The failure of the existing law to provide remedies for the various forms of discrimination inherent in a system of competitive toll making was the fundamental cause of the railroad problem. Since the courts proved inadequate, the parties discriminated against brought their complaints before the legislatures of the various states. Thus railroad reform became a political issue, and so it remained until a series of state and federal statutes returned the problem to the courts or until the legislatures placed it in the hands of specially constructed commissions.

The Granger laws were among the first legislative reactions to the railroad problem and claim particular attention because of their contributions later embodied in the Interstate Commerce Act and its amendments. But they were not the very first such reaction, and their historical importance can only be judged in terms of what other states had done and were doing with the same issue. If we confine our attention to the area east of Lake Michigan and north of the Potomac and Ohio rivers, we find that virtually every state had approached the problem in one way or another before the enactment of the last of the Granger laws in 1874.

The state of Rhode Island, sitting astride the main line between Boston and New York City, was the first to attack the problem of local discrimination. Her grievance stemmed from the fact that her own railroads were charging more per mile for traffic originating within her boundaries than they were for freight passing through the state between Boston and New York. There were complaints of personal discrimination as well, and the whole was flavored with a feeling of resentment against absentee ownership and control, as the railroads of Rhode Island had become a part of trunk lines owned and controlled in the financial centers of New York and Boston.[28]

The leader of the movement to correct these abuses was Rowland G. Hazard, a prominent textile manufacturer and thoroughgoing critic of the American railroad industry. Between 1849 and 1855 he gave voice to nearly every argument advanced against railroads during the post-Civil War era. Railroads, according to Hazard, were monopolies that held the fate of whole sections in their grasp. If they were permitted to fix their charges indiscriminately, they could control the business of an entire community, building up one locality while destroying another, all at the whim of some Wall Street ring. Such perversions of the public interest were violations of the railroad charters and must be prevented. A railroad was a public institution, having been given the right of eminent domain in order to secure its right-of-way. It was subject to the control of the people in whose interest its franchise had been granted, and it could be compelled to fix its rates within limits determined by the legislature.[29] Hazard reasoned that a fair and just standard of rates would be that which existed at points where competition prevailed, and from this he concluded that competitive rates should be made to apply on a prorata basis at all stations along the line. This meant that the lowest ton per mile rate charged anywhere on a given line would have to prevail at every point on that line. As a member of the Rhode Island assembly, he fought valiantly for a hard-and-fast measure that would tie way rates to through rates in this fashion. In 1854 his bill actually passed the senate but was defeated in the house by a well planned counterattack sponsored by the railroad interests.[30] The managers of the roads maintained with the support of the state railway commission, that the through rate would not be a paying rate if charged at way points; furthermore, a reasonable local rate would drive off all their traffic if charged at terminal points. In other words, if compelled to charge on a prorata basis, they could not stay in business. Such mischievous tampering with the laws of trade, they warned, would surely "alarm capital and crush enterprise" if allowed to continue. [31] There would be no further construction of railroads in Rhode Island if the bill passed the house.

The arguments of the pro-railroad forces were as standard to the later controversy as those advanced by Hazard against the roads. The issue was squarely drawn in the very first major encounter. Clearly, the question of constitutionality was not a major factor in the debate. The issue centered on the expediency of control and the effect that it would have upon capital investment within the state. In Rhode Island the forces of "capital and enterprise" emerged victorious, and the prorata movement temporarily disappeared from the legislative scene.[32]

The conflict then shifted to the territory of the trunk lines extending westward from the middle Atlantic seaboard to Chicago. Boston and New York had established rail connections with Chicago in 1852. In 1858 both the Pennsylvania and the Baltimore and Ohio railroads completed their links, and they were followed almost immediately by the Grand Trunk of Canada.[33] As a result of these developments, competitive toll-making on an interstate scale became the order of the day, resulting in gross distortions of the overall rate structure. But in this case it was not only the intermediate points that suffered. The New York State canal system, suddenly unable to compete with overland transportation in the shipment of certain types of goods, added its powerful voice to the general cry for relief.

In New York the bill of indictment against the railroads consisted of four points: (1) the property of citizens of other states was being carried more cheaply than that of New York's citizens; (2) way stations were being discriminated against in favor of major terminals; (3) the people of New York were being deprived of transportation facilities which were used instead to serve the property of western states; (4) losses on through freight were being offset by extravagant local rates.[34]

The prime mover in the New York prorata movement was the rich and powerful Clinton League, an association of merchants and businessmen committed to the prosperity of the Erie Canal.[35] The league had been an antirailroad organization from its founding in 1854, and it had worked tirelessly to protect the canal against rail competition. At first, it worked for a restoration of canal tolls on railroad freight,[36] but after 1858, it turned to the prorata principle. In each case its desire was to raise rate levels on the New York Central and Erie railroads. The low rates charged for through freight on these lines had seriously curtailed canal-boat revenues and had badly damaged those industries, milling in particular, that had established themselves at intermediate towns along the tow paths. The league found willing supporters among the shippers and manufacturers located at way points on the trunk lines; it seems to have been less successful in stirring up the farmers of the state, although the league made much of the fact that low rates were responsible for the growing encroachment of western farmers on the New York market. Opposition to the prorata principle came from the railroads, of course, but also from New York City interests that had profited from the fierce competition in through rates. The city's businessmen argued that a railroad franchise could not be revoked without due process even though it might be altered by the state legislature, but they were soundly rebuffed. More effective was the warning that New York City would lose its place as an export center if rail rates were raised. The fight for the western trade, they pointed out, was interstate as well as intrastate. Philadelphia, Baltimore, and Montreal rail lines would continue to undercut the canal, and the only result would be a drop in New York City's commerce. If the canals could not compete, then it was time that they be abandoned. To try to maintain them by tampering with the laws of trade was a doubtful expedient.[37]

Once again the forces of railroad enterprise triumphed. Although a special investigating committee recommended the adoption of a simple prorata bill of the Rhode Island type, the New York Assembly turned it down during the 1860 session. All the thunder of the Clinton League had been unable to halt the march of progress. The league disappeared as a political power, and the movement was dropped until after the Civil War when it re-emerged under different auspices.[38]

In Pennsylvania complaints assumed a pattern similar to that of New York, but lacking any organization comparable to the Clinton League, the movement for reform attracted far less notice and left a much fainter trace. Discrimination against local stations on the main line of the Pennsylvania Railroad was the central complaint, but special attention seems to have been given to the effect of rate wars on the wholesale trade. The Pittsburgh Board of Trade pointed to the damage inflicted by rate wars in its report for 1858: "Pittsburgh once transacted a considerable produce business, which gave promise of a vast increase. The discrimination against us in railroad charges not only checked the increase but has driven to western points most of that which we formerly had." [39] In other words, western merchants were getting the same rate to and from seaboard points as they were getting to and from Pittsburgh, and the result was disastrous to Pittsburgh's trade.[40]

In pushing their demands for a prorata law, the Pennsylvania merchants were fortunate to possess bargaining power lacked by their New York compatriots: the Pennsylvania Railroad was pressing for the removal of a tonnage tax on out-of-state freight. In 1861 a compromise was effected whereby the tonnage tax and other disabilities were removed, while the railroad agreed that it would not charge more for a short haul than it did for a long haul in the same direction. The need for a general law on the subject, however, caused further agitation, and between 1866 and 1868 the shippers of the state fought vigorously, if unsuccessfully, for a law to prevent all local discrimination. Fearing that it might hamper Philadelphia too much in its struggle with New York and Baltimore, the legislature refused to comply, and the desired reforms were compelled to await the constitutional changes of 1873.[41]

An important alteration in the simple prorata principle appeared in the 1861 contract between the Pennsylvania Railroad and the state. In place of a hard-and-fast rule fixing rates in proportion to distance, the agreement contained what came to be known as a long-and-short-haul clause, which forbade a higher rate for a lesser distance. This was probably the first appearance of such a clause in American law, although it had found its way into at least one unsuccessful bill previous to this time.[42] The long-and-short-haul principle represents the first of several important concessions that had to be made to railroad economics before a satisfactory solution to the rate problem could be reached. A strict prorata formula was incompatible with competitive toll-making and unrelated to the cost of the different services rendered. During this same period the state of Ohio found itself in a position similar to that of Rhode Island. It stood astride trunk lines running east and west, but it did not possess a major terminal that could benefit from a low through rate. Here too the major complaint was based on the fact that business originating within the state received less favorable treatment than business passing through it. In 1863 the Ohio General Assembly passed a weak, ill-defined measure requiring that adequate rolling stock and terminal facilities be provided for local as well as through freight and that charges for both be made pro rata. That the law was not adequate is indicated by the continuance of the demand for legislation, and by the appointment of a special investigating committee in 1867.[43] This committee, influenced by the testimony of coal dealers and other merchants, recommended a law barring all undue discrimination, both personal and local, and suggested the inclusion of a long-and-short-haul clause. The assembly, realizing the complexity of the subject, made provision for further investigation through the appointment of a state commissioner of railroads and telegraphs, but deferred further action until the following session. After a year's deliberation and study, the new official reported his findings. He warned that hasty action on the part of the legislature could very easily drive the through trade of the West to seek rival routes outside the boundaries of the state, thus causing irreparable damage to Ohio railroads. The abuses complained of, the commissioner asserted, were the fortunes of economic war and did not concern the state. As long as all rates were reasonable in themselves, the legislature should not interfere.[44] The findings of the commissioner discouraged the passage of any reform measures in Ohio for the time being.

Other states with trunk lines also attacked the problem with greater or less success before 1874. Maryland, at the insistence of Baltimore merchants, considered a simple prorata law in the late fifties but failed to act.[45] Delaware attempted to amend her railroad charters by the addition of long-and-short-haul clauses in 1873, but the courts found them unconstitutional.[46] Michigan passed a law in 1869 providing that "rates of freight . . . for any shorter distance, shall never exceed that charged and collected for the same class of goods over a longer distance upon the said road; nor shall the rates of freight charged and collected . . . between any intermediate stations upon said road, at any time exceed by more than twenty-five percent, the prorata charge per mile for the same character of freight over longer distances upon the said road, or for the entire distance and length of said railroad." [47] The Indiana General Assembly passed a general act containing a long-and-short-haul clause in 1869, but the governor refused to sign, and it never became law.[48]

Meanwhile, the railway problem reappeared in the halls of New England legislatures. In 1867 a Massachusetts committee reported to the general court that it was amazed by the number of complaints made by businessmen and merchants against the rate-making policy of the state's railroads, and the report led to an act outlawing all unjust discrimination against persons. Two years later an advisory commission was appointed to study the complexities of railroad operation and control.[49] In 1870 the general court adopted a law "declaratory of the general right of the legislature to regulate at its discretion all tariffs of fares and freights on the several railroads of the Commonwealth, without regard to the amount of net earnings." [50] In the following year, at the suggestion of the commission, the legislature enacted a long-and-short-haul measure copied from the Michigan statute of 1869.[51] In spite of the fact that Massachusetts was noted for its policy of informal supervision as distinguished from mandatory control, it had placed three regulatory acts on its statute books by 1871.

The railroad problem in Massachusetts was intensified by the keen rivalry between Boston and New York for the trade of the West.[52] By 1870, to be sure, New York had emerged as the unquestioned victor, but the mad scramble for traffic continued unabated. Extremely jealous of her position of dominance, New York City kept a sharp watch on trunkline rate structures and was not above calling for state aid whenever she appeared to be losing what she believed to be her natural advantage. When, in March 1871, her volume of trade seemed threatened by competing rail and water routes, "five hundred of the most responsible and respectable mercantile firms in every branch of the city trade" petitioned the state assembly to remove the abuses and to regulate the rates of railroads in the state of New York.[53] The move was politically premature, and no concerted effort to obtain relief was made until the late seventies, although the New York merchants continued to press for railway reform.[54] It is interesting to note that their position in 1871 was the complete reverse of what it had been during the prorata movement of 1858–60.

The proposals of the New York City businessmen are indicative of many features of the general rate control movement which had its beginnings in the 1850s. The early suggestions for reform were all crude in principle and lacked any understanding of railroad economics.[55] The apparent iniquities of rate discrimination had produced obvious but unworkable prorata measures that had to be modified into the more flexible long-and-short-haul clauses before they could command serious consideration. If relatively high freights threatened the commerce of the great terminals, the cry went up for arbitrary rate reductions "without regard to the amount of net earnings."[56] The desire for equal treatment was easily expanded into a quest for special advantage at the expense of the railroads. From the very outset, the problems of rate structure were interstate in character and could not be dealt with adequately by local assemblies, but the forces of localism were too strong to be denied. The protection of home industry was as much a cardinal principle of state economic policy as it was of national policy, and it found expression in all of the early reform bills.[57] These bills were designed to protect vested interests in the face of disruptive economic forces engendered by competitive toll-making.

The eastern prorata movements had certain characteristics which will bear comparison with the Granger agitation of the upper Mississippi Valley. In the first place, both were essentially sectional movements, pitting the favored terminals against the unfavored with respect to geographical location. Thus the less fortunate terminals sought to bolster their position against the encroachments of the more favored points, and towns possessing ample but non-competitive rail facilities favored regulation, while the have-nots were opposed to any legislation that might discourage new construction. Divisions along occupational lines were of secondary importance if they existed at all.

Second, leadership in each case was provided by merchants and businessmen. In New York it was the Clinton League and later the city's merchants who assumed the initiative; in Pennsylvania, the Pittsburgh Board of Trade played a leading role; in Ohio, the coal dealers were most conspicuous; in Massachusetts, the Boston mercantile interests provided the initial impetus, and so on. The centers of protest responsible for petitions, printed pamphlets, and lobbying were the boards of trade and other commercial organizations. Although a plentiful amount of propaganda was directed at the farmers of New York State, there is no evidence that they were brought into the movement on any appreciable scale in New York or in any other state.

Third, the debates on the proposed measures turned on economics rather than on law. Lacking any sound constitutional basis of opposition, except where charter provisions were concerned, the railroads tried to justify discrimination on grounds of cost and the requirements of a competitive system. A tariff of strict, prorata charges simply was not feasible in the case of a railroad and could not be maintained without destroying the value of the road. From this basic premise the railroads went on to the more effective argument that any state that destroyed the value of a railroad franchise by imposing an "unnatural" system of rate making upon the operator would never be able to attract additional capital for new railroads or for large-scale industry of any sort. Capital would always seek more favorable fields in neighboring, rival states.[58] As long as the clamor for more railroads continued, and as long as interstate commercial rivalry remained a controlling factor in state politics, the railroads' argument was a convincing one. In many states it was decisive; in others it dictated a compromise or watered-down measure of the long-and-short-haul type. In any case, it made the struggle for control an uphill battle.

A final consideration must be the reaction toward the idea of government control. It is interesting to note that the leaders of the eastern prorata movements were called rash, shortsighted, or unprogressive, but they were never called radical. E. L. Godkin, the conservative editor of the *Nation,* was deeply in sympathy with the five hundred merchants of New York who petitioned the legislature in 1871. To him they were "responsible" and "respectable" businessmen.[59] Nor did anyone accuse the Massachusetts General Court of agrarianism or communism when it asserted its right to control railroad rates, "anything in the charters to the contrary notwithstanding." [60] Legislative rate regulation was too deeply imbedded in American tradition and law to be attacked as radical. In the eyes of its detractors it might be "old-fashioned," "mischievous," and "unwise," but it had not yet become "revolutionary" or "dangerous." [61]

three THE STATES
AND THEIR RAILROADS:
PROMOTION VERSUS
CONTROL

Although the state governments were inter-
vening in many areas of economic life during the antebellum
period, control of rates and prices was less typical of the times than
the promotion of economic growth. The effectiveness of control, in
fact, was severely curtailed by the desire of state governments to
encourage economic development and even to force it beyond
the capacity of private investment. The reins of government regulation were being loosened as a means of inducing economic expansion.

One means of promoting such expansion was to build public
arteries that would enhance the wealth of the state and add to
the business of its principal trade centers. The states of the eastern
seaboard, for example, were interested in tapping the trade of the
great Mississippi Valley which the Erie Canal had placed within
reach of the city of New York, but which could not be reached conveniently by waterway or canal from any other coastal city. In
Boston, Philadelphia, Baltimore, and Charleston railroads were
conceived of as the best means of breaching the mountain barriers
that separated them from the grain and cotton fields of the West.[1]

It was common for the states to assume almost complete responsibility for the provision of public ways; indeed, the construc-

tion and improvement of public highways had long been considered an obligation of the state. In the case of turnpikes, canals, and bridges, private interests had been admitted before 1830, but generally speaking, only when public funds were inadequate. For this reason, it was natural for the states to consider seriously a policy of state ownership of the rail roadway regardless of who operated the carrier. The possibility that individuals might operate cars on the public rails after the fashion of an ordinary highway was not thought to be out of the question.[2] Only after technical and financial considerations had dictated unity of management was the practice of placing the entire operation in the hands of a single agency universally adopted.[3] But the question still remained, should railroads be public or private enterprises?

During the 1820s and 1830s the separate states deliberated at length upon this important issue. In Pennsylvania, Georgia, Michigan, Indiana, and Illinois the decision was finally made in favor of public ownership and operation for all or at least some part of their systems. The rest of the states entrusted the work to private interests, but retained a variety of arrangements for government subsidization and control, thus not breaking completely with the idea of government ownership. Mixed public and private holding of the stock of a company was common and was resorted to during construction of the Boston and Albany, the New York and Erie, and the Balitmore and Ohio railroads. In other cases reversionary rights were reserved to the states, after the example of turnpike grants, which permitted the state to take over the line after a definite period of time or after the entrepreneurs had been rewarded with a fair return.[4] As a rule, the state kept a proprietary interest of one sort or another in a railroad during the first decade or two of construction.

During the 1840s and 1850s, however, this situation underwent a marked change. Many of the public systems were conspicuous failures which led to complete financial ruin for the governments involved. Following the panic of 1837–39, which was part and parcel of the collapse of the internal improvement programs, there was a far-reaching reaction against public enterprise. In a number of states, constitutional prohibitions upon direct state participation in industrial activity, together with restrictions upon the use of state credit, were adopted. There was also a tendency to liquidate state holdings in private corporations. But because of the fact that private capital was as yet inadequate for the contemplated programs of economic expansion which usually centered around railroad construction, the reaction was not toward a hands-off policy. It was rather toward increased subsidization of private incorporated enterprise, as opposed to public works.[5]

The economic debacle of the late thirties resulted in the supremacy of the private corporation as a vehicle for economic activities that were beyond the means of individuals. State assemblies were now more willing than ever to place the problems of railroad operation in the hands of associations of capitalists, giving such indirect financial and political support as was needed, but divorcing themselves more or less completely from the responsibilities of management. This can scarcely be interpreted as a victory for the laissez faire principle, but it contributed to the strength of such a doctrine since it was easily rationalized into an admission of the states' inability to cope with the complex forces of business.[6] The tendency to separate government from the economy was given added impetus even though the principle of positive state action remained. The state as a promoter of industry would continue to "remove obstacles and grant facilities," but it would not participate directly in the public market.[7] It would supervise, direct, and control, but it would not own, operate, or manage.

This decision was not a sudden one growing wholly out of the failure of state-managed internal improvements. It had been formulating bit by bit ever since the foundation of the United States, and the panic of 1837 had merely established it beyond question. From the very beginning of independent existence, the American states had attempted to expand domestic industry by granting corporate charters to groups of capitalists who were willing to undertake economic functions of a public nature. This was particularly true in the fields of banking, insurance, and highways. Traditionally, the charter for a commercial enterprise was obtainable only under extraordinary circumstances. Being a grant of sovereign power, it was reserved for those businesses, such as banking or transportation, otherwise closed to individual enterprise. But in the hands of state legislatures, each endeavoring to surpass its neighbor in the encouragement of home industry, the granting power was used with far less discretion. Elected assemblies vied with one another to attract private capital through promises of limited liability and freedom from government intervention. In the process they greatly expanded the range of their grants, and soon any business thought to serve a public benefit was deemed a suitable subject for a private charter, even though no exercise of public authority was involved. As might be expected once the gates had been opened, there was no stemming the legislative flood. Representative assemblies were opposed to restricting the distribution of public favors to any particular interest. What was available to the turnpike operator was soon placed within the grasp of the shoe manufacturer, and by 1820 the corporation had become simply a form of business enterprise that any competent petitioner could organize.[8]

This rapid multiplication and diversification of commercial charters inevitably contributed to a legal redefinition of corporate status, since the law was as unprepared for the rise of private business corporations as it was for the appearance of competitive highways. The courts were conscious of the fact that they were dealing with a new phenomenon involving new economic relationships. Among the various forms of aggregate corporations, it was possible to discern distinctions as to function and interest. The ancient classification recognized religious and lay, civil and eleemosynary; a later classification separated those that were intended for public government and those that were concerned with private charity. In each case the function was stressed without particular reference to the interest involved, and there was no question as to the relationship of the institution to the granting power. The use of the franchise was always public, the welfare of the community was always paramount.[9]

In commercial corporations, however, there were interests that were definitely private. There was always profit sharing stock which was owned, as a rule, by individuals who therefore possessed a proprietary interest in the franchise as well as fixed property. The use of the franchise—the function of the corporation—remained public, but the interest of the stockholders was clearly private.[10] This fact had been given judicial recognition in

1806 when a Massachusetts court ruled that the charter of a turn-pike company was a contract that the state might not impair unless the power of repeal or amendment had been reserved in the grant itself. The same idea was later expressed by Justice Joseph Story in his concurring opinion in the celebrated *Dartmouth College* case.[11] Taking an even broader position than Chief Justice Marshall, Story made a careful distinction between corporations that were "public" and those that were "private." Unless all the stock belonged to the government or the franchise dealt with the administration of a political or municipal unit, said Story, a corporation was private and stood in a special relationship to the state legislature. Its charter was in the nature of a contract, and for this reason, could not be altered or repealed without the consent of the grantee unless such powers were reserved in the charter or some previous declaration. Unlike Marshall, Story expanded his doctrine to include banks, canals, bridges, turnpikes, and insurance companies. There was no question in his mind that such corporations were private even though their function might be public.[12] The fact that they exercised powers of sovereignty made absolutely no difference to Story. He was concerned with the ownership of the stock, not with the function of the particular agency.

Story's opinion should not be interpreted, of course, as a denial of the state's right to regulate a business enterprise. It simply meant that the courts intended to protect the proprietary interest of the stockholder in a commercial franchise. If the legislature wished to retain the right to alter or repeal the charter it had a perfect right to do so, but the investor of private funds was entitled to know just when and under what circumstances the state could make use of this right. Furthermore, the exercise of the normal police power over the activities of a business organization was not affected in any way by the mere existence of a corporate charter.[13] Unless specific exemptions were included in the franchise, the activities of an incorporated company were subject to the same kind of supervision as those of an individual business-man. In other words, the right of the legislature to regulate prices was not lost unless it was expressly stated in the charter that the company could fix whatever prices it chose.

By 1830 it was established constitutional doctrine that a commercial charter was a contract to be strictly construed by the courts in favor of the state, and not to be impaired by the granting authority without the permission of the grantee. At the same time the private corporation became an accepted means of implementing public policy, on a par with the state itself as a means of carrying out large-scale industrial undertakings of a public nature.[14] Having already been employed for the construction of turnpikes and canals, it was now used for the building and operation of railroads whenever the states themselves did not undertake the task. In effect, the legislatures contracted with private individuals for the construction and operation of public railroads. But in order to stimulate the accumulation of funds sufficient for the completion of various programs, the legislatures often granted railroad corporations privileges not possessed by private persons. In a few cases monopolies of traffic between two terminals were offered as the principal inducement,[15] but monopolies were not consistent with the ideals of the Jackson era. More prevalent were exemptions from taxation and legislative regulation.[16]

It was here, in fact—in the formulation of charter policy— that the promotional and regulatory aspects of state economic policy came face to face. The contractual nature of a charter made possible offers of immunity from legislative regulation of rates, either for a period of years, until the profits of the corporation reached a certain level, or forever. This immunity was eminently desired by capitalists who, with justification, looked upon railroad investment under a competitive system as an extremely hazardous risk deserving of commensurate guarantees. When we examine in more detail the evolution of charter policy in Illinois, the importance of this issue will become evident. Capitalists were demanding, as a privilege and not as a right, the power to fix freights and fares free of legislative interference. The states were compelled to accede to these demands in accordance with their ability to attract investment capital. In short, the states began to promote economic development by promises of ineffectual or delayed regulation, reserving whenever possible the right to regulate but always careful to avoid anything that would "alarm capital and crush enterprise." [17]

The widely varying rate provisions of early railroad charters and statutes were the result of this policy. They asserted the traditional right of the legislature to regulate the price level, but they were designed to encourage rather than restrict railroad earnings. Where maximum freights were actually fixed, they were placed above those which the operators themselves expected to charge; where the power to reduce rates was reserved, the promise of a ten to fifteen percent profit was usually included. These charters and statutes revealed the relative strength of both the capitalists and the states in the bargaining process. New York and Massachusetts, for example, stoutly maintained their right to regulate, and their power was actually exercised in such a way as to affect the management of the roads. Ohio, on the other hand, maintained but did not enforce a theory of control, and Maine denied outright the power of regulation.[18] The ability of the various states to attract capital is clearly evident in the character of their railroad charter policies. The strong made limited concessions, while the weak virtually allowed the roads to govern themselves.

Bargaining strength was also revealed in the different attitudes toward prorata legislation assumed by the states after 1850. The Rhode Island law was defeated because it might "alarm capital," and the same was true of the Indiana bill of 1869. In Massachusetts and Pennsylvania, however, control legislation was adopted. Although the failure of New York to pass a prorata bill would appear to be an exception, it must be remembered that the legislative committee did strongly advise the passage of a control measure, and it failed to carry its point only because of the prevailing prosperity of New York City interests. It is interesting to note that in the case of New York considerable attention was given for the first time to questions of constitutionality. This was the last refuge of railroad owners when the "alarmed capital" argument failed.

The question of legislative control, particularly after the failure of the state lines and before the panic of 1873, was inextricably intermeshed with the promotional activities of the states. The decision to stimulate internal improvements by the infusion of private capital led to a period of business freedom, more from economic necessity than from philosophical conviction. This fact can be fur-

ther demonstrated by an examination of the history of railroad
policy in Illinois.

Illinois was the only state of the upper Mississippi Valley to embark on a program of railroad construction prior to the
panic of 1837. For obvious reasons some account of her early
efforts to formulate a workable policy of promotion and control
is useful to an understanding of later Granger legislation. But the
history of early Illinois policy is valuable for a second reason: it
reflects in bold relief the broad developments in American railway
policy during the period before the outbreak of the Civil War.
If we divide the prewar era into two parts, one being the period
of public works when the states retained a proprietary as well as
a promotional interest in their roads, and the second being the
period of the private corporation, publicly subsidized but not publicly owned, we find that Illinois provides us with an extreme
example in each case.

During the internal improvement boom of the thirties Illinois,
together with her sister states, debated the problem of public
versus private or semi-private ownership of railroads. In 1835 and
1836 an effort was made to promote a program of public works
through incorporated associations of private capitalists, and the
legislature granted a number of charters for railroad companies
including the Galena and Chicago Union and the forerunner of
the Illinois Central.[10] It seemed that the state had abandoned the
notion of public ownership that it had adopted previously for the
Illinois and Michigan Canal.[20] The charters of 1835 and 1836
were typical of the period in that they permitted public ownership
of stock, contained either reversionary rights or permitted the
state to purchase the road under certain conditions, and provided
for legislative reduction of rates once the profits of the company
exceeded a certain percentage. But the inability of private corporations to attract a sufficient fund of risk capital in a frontier community limited the success of this early program.[21] In order to
acquire the desired rail system, the state was compelled to adopt
public ownership.

Between 1837 and 1839, Illinois launched the "most stupendous, extravagant, and almost ruinous folly . . . that any civil community, perhaps ever engaged in." [22] With a population of some 300,000 people, she committed herself to a liability of approximately $20,000,000 to obtain a system of railroads, turnpikes, and river improvements that had little relation to the transportation needs of the time and could never have proven successful even if completed. The plan was the result of logrolling on a magnificent scale and contemplated about 1,300 miles of railroad, confined almost entirely to the southern half of the state. The system of finance was to be the same as that developed by New York for the construction of the Erie Canal, and it provided for the payment of all obligations out of general income from taxes and not merely from revenue derived from the works themselves. The complete recklessness of the scheme was matched only by its failure. The plan was scarcely conceived before the panic and depression of the late thirties laid it low. Construction work on all but one small part of the railroad system, the so-called Northern Cross, was suspended in 1840. The Illinois Commission of Public Works, in whose hands the management of the system had been placed, was able to put a grand total of fifty-five miles of road in operation, but finding that the income from its business was inadequate even for repairs, it sold this last remnant of a glorious dream in 1847 for $21,000 in state bonds. Needless to say, the government found the running of a railroad a most wearisome task and was glad to be rid of it.[23] The public, meanwhile, had become thoroughly convinced "that works of this character never ought to be under the control of the State." [24]

The end result of the Illinois internal improvement program was a crushing debt of over $14,000,000 to be paid entirely out of taxes.[25] "Among all the States of the Union which succumbed to the financial storm of 1836–40," commented *Hunt's Merchants' Magazine*, "none had more canvas spread, or so little ballast, as that gem of the West, Illinois." [26] By July 1841 the treasury was empty, and the state was forced to default on its interest payments. Failing to meet her obligations, Illinois found herself blacklisted by every financial center in the United States and western Europe.[27]

The reaction against public ownership was greater in Illinois, perhaps, than in any other state in the nation. Having attempted one of the most ambitious programs of railroad construction, she had also tasted the most bitter defeat, and was now ready to abolish all her proprietary interests in industrial undertakings.[28] The new constitution adopted in 1848 provided that "the General Assembly shall encourage Internal Improvements, by passing liberal general laws of incorporation for that purpose." It also stipulated that "the Credit of the State shall not, in any manner, be given to or in aid of any individual, association or corporation." [29] Henceforth, all railroads were to be built and managed by private corporations without any direct financial aid from the state.

The Illinois Constitution of 1848 was also conspicuous for its failure to include a reservation clause. At virtually the same time, New York (1846), California (1848), Wisconsin (1848), Michigan (1850), Ohio (1851), and Pennsylvania (1851) adopted constitutional provisions that safeguarded the right of the legislature to alter or repeal all subsequent corporate grants. In the absence of full reports on the debates of the Illinois Constitutional Convention of 1847, it is impossible to assign a definite reason for this omission, but it is probable that the clause was left out in the hope of attracting out-of-state capital which had shown itself extremely reluctant to migrate to the blacklisted "gem of the West" after the failure of 1841. The Wisconsin Constitutional Convention debates of 1846 reveal the adverse attitude of eastern capital toward charter reservations,[30] and there is good evidence for the belief that English investors were extremely reluctant to put their money into western railroads for fear of what the state legislatures might do to the franchises once the roads became prosperous.[31] In view of Illinois' extremely low credit rating during the 1840s and her intense desire to foster private railroad development,[32] it is likely that the power to amend and revoke corporate grants was purposely excluded.

The constitution of 1848 directed the legislature to encourage internal improvements by adopting "liberal *general* laws of incorporation." [33] There was considerable reluctance on the part of the general assembly, however, to pass a general railroad act, and as a matter of fact, only New York had passed such a law previously, and this not until 1848. At the regular legislative session of 1849, the Illinois House Committee on Incorporation reported that a general law was not applicable to railways. In the first place, they insisted, the state must reserve its right to locate the termini of each line; in the second place, it would be impossible to fix a uniform maximum rate for all roads under all conditions since the maxima would depend upon the nature and concentration of traffic. The idea of surrendering control of the roads to capitalists who had no other interest than the collection of tolls was repugnant.[34]

The general assembly failed to pass a railroad law during the regular term of 1849, but in the fall of the same year a special session was called from which there emerged a general act of railroad incorporation patterned after the New York law of the previous year. It permitted the directors of the roads to fix whatever rates they chose, provided that passenger fares be no more than three cents a mile. It also stated that the legislature might reduce the rates of freight on each road so long as such reductions did not bring the company's profits below fifteen percent per annum on the paid-in capital. To pacify those who had insisted upon the right of the assembly to locate the termini of each line, the law required that a special grant of the right-of-way be secured from the legislature by each company. The General Act of 1849 was liberal only to the extent that it permitted stockholders a return of fifteen percent per year instead of a more conservative ten or twelve percent, but it failed to encourage internal improvements. The record shows that prior to 1870 not a single Illinois railroad that actually reached the operational stage was incorporated under the general law.[35] As long as it was possible to obtain special charters from the Illinois legislature vesting exclusive rate-fixing powers in the directors of the road, no one wanted to incorporate under an act that provided for legislative regulation. The situation is illustrated by a brief episode in the history of the Chicago, Burlington, and Quincy Railroad.

In February 1851 a group of citizens from Galesburg, Illinois, obtained a charter for a line to be known as the Central Military Track Railroad, which was to provide the town with through connections to Chicago. The enterprise was begun as a purely local undertaking, but it soon became evident that eastern financial assistance would be necessary. To secure this aid Chauncey S. Colton, the leading merchant of Galesburg and one of the directors of the C.M.T., went to Boston to bring the project to the attention of John Murray Forbes. Forbes, the great railway builder of the time, was looking for western connections for his Michigan Central and was gradually putting together the future Burlington system out of available roads west of Chicago. After brief negotiation it was agreed that if the Galesburg charter could be brought into conformity with Forbes's wishes, the Central Military Tract Railroad with full eastern backing would become a part of a through route from Lake Michigan to the Mississippi River.[36]

The C.M.T. charter had been granted under the general law of 1849 and was governed, of course, by all of its provisions including those dealing with rates. Forbes and his associates, however, were aware that the Illinois Central had obtained a charter that gave its board of directors the right to establish rates without any legislative restriction whatsoever. This valuable privilege had been gained through a special charter granted without reference to the law of 1849. The Forbes interests may well have made a similar privilege the sine qua non of their support for the C.M.T., because Colton hurried back to Galesburg and impressed upon his own associates the need for a revised charter based upon that of the Illinois Central.[37] As he himself wrote at a later time, "I contended that the most important feature in our charter should be *absolute self control* as to rates and fares, for our company *free from all subsequent legislation*." [38] In June 1852 Colton went to Springfield in an effort to get the charter amended. According to his own account, he found

many influential members opposed strongly to the idea of granting a charter which should be beyond their control, by future legislation, in regard to *establishing rates and fares*. This matter I wish to have understood for all time to come. viz That the subject of fixing *rates and fares,* was made a square open issue in the Legislature, in obtaining this foundation charter, of the CB & QRRd. I told the members and committee that we could not raise money to build a railroad upon the uncertainties of future legislation on the subject of fares & rates! I told them that, under the old style of charters, we could not build a road, but under the principle of *no future legislation,* we *could;* and that it was a question of a road or no road. Upon this plain distinct understanding we secured the grant of a charter subject to no legislative control.[39]

Under similar pressure the Illinois General Assembly granted special charters to other railroad corporations. Reluctantly at first perhaps, but with ever increasing boldness, it bargained away its sovereign right of toll regulation in exchange for the capital necessary to provide the state with a network of railroads. By 1853 the last resistance to privileged charters was melting away under the warming influence of prosperity induced in large measure by the railroads themselves. The governor of Illinois, Joel A. Matteson, saw no cause for alarm when he reviewed the state's policy in his inaugural address of that year. He noted that "this state has wisely abandoned the policy of embarrassing the treasury by engaging in works of internal improvement" and has instead "granted charters with a liberal hand and afforded every proper encouragement." Such a policy had proved to be "of such manifest advantage, [that] sound policy would seem to dictate the same liberality should continue as long as capital can be obtained to bring new fields of labor into market." [40] Between 1853 and 1859 the general assembly granted special charters by the score in the form of omnibus bills, which were not even read on the floors of the two houses.[41] Having placed the development of her internal improvements in the hands of private capitalists, the state gave away her powers of control with a rashness equal to that demonstrated in the formation of her public works program.

It is apparent that during this second phase of railroad promotion in Illinois, the efforts of the state to encourage construction completely obliterated the traditional policy of restrictive control. The same was true to a lesser degree of the other Granger states and of American policy in general. The intense demand for more and more railroads that marked the period from the middle forties to the middle fifties forced the traditional forms of regulation into abeyance. As the harbinger of prosperity, the private railroad corporation had been given its head and had been allowed to run relatively free of legislative restraint.

The early prorata movements marked the beginning of a general reaction against the policy of unlimited freedom for railway corporations. Once again the legislatures weighed the advantages and disadvantages of state control over rates and services, and although the desire to promote new enterprise was strong enough to offset the pressure for reform in many instances, the advocates of public regulation ultimately prevailed. The legislatures of the several states had granted extensive liberties to the proprietors of railroad corporations, but always on the assumption that private operation would improve the industrial and commercial opportunities of the states. In spite of a desire to divorce government from business, the assemblies remained very much alive to the needs of their local economies. In no sense were they intentionally subordinating state interest to the demands of private capital; they were assuming, rather, that the two interests would be identical.

The first corporations formed to provide rail transportation had all been promoted by local mercantile and industrial interests. The roads were designed to serve existing commercial centers, and care had been taken not to extend their benefits to competing centers. Charters for lines with terminals outside the state were often denied,[42] and in many cases different gauges were deliberately adopted to prevent the formation of through connections. As late as 1870 the rail net of the United States was still a disconnected, uncoordinated tangle of separate systems reflecting local jealousies. But there had always been a close identity of interests between the owners of the railroads and the other businessmen and producers in a given area; the success of a railway company was measured as much by its contribution to these other interests as it was by its own profits.[43]

During the 1840s and even more noticeably in the 1850s, this close interrelationship of local economic interests began to change. By this time railroads were looked upon as worthwhile investments in themselves, and capitalists were buying into strategically located companies purely for speculative purposes. The ownership of American railroads was becoming increasingly capitalistic, and the value of railway properties was being measured more and more by their ability to produce dividends. While it is clear that this infusion of outside capital made possible the completion of most American railroads—particularly those in the West—the growth of absentee ownership was a potential source of mischief. The new railroad proprietors were often interested in the development of regional transportation and marketing systems, and they were not inhibited by state boundaries or by particular local interests.[44] The boldness of their objectives surpassed anything yet conceived of in the business world, and their plans could not be carried out within the limits of the established mercantile order. A clash of interests was unavoidable, and it was this clash that precipitated the movement for state legislative control of railroad rates.

As already noted, there was a close correlation between the beginning of political agitation for rate-law reform and the introduction of interstate rail service. The first attempts to integrate separate state railroads into larger regional systems took place in New England, where through connections between Boston and New York were established by capitalists at either end of the line. Rowland Hazard's first demands for rate regulation in Rhode Island came soon after the completion of a right-of-way through the city of Providence. Rhode Island railroads were now being used to serve Boston and New York to the disadvantage of local business. The most spectacular early combinations of railroad properties, however, took place in the West. During the 1840s John Murray Forbes and his Boston associates began to assemble a series of lines linking Boston with the upper Mississippi Valley. Starting at the western end of the Boston and Albany, Forbes purchased a major interest in the New York Central and acquired control of the Great Western of Canada and the Michigan Central. By shifting the western terminus of the latter road from St. Joseph, Michigan, to Chicago, he was able to forge a continuous chain between Boston and the West by way of Buffalo and Detroit. Continuing westward, he put together the Chicago, Burlington, and Quincy and acquired a controlling interest in the Hannibal and St. Joseph Railroad of Missouri and the Burlington and Missouri River Railroad of Iowa. By 1860 Forbes's properties stretched across seven states and British North America, from the Atlantic seaboard to the Missouri River.[45]

Meanwhile, a group of New York capitalists put together a

second trunk line from New York to Chicago along the southern shore of Lake Erie. For this purpose they shared control of the New York Central with the Forbes group, but west of Buffalo they struck off on their own. They combined separate lines in New York, Pennsylvania, Ohio, Michigan, Indiana, and Illinois into the Lake Shore and Michigan Southern and pushed their tracks into Chicago simultaneously with those of the Michigan Central in 1852. In the following years the New York syndicate advanced across Illinois and Iowa by buying into the Chicago and Rock Island and the Mississippi and Missouri.[46]

The ownership of the various companies that made up these two western systems continued to change hands, and during the sixties and seventies, the Forbes properties east of Chicago together with the Lake Shore and Michigan Southern all came into the possession of the Vanderbilt group of New York. Forbes had decided to trim his holdings and to concentrate on the development of the Burlington. The Vanderbilt organization, on the other hand, proceeded to enlarge their western connections by assembling and extending the Chicago and North Western. By 1873 they were in control of a vast and unwieldy network reaching from Boston and New York to Nebraska and the Dakotas.[47]

Efficient service on these and other east-west systems developed slowly because of breaks in the lines at major river crossings and at points where gauges changed. With the stimulus of new competition in the late fifties, however, the service was improved. Through freights east of Chicago became a reality and complaints of discrimination began to be heard in New York, Michigan, Ohio, and Indiana. Since the new managers were guilty of charging higher rates for local traffic than they did for interstate trade, the forces of particularism were aroused.[48] Absentee ownership of the major rail lines introduced another element of tension into the political and commercial life of the states. There was no longer an immediate identity of interests between the proprietors and the communities they served. The states could not rely on a common purpose to secure favorable treatment as to rates; the railroad owners could not rely on a common purpose to prevent political harassment. The point is not that they were unconcerned about one another's welfare, but that the relationship between

the states and the roads was almost entirely a matter of contract—
a matter of law. The adjustment of their differences often resulted
in a major political contest.

The builders of interstate rail systems stoutly resisted the movement for rate-law reform. They looked upon the prorata and the
long-and-short-haul principles as serious limitations upon their
freedom of action. The necessity of conforming to local state
interests, moreover, seriously impaired the value of their regional
properties. They had relied heavily on promises, real and implied,
of freedom from legislative interference, and they resented the
efforts to change their contracts without their consent. Lacking
adequate political backing in local assemblies, the owners played
upon the fears of the have nots, warning the areas still in need of
rail facilities that restrictive legislation would "alarm capital and
crush enterprise." [49] The result was a series of prolonged political
battles.

The progress of rate-law reform, in other words, was greatly
impeded by the conflict of interests between the suppliers of capital and the suppliers of corporate privileges. The states were not
ready to condone the subordination of their local economies to the
requirements of the new industrial order, and they sought to
maintain their local mercantile interests through legislative action.
The capitalists, at the same time, were reluctant to accept the
necessity of operating within the separate jurisdictions of the several states, and they sought to establish barriers against the claims
of the state assemblies. The resulting political and judicial struggles had begun in the east where interstate railway service had
first come into being, but they reached a climax in the west where
the largest interstate systems existed. The efforts of the four states
of the upper Mississippi Valley to regain control over their railroads through rate-law reform led to the Granger laws; the efforts
of the larger interstate systems to break free of state restrictions
and to find some measure of security under federal jurisdiction
led to the Granger cases.

four   ILLINOIS:
THE TRIUMPH OF
JUDICIAL REVIEW

I N 1860 THE TOWN of Belvidere, Illinois, some seventy-five miles west of Chicago, was a community of 1,114 persons and a way point on the Galena and Chicago Union Railroad. As a way point on an important trunk line between the Mississippi and Lake Michigan, it was susceptible to all the economic pressures caused by rate discrimination and therefore became one of the many centers of protest against the railroads. Its size and location scarcely entitled its representatives to more than a minor role in state politics, but during the course of the 1860s and 1870s it sent to the state legislature three men of preeminent importance in the movement to impose governmental controls upon the railroads of the state. Between 1861 and 1873, one or another of these men was at the forefront of the drive to reform railroad rate law in Illinois.

First in point of time and national prominence was Stephen J. Hurlbut, elected to the state House of Representatives in 1858, 1860, and again in 1866. He was born and raised in South Carolina and had received his legal training from James L. Pettigrue, one of the leading lawyers of the South. Hurlbut, like his teacher, was a southern Whig with strong antislavery leanings, and after his removal to Belvidere in 1845, he became associated with Lin-

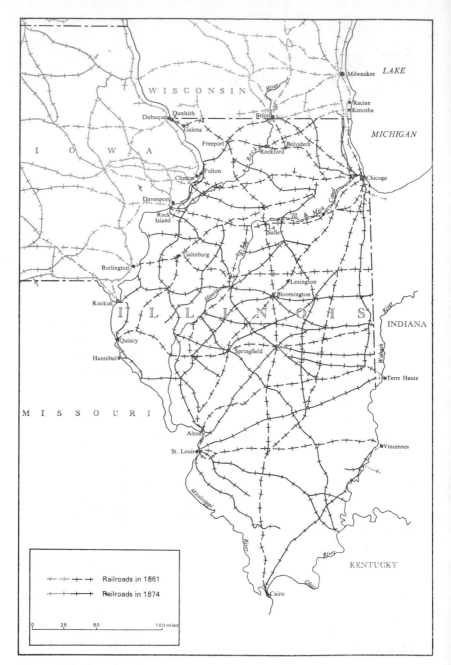

Map 1. Illinois Railroads, 1861 and 1874. (Map by University of Wisconsin Cartographic Laboratory.)

coln and the founders of the Republican party in Illinois. In 1861 Lincoln sent him as one of two special emissaries to measure the depth of secessionist feeling in South Carolina. On the completion of this mission Hurlbut returned to Belvidere and became one of the first to volunteer for military service. He served with distinction and in 1867 returned to the Illinois house where he concentrated on the railroad problem and became the recognized leader of the antimonopoly forces. The Democratic *Chicago Times* called him the ablest lawyer, best scholar, and readiest debater in the house. As a Republican, an ex-Union general, and a founder of the Grand Army of the Republic, Hurlbut was indeed a power to be reckoned with. After his career in local Illinois politics came to an end in 1867, Hurlbut was appointed minister to Colombia by Grant, served a term in Congress, and became minister to Peru under Garfield.[1]

The second representative from Belvidere was Allen C. Fuller, lawyer and banker, who served as speaker of the Illinois house in 1865 and as state senator from 1867 through 1871. Fuller was born in Connecticut and studied law under David Wilmot of Pennsylvania and James Doolittle, later senator from Wisconsin. He moved to Belvidere in 1846, and from the beginning of his residence, he took an active interest in the Boone County Agricultural Society. A contemporary biographical sketch declares that he helped to organize the Republican party in his district. Fuller, like Hurlbut, was a warhawk on the secession issue and worked hard to organize the first company of Illinois volunteers taken into federal service. When war broke out he was appointed adjutant general of the state, in which capacity he served until 1864. In that year he resigned his post and ran for the state legislature. After serving one term in the lower house he was elected to the senate, where for the next three sessions he was the leader of the more radical wing of the antimonopoly faction. His active political life came to an end following the session of 1871.[2]

The third man from Belvidere was Jesse S. Hildrup of Connecticut, also a lawyer. He received his legal training at the State and National Law School in Poughkeepsie, New York, and began his practice in Belvidere in 1860. The *United States Biographical Dictionary* calls him a worthy example of an independent, self-made man and credits him with fostering much of the important railroad legislation in the country up to that time. As a delegate to the Illinois Constitutional Convention of 1869–70, as a member of the state general assembly in 1871 and 1873, and later as a member of Congress, Hildrup contributed to the solution of legal problems arising out of the growth of corporate power.[3]

Hurlbut, Fuller, and Hildrup prepared or helped to prepare most of the key railroad regulation bills presented to the Illinois General Assembly between 1861 and 1873. Of the three, Fuller probably made the greatest individual contribution, but Hurlbut had the distinction of introducing the first antidiscrimination bill, and Hildrup played a central role in framing the Illinois Granger law of 1873. These three lawyers from the Boone County seat dominate the legislative history of the Granger laws in Illinois.

The early years of the Illinois movement to impose legislative restrictions upon railroad rates cannot be described in depth; the evidence is scattered and entirely too meager to give more than a general impression of events. In the late fifties and early sixties complaints of unjust discrimination against persons and localities began to appear in the press, in state conventions, and on the floors of the state legislature. In May 1858 the businessmen of Rockford, Illinois, held a mass meeting to protest the rate-making policy of the Galena and Chicago Union Railroad.[4] In 1861 certain coal mining companies prevailed upon Stephen Hurlbut to introduce in the state legislature a bill to prevent and punish any fraudulent discriminations by railroad companies chartered under the laws of Illinois.[5] Without fanfare, the house adopted the bill by an overwhelming vote of 50 to 8, but the session ended before the senate had time to act.[6]

During an abortive constitutional convention in 1862 the rate problem received considerable attention, but again without much dispute and with practically no publicity. A delegate from the Grand Prairie region south of Chicago offered a resolution to the effect that railway companies be required by the constitution to adopt a uniform rate per mile for both passengers and freight, from and to way points, in proportion to the distance traveled. Another member representing the rich corn-growing area of the upper Illinois Valley suggested the creation of a board of commissioners to supervise passenger and freight rates and to regulate the time tables and connections of the various railroads in the state. A third delegate from the Central Military Tract wanted to require the assembly to fix a schedule of reasonable maximum freight rates.[7] The convention did not see fit to write a special section on railroad rates into the constitution, but it is interesting to note that it did provide for "amending, revising, renewing, extending and enlarging existing charters."[8] There is no positive indication that the delegates had restrictive amendments to railroad charters in mind, but apparently the corporations were sufficiently alarmed to work for the defeat of the proposed provision. In the end, the entire constitution was rejected because of the Copperhead character of its framers.[9]

During the early war years the people of Illinois were faced with a transportation problem growing out of the closing of the Mississippi River as a result of southern secession. The entire grain surplus of the valley now had to find its outlet in the East, and consequently, most of it had to be moved by rail at least as far as Lake Michigan. At the same time, certain railroads were compelled to devote much of their capacity to military requirements, and the resulting burden on western carriers was unprecedented. In the face of traffic that was simply too heavy to handle, the railroads raised their rates wherever possible. Increased transportation charges were made all the more burdensome by a sharp financial crisis in Illinois resulting from the collapse of a number of state banks whose notes had been backed by southern bonds and from unfavorable market conditions at the lake ports. The increased grain production of the western states plus the closing of the Mississippi River had temporarily flooded the Chicago and Milwaukee markets and depressed prices. In view of the fact that eastern prices were rising because of war needs and the increased demands of Great Britain, the feeling of frustration among every element of the grain trade from Chicago westward was understandably great. Neither the farmer, the country shipper, nor the Chicago trader derived the slightest benefit from boom conditions in the eastern market. On the contrary, their returns were actually diminishing, and it seemed perfectly obvious, in the face of higher rail rates, that the difference between high and low prices was being eaten up by exorbitant transportation charges.[10]

The principal outlet for western wrath was the movement for more and improved water routes to the eastern seaboard, a movement in which some of the western railroad leaders participated. But the concern over high transportation costs also focused attention on the railway rate problem and stimulated the demand for reforms. The Illinois Constitutional Convention of 1862 reflected the growing strength of this movement. The complete dependence of the state upon railroads that were owned by and operated for "foreign" capitalists had been brought home with telling force. As a result of war conditions, the former harbingers of prosperity had suddenly become oppressive monopolies levying arbitrary tolls upon helpless producers and shippers. The existence of a Copperhead majority in the convention of 1862 indicated the intensity of this regional antagonism. Although the convention contributed nothing to the substance of rate-law reform, it pointed up the sectional overtones of the movement. The railway problem was fast becoming an issue of political importance.[11]

During the 1863 session of the Illinois General Assembly a number of petitions praying for the redress of grievances were received by members representing the Central Military Tract. In the senate, William Berry of McDonough County offered a resolution requiring the judiciary committee to report whether or not the "present exorbitant and ruinous rates of charge" could be restrained by law. Albert C. Mason of Knox County presented a bill that provided for the appointment of three commissioners to regulate rates so as to limit the net income of railroad companies to ten percent per year. Although the latter bill was passed by the senate by a vote of 15 to 9, no action was taken in the house. The lower chamber also considered creating a regulatory commission as proposed by Henry R. Peffer of Warren County, but this bill too failed to come to a final vote.[12]

Before the house reconvened, the depression of the early war years had given way to boundless prosperity. With the issuing of Greenbacks and the establishment of a national banking system, the local shortage of currency soon disappeared. The railroads and lake boats were again able to handle the huge eastbound traffic, and some semblance of order was restored to the grain trade. By 1864 it seemed that unparalleled good times had come to Illinois.[13] In that year the president of the Illinois State Agricultural Society wrote:

See the railroads pressed beyond their capacity with the freights of our people . . . every smaller city, town, village, and hamlet within our borders all astir with improvement; every factory, mill, and machine shop running its full complement of hands; the hum of industry in every household; more acres of fertile land under culture, fuller graineries, and more prolific crops than ever before; in short observe that this state and this people of Illinois are making more rapid progress in population, development, wealth, education, and in all the arts of peace, than in any former period and then realize if you can, that all this has occurred and is occurring in the midst of a war the most stupendous ever prosecuted among men.[14]

But the demand for cheap freights seemed to keep pace with the volume of trade. Strangely enough, prosperity did not bring contentment. In February 1865 the *Chicago Tribune* declared that the "question of cheap freights from the West to the East is next in importance to the suppression of the rebellion itself." High railway rates, it complained, were amounting almost to a blockade of commerce.[15] And so the plea for more canals and railroads and limitations on the rate level of existing roads continued. The general assembly of 1865 received a large number of petitions asking for the regulation of freights and fares. A good share of them had been printed in quantity and circulated prior to the beginning of the session, and it was claimed that they came from the industrial classes.[16] The agency responsible for their distribution was not indicated, nor was its name revealed in the course of the debates. It is interesting to note, however, that the demands endorsed by the farmers were identical with those put forward by merchants and shippers. As yet, there appears to have been no sharp division between producers and middlemen on the question of railroad tariffs.

As a result of such agitation, the house appointed a special committee to frame a bill "restricting and regulating tariffs on freight and passengers on all the railroads of this State." In due course the committee reported a measure limiting passenger fares to three cents per mile and another creating a board of railroad commissioners. The commission bill passed the house by a vote of 62 to 1, a good indication that the bill granted the commission no more than investigatory powers. The fare bill also passed by a comfortable margin, 46 to 18, but neither measure came to a vote in the senate. It is not likely, however, that either bill would have survived the upper house, because the senators were proving most reluctant to include rate restrictions and reservation clauses in the new charters. Nonetheless, the house was making a concerted effort during this session to assert the power of the legislature over corporate franchises. The house had placed various limitations upon the rate-making powers of the new roads in all new charters, but the upper chamber steadily refused to accept them.[17]

Those opposed to placing restrictions upon the new railroads maintained that such controls would either prevent construction or so weaken the new lines that they would fall easy prey to the established companies. In either case the problem of monopoly would be aggravated instead of solved. Many expressed disappointment that reservations had not been imposed from the very start, but they refused to penalize communities without rail service by discriminating against new lines. The supporters of restrictive clauses insisted that regulatory provisions would not crush the new roads, and they asserted confidently that such clauses would act as regulators for all roads since the established lines would have to compete with the new ones on the latter's regulated terms. But the defenders of the have-not areas were in the majority, and although a few restrictive charters were passed, the general policy of reservation clauses for all new railroad franchises was defeated.[18]

During the winter of 1865–66, the northern part of Illinois was swept by an antimonopoly revolt. In the first year of peace since 1860, grain prices had fallen off from their wartime highs, while rail rates tended to rise. Farmers, grain dealers, and merchants assembled in conventions at Morris, Bloomington, DeKalb, Sterling, Rockford, and other leading collecting points to demand relief from the oppressive charges of railroads serving their parts of the state. Here again the remedy most frequently mentioned was improved water routes, but the demand for legislative regulation of railroad rates was also heard frequently.[19]

Chicago, sharing the sentiments of these rural centers, urged both improved water routes to the eastern seaboard and lower rail charges west of the lakes. An added reason for Chicago's concern was the revival of competition with St. Louis following the reopening of the Mississippi River at the end of the war. Peace ended the monopoly of the eastern market and threatened to deprive Chicago and Milwaukee of their dominant positions. With freight rates rising as a result of postwar conditions, the river route was able to capture an alarmingly large part of the 1865 harvest of Iowa and Minnesota. In December of that year the *Chicago Tribune* complained: "If the officers of the railroad corporations of the Northwest were under the immediate pay of St. Louis, they could not work more effectually to build up that city than they are doing at the present time. By charging exorbitant rates of freight on the various lines leading into Iowa and Minnesota, for the past two or three months they have driven the great bulk of the produce of those States to seek a market down the Mississippi River." [20]

The St. Louis Chamber of Commerce was quick to exploit its opportunity. It sent delegates to the antimonopoly meetings in Illinois to urge support for improvement of the Mississippi as an outlet for western grain. The antimonopolists, in turn, played one city off against the other, and by the beginning of 1866, they had Chicago firmly on their side. The Chicago Board of Trade, Mercantile Association, and Board of Real Estate Brokers converged upon the railroads and demanded that rates be reduced. If they were not lowered, the Chicago business community threatened to support legislative action that would compel reductions.[21]

The revolt smoldered through the summer of 1866 and with somewhat diminished fury broke out afresh after the harvests for the year were in. Once again the rural collecting points, with the support of Chicago businessmen, demanded additional waterways to break the hold of railroad interests on the western trade. They also asked for legal restrictions on rates and fares. During the elections of 1866 particular attention was paid to the transportation problem, and as the new state legislature assembled in January 1867, the antimonopoly forces met in convention in Springfield to press their demands. Their program included restrictions on railroad combination and consolidation, uniformity of freight rates, a three-cent maximum on passenger fares, and annual reports from every railroad corporation operating in the state.[22]

The program of the Springfield convention included an important clarification of the railroad issue. In the antimonopoly meetings held prior to this time, the demands for state regulation had been couched in terms that clearly implied that cheap freights as well as uniform rates were the objectives of control. There is abundant evidence to support the supposition that rate levels were a matter of grave concern in the immediate postwar years.[23] But as the pinch of depression began to ease and the railroad problem was discussed in less passionate terms in the press and legislature, it became increasingly apparent that uneven rate structures were the one major problem with which the state assembly would concern itself. The movement for cheap transportation tended to separate out and go its own way, taking the form of nationwide drives for various federal internal improvements such as canals and cheap-freight railroads.[24] The cry for legislative reform came to center on the question of discrimination. The request of the Springfield convention for uniformity of rates indicates a more precise conception of the nature of the railroad dilemma.

In the 1867 session of the general assembly the railroad problem received its first thorough airing in open session. Stephen Hurlbut, again a member of the house of representatives, was chairman of the railroad committee. The corresponding position in the senate went to Alonzo Mack of Kankakee, known to be a moderate on railroad questions, but pledged to back a restrictive control measure. His committee included Allen Fuller of Boone County, a strong advocate of the antimonopoly program. The debates of this session centered around bills introduced by these three men. Hurlbut's bill provided for restrictions upon consolidation, a three-cent passenger fare, maximum rates on grain and coal, compulsory reductions on other rates amounting to 33⅓ percent of those in force on January 1, 1867, and a stipulation that all rates must be in strict conformity with the distance traveled. The bill was to apply to all railroads operating within the state, regardless of their charter stipulations. Hurlbut insisted that the creator was above the created, and that a corporation had no vested right to oppress the people; he denied that the *Dartmouth College* decision contradicted his intended reforms.[25]

Fuller's bill was a maximum-rate measure designed to reduce passenger rates to three cents a mile and to cut freight rates 20 percent from the level of January 1, 1867. It further provided that if a railroad was dissatisfied with such rates it could appeal to a board composed of the governor, the auditor of public accounts, and the treasurer, which was empowered to raise the maximum set by the bill if it saw fit, but not above the level of rates in effect on January 1. The legislature, however, could review the findings of the board and would have the last word in every case. Fuller was also undisturbed by the cry of vested rights. Unless the power of the legislature over rates had been expressly relinquished—and he was satisfied that it had not been—the assembly was perfectly free to impose reasonable restrictions.[26]

Alonzo Mack, by contrast, was a staunch defender of vested rights. Nevertheless, according to his own account, he was "a sincere friend of regulation." He held both Fuller's and Hurlbut's bills to be unconstitutional on the grounds that they impaired obligations of contract. He also pointed out that Hurlbut's strict prorata formula would make long hauls uneconomical for the railroads. Rather than attempt to exercise the police power, he sought to reenforce the common law requirement of reasonableness as interpreted by the courts. The Mack bill of 1867 proposed a board of three commissioners who would study the rate problem and, wherever necessary, suggest reductions. The commission could not order compliance, but if a railroad refused to follow its suggestions, the board could apply to the state supreme court for a writ of mandamus requesting the company to show cause. The court could order the reduction after hearing the case.[27]

Mack's bill was a compromise, unsatisfactory to extremists on both sides in the legislature, but it was probably acceptable to the railroads. The antimonopolists denounced it as completely ineffectual and condemned its author as a tool of the railroad interests. Mack replied publicly that he was not trying to please the antimonopolists, but he also denied that any railroad had a hand in framing the bill. The Hurlbut and Fuller bills were acceptable to the antimonopolists, but they aroused the opposition of the have-not areas in central and southern Illinois. Every member of the assembly who sought a charter for a new railroad in his home district was carefully reminded by the corporation lobby that such a line would never be constructed if a restrictive control bill was passed.[28]

The result was a division of purpose that prevented any action from being taken. Mack's middle-of-the-road position was too strong for the have-nots and too weak for the antimonopolists. No one was willing to compromise, so the have-nots won by default. Hurlbut's bill, slightly modified to incorporate some of Fuller's maximum rate provisions, passed the house but was easily sidetracked by Mack in the senate, despite the fact that it was strongly supported by the Chicago press of both parties and by the Chicago delegation in the assembly. Fuller refused to accept amendments that would protect new or weak roads from the rigid restrictions of his maxima, and as a result, failed to bring his measure to a vote.[29] In the midst of the proceedings, the *Chicago Times* boldly announced that senators were selling out to the railroad lobby in wholesale lots. The paper even went so far as to quote a price list.[30] But the fundamental reason for the failure of 1867 was the opposition of the have-nots and the inability of the friends of regulation to compromise their differences. After the Civil War the demand for new railroad construction overtook the cry for regulation, and as a result, the antimonopoly revolt failed to spread into central and southern Illinois. Due to its sectional limitations, its failure to produce a clearly defined program, and perhaps because of its inability to arouse the agricultural population to more than sporadic political action, the revolt collapsed without producing any tangible results.[31]

Between the end of the legislative session of 1867 and the beginning of the next one in 1869, the railroad question virtually disappeared from the pages of the Illinois press. The only continuing remnant of the antimonopoly movement was an occasional reference to the need for improved transportation routes to the seaboard, particularly in the form of river improvements and canals. With a few exceptions, the election campaigns of 1868 were fought without reference to the transportation issue. The retiring governor, Richard Oglesby, spoke only of prosperity and contentment in his final message to the new legislature in January 1869. Thus it came as a surprise when the new governor, John M. Palmer, devoted a large part of his inaugural address to the need for railroad-law reform. Palmer, an ex-Union general, was a Republican with heretical views on the question of state's rights. In his opening address to the general assembly he used the railroad problem as a vehicle for his so-called Copperhead notions, deploring attempts to involve the federal government and insisting on vigorous state action to prevent existing abuses. Although there had not been any considerable movement for federal regulation in Illinois, the matter was being given serious thought elsewhere and had recently become the subject of debate in Congress. Palmer was less concerned with the railroad problem than with the expansion of federal power, and he used railroad regulation as one example of a state function that should not be allowed to pass into the hands of the federal government.[32] "Fixed tolls are permitted," he concluded, "not to authorize unreasonable rates to be demanded, but that reasonable charges may be conveniently ascertained and collected, while the whole matter must, in the nature of things, be subjected to the final control of the state."[33] The governor's recommendations were clumsy and extremely vague, and they were almost forgotten in the indignant reaction of his own party to his surprising espousal of Democratic principles.[34]

But the stage was set for another attempt at reform. Despite the apparent slackening of public demand for rate regulation, Allen Fuller returned to his seat in the senate with a determination to put the constitutionality of legislative control to a test. The railroad lobby was strangely absent, possibly because the corporations were unprepared for this new effort, but more likely because they felt secure in their belief that the courts would protect them. As a result, the assembly of 1869 was able to approach the railroad problem in a spirit of relative calm. In order to obtain a test case with the least possible delay, Fuller introduced a maximum passenger-rate law that would limit fares to three cents per mile. In order to assure its passage, an exemption clause was added freeing new roads from the bill's provisions for a period of ten years. Although the have-nots still objected, their numbers had been considerably reduced by new construction in central and southern Illinois during the preceding two-year period. This factor, plus the inclusion of the exemption clause, insured the adoption of the measure by comfortable margins in both houses. Toward the end of January the bill went to Governor Palmer for his signature.[35]

The unpredictable governor promptly returned the bill to the assembly with his veto. A charter, he said, was a contract and could not be impaired by the legislature without the consent of the grantee. Although he agreed that some form of regulation was necessary, that the states should have ultimate control over corporations they created, and that three cents per mile was a reasonable maximum fare, he could not accept a law that arbitrarily imposed a maximum rate on companies that were specifically authorized to fix their own rates. Furthermore, Palmer did not believe it was the duty of the legislature to pass on the reasonableness of rates; that was a judicial function. The assembly, the governor maintained, should pass a law requiring that all rates be reasonable, and it should then establish a tribunal that was qualified to enforce those rates.[36]

Rebuffed in his efforts to put a rate-fixing law before the state courts, Fuller agreed to work for a general law in compliance with the governor's suggestion. When a bill limiting railroads to just, reasonable, and uniform rates was reported to his railroad committee, Fuller used it as a model but reworked it and reported a substitute embodying his own ideas. In its final form the second bill did little more than echo the existing common law, but it is clear from Fuller's own statement that it was designed to curb discrimination against persons and places through a stipulation that all rates must be uniform.[37]

During the debate over Fuller's experimental passenger fare bill, protesting members had stated repeatedly that freight rates, not passenger fares, were the chief concern of the people, and that personal and local discrimination, not the rate level, was the principal abuse. The need for antidiscrimination laws had been repeatedly expressed by representatives of the major northern collecting points, including Chicago, and a number of prorata bills were introduced in the house. A rigid prorata law, however, was too strong for the railroad and judiciary committees. Representatives of the railroad companies appeared before the senate judiciary committee, and by explaining the economics of railroading, proved beyond question that prorata rates were totally impractical. The Chicago press, which had been clamoring for some sort of regulation, woke up to the fact that Chicago had been built on favorable through rates. The second Fuller bill, therefore, used the more nebulous term *uniform* instead of prorata, but it specifically outlawed rebates and drawbacks. In this shape the bill passed with the tacit approval of the railroads, but over the continuing objections of the southern have-not areas. With the signature of Governor Palmer, the bill became law.[38]

By 1869 repeated efforts to reform the law of railroad rates in Illinois had brought only meager results, but the issue had been clarified and the lines of division drawn. The old law held that rates for the use of common carriers must be reasonable and non-discriminatory, terms which could be defined by the legislature as long as it had not deprived itself of this right by provisions in its charter contracts with the carriers. In the absence of specific statutes, or whenever the legislature had bargained away its power of control, the courts enforced the law according to custom and such rules of evidence as the legislature might establish. In Illinois the legislature had renounced its power of control in all but a few cases; the effective agencies of governmental control, according to the predominant legal opinion, would have to be the courts. Most of the bills introduced in the Illinois General Assembly between 1861 and 1869, however, contemplated direct legislative regulation of rates. The Mack bill of 1867 is virtually the only example of a measure designed to stengthen judicial control. In the face of public necessity, the antimonopolists simply denied the force of the *Dartmouth College* decision, and they were able to carry a majority of the assembly with them. The same senate that rejected the Hurlbut and Fuller bills of 1867 adopted the Fuller resolution which declared the right of the legislature to limit fares and freight rates, even though it refused to take such a step at that time.[39] The representatives of the people of Illinois were determined to solve the problem of discriminatory rate making by direct exercise of the legislative power.

The means suggested for the accomplishment of their purpose can be classified under two headings: schedules of maximum rates and prorata restrictions. The first contemplated lowering rates at way points in order to bring them into closer conformity with through freights. Fixed maxima were also a means of influencing the direction of traffic since enforced, low intrastate rates would help prevent the diversion of trade to out-of-state terminals. For this reason the idea appealed to trade centers like Chicago where prosperity depended more upon the volume of business than upon the price of commodities.[40] The plan possessed the political advantage of not alienating competitive centers by threatening to raise their rates, but it also possessed the political drawback of discriminating against new and weak roads that could not survive under schedules designed to curb trunk lines. Therefore, certain areas in central and southern Illinois were unwilling to support this form of control regardless of the discrimination practiced against them.

Prorata limitations were designed to extend the advantages of competition to way points by making the lowest competitive rate on any given line the basis of the rate schedule for the entire line. This principle was calculated to please the way points, but because of its tendency to raise rates at rail centers as a means of evening out the rate structure, it was unpopular with competitive points. It had the further disadvantage of raising long-haul rates to such an extent that it radically reduced the size of existing markets and therefore was unpopular with major terminals. Politically, its chief drawback was the uncompromising hostility of the railroads, and the have-nots were unwilling to antagonize railroad capital by voting for such a law.

The voting pattern for the rate control bills of the 1860s shows a regional economic influence. The communities with railroads, located in the northern part of the state, were the leading exponents of control; the unserved communities in the so-called Egypt area to the south were its bitterest opponents. Occupational divisions were of no apparent consequence. Despite frequent references to the plight of the producing classes, the important bills were framed on behalf of the supposedly disadvantaged collection and distribution centers, including the great terminal of Chicago.

The law of 1869, sometimes considered the first Granger railroad law, was of so little consequence that it was perfectly acceptable to the railroad interests.[41] The *Tribune* called it "an apple dumpling with the apple left out." [42] Because the bill was largely an innocuous restatement of the common law it was approved. True, it outlawed rebates and drawbacks, but its enforcement depended upon the willingness of an individual shipper to challenge a railroad corporation in a court of law. So unequal a contest was not apt to be attempted, particularly when the shipper remembered that he was dependent upon the good graces of the railroad for the successful pursuit of his business. The first of the Granger laws contributed little, if anything, to the solution of the railroad problem.

During the winter of 1869–70 delegates assembled at Springfield to frame a new constitution. Dissatisfaction with the basic law of 1848 had developed largely as a result of the irresponsible behavior of the general assembly. One critic lamented that the legislature "meets in ignorance, sits in corruption and dissolves in disgrace every two years." [43] The calling of the convention was only indirectly connected with the railroad question, and the unrestricted granting of special railway charters in defiance of the constitutional prohibition against such action was but one of many similar abuses calling for reform.[44]

Among the delegates were Joseph Medill of Chicago, part owner of the powerful *Tribune* and an active supporter of railroad regulation during the antimonopoly revolt; Lorenzo Whiting of Bureau County, a prosperous farmer and leader of the movement for rural organization; Reuben Benjamin of Bloomington, a Harvard lawyer who later helped prepare the brief for the state in the case of *Munn v. Illinois;* Orville H. Browning of Quincy, a distinguished lawyer, former United States senator and secretary of the interior; and Jesse Hildrup of Belvidere, third of the dynasty from Boone County. The convention was notable for its even division between Democrats and Republicans and for its large preponderance of lawyers, fifty-six out of eighty-five delegates being members of the Illinois bar. The remaining twenty-nine seats were divided equally among farmers, professional men, and business-men.[45]

In spite of the cooling of passions since the collapse of the anti-monopoly revolt in 1867, it soon became evident that the railroad problem was one of the leading questions on the minds of convention delegates. "I say if there is anything like unanimity in this State upon any one thing," said one member, "it is upon restricting these railroads, these immense corporations. . . ."[46] Another claimed that the people expected the convention to inaugurate a contest between the railroads and the state.[47] Whenever the debate turned to internal improvements, municipal indebtedness, corporations, or railroads, the question of unreasonable and discriminatory rates was raised. Although the subject matter of petitions sent to the various delegates indicates that warehouse frauds and abuses in the weighing and shipment of grain were issues of more immediate concern in 1869–70,[48] the rate problem would not down. It was readily apparent that a separate railway article would have to be framed and submitted to the people for their approval.

During the course of the proceedings the full range of opinion on rate regulation was covered. A few delegates believed that competition was the only effective means of control, and they urged the construction of more railroads, canals, and improved waterways, with provision against the consolidation of parallel lines. Moderates asserted that the common law requirement of reasonableness, enforced through the courts, set proper limits to state action. These views were commonly expressed by members from southern Illinois who opposed any restrictions that might alarm capital. The more outspoken representatives of have-not communities accused the delegates from major rail centers of deliberately seeking to prevent new construction that might divert trade away from or around these centers, but a majority of the delegates were ready to endorse direct legislative regulation of rates. A proposal for expanded and intensified judicial control received no consideration whatsoever, and the suggestion of a purely supervisory commission was decisively rejected.[49]

This brought the convention face to face with the problem of vested rights. Virtually all the railroad corporations of Illinois had charters granting their directors and managers full powers of control over rates. Charters, according to the *Dartmouth College* case, were contracts that could not be impaired through the unilateral action of the state unless they were granted subject to a reservation clause. How then could the Illinois General Assembly place restrictions upon the rate-making powers of railroad corporations without violating the constitution of the United States? The answer of the majority of the delegates was given in extreme form by James C. Allen of Crawford County when he declared, "I do not intend, sir, by any act or acquiescence of mine, to recognize the decision of a former age in reference to the rights of corporations, when that recognition leads to a standing wrong upon the rights of the people; and whatever may have been the decisions of the courts upon this question, in an age and at a time when the people's rights were not so fully settled, they must give way to that overpowering sentiment in this country that is rising against injuries from these monopolies." [50]

Legal minds were able to put the same radical intent into more conservative language. During the final two weeks of the convention when the draft of the railroad article was under consideration, they advanced a two-pronged doctrine of legislative supremacy, amply supported by citations from federal court cases and legal treatises. The first and greatest single contribution to this doctrine was made by Reuben Moore Benjamin of McLean, a student and teacher of American constitutional law. Benjamin expounded a theory of inalienable sovereignty that restricted, without challenging, the force of the *Dartmouth College* decision.

All privileges rightfully granted to corporations, said Benjamin, are vested rights that cannot be impaired without the consent of the grantee; yet there are certain powers inherent in sovereignty that no legislature has a right to bargain away beyond the recall of its successors. Among these is the power to regulate business enterprise. Benjamin, in masterful fashion, reviewed the history of legislative restrictions upon common employments in the United States and asserted that such exercises of the police power could never be rendered invalid by mere default. The failure of the Illinois legislature to fix by law the rates of its railroads had not in itself deprived the state of its constitutional power to do so in the future. Rate fixing was undeniably an attribute of sovereignty vested by the state constitution in the general assembly. But could not the legislature relinquish its police power by a charter contract? Here was the crux of the problem. Benjamin denied that a legislature could in any way diminish its own powers by grant or otherwise. The ultimate source of all governmental authority, he insisted, was the people, and they alone could relieve the assembly of the responsibility for exercising its constitutional duties. Legislative power is not a subject for contract or sale. The general assembly "cannot change the Constitution or make a new Constitution, and yet it would be doing just this, if it could limit the governmental powers of a future Legislature." All provisions in railroad charters giving the directors sole power to regulate rates were, therefore, unconstitutional and void. "Let the next Legislature enact substantially the railway laws of England, regulating and limiting the rates of freight and passenger tariffs, and I firmly believe that the courts would hold that such reassertion of government control over railroad rates, is not any interference with vested rights." [51]

Benjamin's logic seems to have satisfied most members of the convention. They proceeded to frame a railway article of unprecedented stringency. It declared that all railroads in the state were public highways "free to all persons for the transportation of their person and property . . . under such regulations as may be prescribed by law." It gave the general assembly the right to establish "reasonable maximum rates of charges" and to subject railroad property "to the public necessity." A third section empowered the general assembly to "pass laws to correct abuses and prevent unjust discrimination and extortion in their rates." The article also included a section banning the consolidation of parallel or competing lines, and it attempted to deal with absentee ownership by requiring that a majority of the directors of any railroad corporation chartered by the state be citizens and residents of Illinois. To provide future legislatures with a reserve weapon for the coming battle, a second doctrine of legislative supremacy was written into the same article. On the day following Benjamin's statement of inalienable sovereignty, Jesse Hildrup of Boone County expounded a theory of eminent domain. The police power, he maintained, was too limited. It left the railroads free to discourage legal action by a threat of prolonged litigation that no individual shipper could afford. What was needed was a whip to compel the railroads to obey, something capable of destroying them if they chose to persist in flaunting the public interest. Such a power was eminent domain.

The doctrine of vested rights, said Hildrup, does not deny the right of the state to appropriate for public use, after just compensation, the property and franchise of a railroad company. While the government cannot take private rights for private use, it may appropriate them for public use whenever the necessity arises, the judge of such necessity always being the legislature. Thus the general assembly may condemn all or any part of a corporate franchise under a proper exercise of the right of eminent domain without interfering with the inviolability of contracts. The substance of this position became section 14 of the railroad article.[52]

A parallel effort was made by the convention to bring Chicago grain elevators under public control. Complaints of abuses in the receipt and handling of grain by the warehouse monopoly persisted despite earlier attempts at state regulation. Because Chicago grain dealers were the principal victims of elevator frauds, the Chicago Board of Trade was the dominant force in this movement. Largely through its efforts, a warehouse article requiring close supervision and control of all Chicago elevators was inserted in the new constitution.[53]

The legal doctrines put forward by Benjamin and Hildrup to circumvent the protection given to corporations by the *Dartmouth College* decision were carefully constructed and fully substantiated by legal opinions. In point of fact, no part of their argument has since been refuted by the United States Supreme Court. And yet, in light of repeated previous assertions by the courts of the right of the legislature to deprive itself of the power of control over rates,[54] the notion of legislative supremacy would seem to mark a radical change in constitutional thought. There is no question but what the Illinois General Assembly had consciously bargained away its power of legislation on the subject of rates during the decade of the fifties, nor that the railroads had been given to understand that their privileged charters were unalterable. The denial of the sanctity of such contracts, therefore, was a fundamental departure from existing legal principles.

This apparent manifestation of western radicalism was but part of a nation-wide reaction to the growth of corporate power that appeared first where corporate power appeared first—in the East. It was apparent to a certain extent in the arguments of Rowland Hazard of Rhode Island in 1849; and it was explicit in the Massachusetts Declaratory Act of 1870. The growing awareness of the dangers of corporate wealth and power is quite apparent in the pages of the *Nation* and in the writings of Charles Francis Adams, Jr. The eminent naturalist and railroad commissioner for Vermont, George P. Marsh, maintained in his report of 1858 that jurists were modifying their views as to the sanctity of corporate franchises, and that legislatures were now recognized to have full power, regardless of charter provisions, to pass any necessary regulation for public moral or material interests.[55]

In the law journals and legal treatises of the period, the question of corporate immunity was also receiving careful attention. Isaac Redfield questioned the absolute sanctity of charters without coming to any clear cut decision in his *Practical Treatise on the Law of Railways* (1858),[56] while Thomas M. Cooley recognized the pertinence of the question in his *Constitutional Limitations* (1868). Questioning the right of legislatures to bargain away their sovereign powers in the form of corporate charters, Cooley asserted: "If the legislature has power to do this, it is certainly a very dangerous power, exceedingly liable to abuse, and may possibly come in time to make the constitutional provision in question [the contract clause] as prolific of evil as it ever has been, or is likely to be, of good." [57] In 1873 the *Legal Gazette* reported an address by James A. Garfield in which the future president declared that those features of the *Dartmouth College* case that stood in the way of public control of corporations, and particularly of railroad corporations, would have to be changed. In the *American Law Register* for January 1874 Judge Redfield stated more definitely his opinion that state legislatures could regulate railroad rates regardless of charter provisions.[58]

The comments of eastern journals upon the Illinois railway article also belie the agrarianism of the convention. The *Nation* feared that the Supreme Court might deny its applicability to past charters, but its editor was not hostile to the railway article's motives; Charles Francis Adams, Jr., in the *North American Review* asserted that the article was an important step in the right direction; and the *Commercial and Financial Chronicle,* unquestionably the leading Wall Street organ of the day, claimed that the railroad provisions guaranteed to the corporations all their legal rights, while exercising "a judicious care . . . that they may not entrench upon the rights of the people of the State." [59] The railway article of the proposed Illinois constitution was in accord with the trend of American constitutional thought during the 1850s, 1860s, and 1870s, and it is interesting to note that its example was followed by Michigan in 1870 and by Pennsylvania in 1873.

The railroad article, along with several other controversial sections of the new document, was submitted to the people separately for special consideration. Consequently, the question of railroad rate regulation in Illinois became the subject of a popular referendum, and it is possible to determine with a fair degree of accuracy just where support and opposition were located. The article was adopted by a vote of 144,750 to 23,525, which showed a majority of six to one in favor of regulation, but judging by the smallness of the vote, an amazing lack of interest in constitutional reform.[60] The distribution of votes indicates that local interest was still the chief determining factor. The centers of opposition were in the south and west where the demand for more railroads was greatest. The area of most solid support was the northern third of the state, including Chicago, where the antimonopoly movement had always been strongest.[61]

The Chicago vote was overwhelmingly pro-control, being more than twenty to one in favor of the article. Although the city press had cooled considerably toward the issue since 1867, the fear of losing trade as a result of arbitrary rate making had not diminished among the businessmen of the community. The diversion of trade from Chicago was a constant source of editorial comment during 1869, largely because of increased efforts by St. Louis and country shippers to develop the Mississippi as a cheap outlet for grain, but also because of the growing use of through rail shipments to eastern points under the influence of favorable long-distance rates on the fast freight lines. The volume of the grain trade of Chicago in 1869 was a decided disappointment to the board of trade, and this undoubtedly accounted for the activities of its members in behalf of rate control. At the meeting of the National Board of Trade in Richmond, Virginia, during December 1869 and at the so-called farmers' convention at Bloomington, Illinois, during the following April, the Chicago grain interests were leading advocates of government regulation.[62]

The Bloomington convention seems to have been the only mass meeting of consequence which attempted to stimulate a general interest in the railway problem during the time the new constitution was being considered. During 1869 and 1870 there was no groundswell comparable to the antimonopoly revolt of 1865–67. The effort of the Bloomington meeting to organize the farmers in support of internal improvements and restrictive railroad legislation seems to have been a failure. Nevertheless, as an expression of the discontent of leading commercial farmers and grain dealers, the meeting may have had some influence upon the outcome of the referendum. But, generally speaking, there was no need for a highpowered campaign in behalf of the railway article. A good majority of the population, regardless of occupation or party, was convinced that its interests could be served by legislative curbs upon the rate-making policies of the state's railroads.[63] The general assembly, under the new constitution, had received a mandate for further reform of the rate law of Illinois.

In his address to the 1871 assembly, Governor Palmer once again stressed the need for effective control of the state's railroads. He spoke of the failure of competition to regulate rates, evidencing an obvious familiarity with the writings of Charles Francis Adams, Jr. Competition, he explained, was the very cause of existing oppression, and without restraints, could never be counted on to correct unequal treatment. "Deprive railroad corporations of the power to impose discretionary rates upon their traffic, and the business community would suffer far less from the selfish contests of competing lines, that in their effect unsettle values, to the confusion of business and the disappointment of the most prudent calculations." [64]

As in 1869, both houses of the assembly had solid Republican majorities and a heavy preponderance of business and professional men. The railroad committees were presided over by Allen Fuller in the senate and Jesse Hildrup in the house; the Boone County contingent was in full command. In view of the historical reputation of the Granger laws, however, it is well to recognize the existence of a new political factor. To look after the interests of the farming population, a new organization among the members of the assembly appeared during the session of 1871. It was known as the Legislative Farmers' Club and was composed of representatives from both parties in both houses. Strangely enough, the list of subjects with which the club claimed to be most vitally concerned did not include the railroad problem. Apparently, the Legislative Farmers' Club of 1871 was sharply divided on the control issue, and for this reason, assumed a passive attitude toward railroad legislation throughout the session. Although Fuller tried to gain its support, he does not appear to have succeeded.[65]

At the first meeting of the assembly following the adoption of the new constitution, it became apparent that the battle lines had shifted slightly from those of 1869. The have-nots were no longer a political power. The conflict was now between the strong-road and weak-road men, with the former supporting measures of sufficient severity to restrain the established trunk lines and the latter out to safeguard the new, less powerful roads. Fuller, as might be expected, was the leader of the strong-road forces; the champion of the weak-road group was Senator William Underwood, a lawyer from Belleville.

Underwood was aware of the difficulty of regulating all railways by a general law. What might be an excessive rate for one road could easily be unremunerative for another. He warned that hasty or ill-advised legislation of a general sort would ruin the weak roads and most certainly prevent any new construction. Furthermore, the senator was not at all convinced that the assembly had a right to withdraw vested rights, and for what seems to be the first time in an Illinois debate, he suggested that rate regulation would be unconstitutional on the grounds that it deprived the railroad corporations of property without due process of law. All these difficulties could be avoided if the state formed a commission with power to fix rates. Such a board of experts could devise a system of railroad classification that would solve the strong-road–weak-road impasse, and it could also serve as a court for the corporations. This system would prevent the destruction of the smaller companies and would provide the due process of law necessary to safeguard the property rights of the railroads. Both in its spirit and its provisions, the Underwood proposal of 1871 was akin to the Mack bill of 1867.[66]

Fuller countered Underwood's arguments by reminding the senate that the constitution had given the power of rate regulation to the general assembly and not to a board of commissioners. To delegate this power would clearly be an unconstitutional act. Some sort of a commission, he admitted, would be useful in an advisory capacity, but it would not obviate the need for statutory limits on both fares and freights. As far as classification was concerned, he doubted that any satisfactory system could be devised.[67]

To meet the requirements of his own program, Fuller introduced a passenger fare bill restricting rates to three cents per mile; a freight rate measure with a long-and-short-haul clause and a provision forbidding a railroad to charge higher rates in any one month than it had charged during the same month of 1870; and a commission bill that provided for three officials to supervise the railroads and warehouses of the state. The freight rate bill was designed as a stopgap measure pending further study of rate problems by the commission. Its key provision was the long-and-short-haul clause designed to protect way points against local discrimination. Rate limitations were added to prevent the railroads from raising their competitive rates rather than lowering their way rates as a means of complying with the antidiscrimination clause. The commission was empowered to study, investigate, and report, and as its first duty, to pay special attention to the problem of classification. If, in the course of its investigations, the board found any railroad company acting in violation of the laws of the state, it could direct the attorney general and the state's attorneys to institute legal proceedings in the name of the state. In this way the inordinate power of a corporation in a lawsuit initiated by an individual shipper would be largely overcome.[68]

After a prolonged debate the senate rejected the Underwood proposal and adopted Fuller's program in its entirety. As might be expected, the rigid passenger fare bill met vigorous opposition from the weak-road group, but the other two measures passed by overwhelming majorities. The antimonopoly faction, under Fuller's earnest leadership, had finally succeeded in getting its program past the senate without amendment, but it should be pointed out that the railroads themselves had made no effort to block it,[69] and that Fuller, whether he realized it or not, had made important concessions. He had replaced the prorata principle with a long-and-short-haul clause, and he had consented to the appointment of a commission that promised to attempt to resolve the weak-road problem. From the standpoint of substantive law, these were considerable modifications, actual and potential, of his original position.

When Fuller's program was presented to the house, the strong-road–weak-road controversy was renewed with even greater vigor. The weak-road supporters drew added strength from the fact that Jesse Hildrup, though a staunch supporter of the antimonopoly program, did not share Fuller's belief that a system of classification was impractical as a basis of regulation. As a result of correspondence with Charles Francis Adams, Jr., he was inclined to sympathize with the demands of the weak-road interests on this vital point. He agreed that Fuller's passenger fare bill was unnecessarily harsh on new and lightly patronized roads, but he also held that it was too lenient on the trunk lines. The house committee on railroads prepared a separate bill dividing the railroads of the state into four classes, based on earnings, and imposed different maxima upon each class, ranging from $2\frac{1}{2}$ cents per mile to $5\frac{1}{2}$ cents. With almost no debate the Hildrup bill was rushed through the house and sent to the senate, even before house action was taken on any of the Fuller proposals.[70] The house, with its large weak-road faction, had placed itself in a position to bargain.

Fuller's committee proceeded to report the house bill unfavorably, but after a proper show of resistance, was perfectly willing to compromise. A conference committee produced the obvious recommendation that the senate accept the house passenger fare bill in return for the house's concurrence on the senate's freight rate and commission bills. The committee's suggestions were adopted, and without any change, the two acceptable Fuller bills plus the Hildrup maximum fare measure were passed and sent to the governor for his signature.[71] Palmer found no reason to exercise his veto, and the intent of the framers of the new constitution was complied with in every respect.

The Illinois legislation of 1871 made important changes in the railroad rate law of the state. Through a direct exercise of the police power it did for local discriminaton what the law of 1869 had done for personal discrimination. Railroads were compelled to adjust their freight rates in relation to the distance traveled within limits imposed by the schedules in actual operation during 1870. Passenger fares were limited to specified statutory maxima in accordance with a classification table based upon earnings.[72] From the standpoint of principle, a more decisive exercise of the police power would be hard to imagine. Yet the long-and-short-haul clause was merely a slightly modified version of laws already in force in Michigan, Pennsylvania, and Massachusetts, and the rate maxima were clearly in the tradition of statutory restrictions upon the charges of common carriers. The second of the Illinois Granger laws made no real substantive contribution to the theory of American railroad rate law.

The reaction of the state press to the laws of 1871 was decidedly mixed in tone. The *Belvidere Standard,* probably expressing the viewpoint of intermediate collecting points, gave its wholehearted approval. The Chicago press, by contrast, disliked the long-and-short-haul feature. It feared that it would hamper the city's struggle for the trans-Mississippi grain trade. The *Prairie Farmer* paid little attention to the rate problem during the session of 1871 but gave its general approval after the publication of the laws. The *Railroad Gazette,* on the other hand, deplored the bungling efforts of uninformed legislators to deal with a problem about which they knew nothing. Although it did not deny the existence of abuses in rate-making practices, it could not condone the attempt to cure them by legislation. It recommended a Massachusetts-type commission (apparently without the accompanying Massachusetts legislation) as the best method of control.[73]

With respect to its authority over railroads, the new Illinois commission was similar to those employed by other states, but it had the added power of being able to institute legal proceedings against railroads that violated state law. Although no evidence of a direct connection has been found, it seems to have been patterned after the Rhode Island commission established in 1839 to supervise the railroads of that state and to oversee the enforcement of state laws and charters.[74] The Illinois board was empowered to serve as plaintiff in behalf of shippers who would not venture to challenge a railroad corporation on their own, and as such, it was an important innovation in legal procedure.

The general assembly of 1871 also sought to fulfill its constitutional obligations with respect to Chicago grain elevators. A Warehouse Act declared that all elevators in cities of more than 100,000 (Chicago was the only one) were public warehouses. New machinery was established for the inspection and regulation of elevator facilities, maximum storage rates were imposed, and the whole procedure for issuing and redeeming warehouse receipts was prescribed in detail. The Railroad and Warehouse Commission was charged with the enforcement of the law. The act carried out virtually every declared wish of the Chicago Board of Trade.[75]

The testing of the railroad laws of 1871 began almost immediately. In Kankakee County the Illinois Central Railroad was charged with demanding passenger fares in excess of the three cent per mile maximum. In the resulting suit, the circuit court found that maximum rates were in violation of the contract clause and therefore void. The commission made no effort to appeal the decision, but in a similar action involving the Chicago, Burlington, and Quincy Railroad the principle enunciated by the circuit court was reversed. The crucial test of the new legislation, however, came in the so-called *McLean County* case. At the December 1871 term of the circuit court for the eighth judicial district, State's Attorney J. H. Rowell together with special counsel Hamilton

Spencer and Reuben M. Benjamin filed quo warranto proceedings against the Chicago and Alton Railroad Company for violating the act of April 7, 1871.[76]

The Alton was charged with setting a higher rate for the transportation of lumber between Chicago and Lexington, Illinois, than it did for the same service between Chicago and Bloomington, a greater distance. The case was argued in July 1872. The railroad admitted the alleged facts, but claimed that its charter permitted it to ask whatever rates it pleased as long as such rates were reasonable. The charge from Chicago to Lexington was reasonable; that from Chicago to Bloomington was unreasonably low due to competition between the Alton and Illinois Central railroads. The right to reduce rates under such circumstances had never been challenged in a United States court and had always been stoutly upheld in England. Furthermore, the railroad's attorneys argued, the act of April 7, 1871, was void because the reasonableness and justness of rates became a judicial matter once the power to fix rates was granted. The counsel for the Railroad and Warehouse Commission repeated Benjamin's argument on inalienable sovereignty, declaring that a grant of rate-fixing power does not remove a corporation from the operation of the police power. It was also maintained that the *Dartmouth College* decision did not apply to railroad charters that contained grants of political power. A railroad was a public institution and therefore subject to legislative control in spite of its charter. In either case, the long-and-short-haul clause of the act of April 7 was constitutional and applicable to the Chicago and Alton.[77]

Judge Thomas F. Tipton, a former resident of Lexington and more recently an associate of Reuben Benjamin in Bloomington, agreed with counsel for the plaintiff. To say that a corporation created for the public good was beyond legislative control and that it might become destructive of the purpose for which it was created was untenable. It was the duty of the legislature to protect the public against unreasonable and unjust discriminatory rates. In the opinion of the court, the law of 1871 conformed exactly with the provisions of the constitution of 1870. For violation of the act of April 7, Judge Tipton declared all the corporate franchises and privileges of the defendant forfeit.[78]

From the circuit court of the eighth judicial district, the *Mc-Lean County* case went on appeal to the state supreme court. The case was argued in January 1873, and in February an opinion was delivered by Chief Justice Charles B. Lawrence. Lawrence wasted no time discussing the right of the legislature to regulate rates. While admitting that a charter was an inviolable contract, he held that the legislature still had "the clearest right to pass an act for the purpose of preventing unjust discrimination in railway freights whether as between individuals or communities, and to enforce its observance by appropriate penalties." [79] All common carriers were subject to the provisions of the common law regardless of the terms of their charters, and one of the principles of the common law enforceable in the Illinois courts was that there may not be any unjust discriminations as between persons. The court saw no difference between discrimination against indivduals and that against communities. Certainly the competition of another railroad was not an adequate reason for charging a greater rate for a lesser distance. The case in question was an obvious example of unjust treatment against the less-favored community, and the legislature had a perfect right to prevent such practice. An act intended to enforce a common law duty does not impair the obligation of a contract in any way. Up to this point the court, although seeming to uphold the validity of the law, had not chosen to follow either line of reasoning advanced by counsel for the commission. It assumed that the assembly was merely trying to enforce an existing common law obligation, but that was not the case at all. The act of 1871 was a bold assertion of the legislative police power designed to enforce principles of justice as determined by the legislature, not as established by the courts. Chief Justice Lawrence, for the court, took the position that reasonableness was entirely a judicial matter, and that the validity of the law would depend upon its faithfulness to common law principles.

In spite of the court's obvious sympathies with the intent of the legislature, the law was doomed by the court's assumption. Lawrence pointed out that the constitution of 1870 authorized the legislature to prevent only unjust discrimination; the act of 1871 prevented all discriminations against localities, whether just or unjust. Thus the legislature had exceeded its constitutional powers, and the law was void. But the chief justice did not stop there; he was ready and anxious to instruct the General Assembly on the proper fulfillment of its duties. The law of 1871, Lawrence declared, had defects, "but they are susceptible of easy amendment." [80] The fact that a railroad company charged more for the same class of freight over a given distance on another part of the road was not in itself conclusive evidence of unjust discrimination. Conceivably, it might be an act of wise discretion beneficial to the people of the state, and the railroads should be given a chance to defend themselves. The legislature should regard the act of charging more for a lesser distance prima facie, instead of conclusive, evidence of unjust discriminaton. In this way, a jury might determine not only the fact of unequal treatment by a common carrier but the justice of it as well.[81]

The opinion in the *McLean County* case was handed down during the legislative session of 1873. Perhaps the most surprising thing about it was the air of complete calm with which it was received both by the members of the general assembly and by pressure groups working for even more drastic restrictions. There seems to have been no general realization of the damage it inflicted upon the doctrine of inalienable police power which lay at the basis of the constitution of 1870 and the law of 1871. The executive committee of the Illinois State Grange adopted a resolution declaring "that the recent decision of the Supreme Court of the State in the railway case for McLean Co., so-called, seems dictated by patriotism and wisdom, and so far as we understand its reasoning and suggestions, they are accepted with satisfaction and approval." [82] The common reaction seemed to be gratitude toward the court for putting the legislature back on the right track.[83]

The general assembly of 1873 met in the hectic atmosphere created by the farmers' uprising of the winter of 1872–73. The Granger movement first manifested itself on the Illinois prairies in the fall of 1872. In October a meeting of the representatives of various agricultural clubs and granges was held at Kewanee; the following January a much larger convention assembled at Bloomington. From these meetings there emerged the Illinois State Farmers' Association, a frankly political organization with a legislative program. The association favored strict legislative regulation of all corporations, regardless of their charters, and vigorous enforcement of the railway laws of 1871. Under the leadership of men like Willard Flagg, S. M. Smith, and Lorenzo Whiting and with the legal advice of such prominent lawyers as J. H. Rowell and Reuben Benjamin, the association exerted constant pressure upon the assembly of 1873. Further pressure was brought to bear by the many reports of farmers' conventions during the winter of 1872–73 which fill the pages of the *Prairie Farmer* and the *Chicago Tribune*. A study of the officers and speakers at these meetings, however, indicates that merchants and businessmen were frequently among the leaders, and there is no evidence of any distinction between the farmers' demands and those of the commercial interests on the general question of rate-law reform. The differences that did appear during the session of 1873 were concerned with methods, not aims.[84]

The assembly, to be sure, had not been elected on the issue of farmers' rights and was no more a farmers' legislature than its predecessor. According to Willard Flagg, president of the Illinois State Farmers' Association, there were only about eight real farmers in a senate of fifty-one members and forty in a house of 153 members. Flagg characterized it as a conclave of lawyers.[85] Nevertheless, the militant farmers were able to influence the appointment of members to the second Railroad and Warehouse Commission, and through the reorganized Legislative Farmers' Club, were able to bring their demands before the two houses.

It should not be assumed, however, that the cries of organized shippers and merchants were drowned out by the new farmers' movements. In January 1873 the Chicago merchants were complaining bitterly of trains that rumbled through the railroad capital of the West without breaking bulk. By means of their favorable through rates to the seaboard, the fast-freight lines were enabling eastern wholesale houses to undersell the Chicago merchants in Champaign, Decatur, Peoria, and other local distribution points. The commercial interests were still in the thick of the fight, and the principal issue was still discrimination despite the more flamboyant cry of extortion in the rural meetings.[86]

When the *McLean County* decision was announced, the railroad committees of both senate and house turned to the task of framing a measure that would comply with the recommendations of the chief justice. With Fuller no longer present, the senate committee was presided over by Michael Donahue, a Republican lawyer from DeWitt County; Hildrup was again chairman of the committee in the house. In the following weeks, a number of bills representing various shades of opinion were referred to both bodies, and although the picture is somewhat confused, it is possible to separate the "assembly men" from the "commission men." Both groups accepted the idea that the legislation of 1871 must be completely scrapped and replaced by laws based on the new principle of judicial review. With respect to the long-and-short-haul clause, Chief Justice Lawrence had been sufficiently clear, but the question of where and how to peg the rate level of each road in order to protect the competitive points against excessive increases was still to be solved, as was the question of whether the legislature or the commission should make up the table of rates.

There was a strong faction in favor of abolishing the commission entirely. A member of the railroad committee of the Farmers' Legislative Club referred to the board as a fraud and a humbug, easily controlled by the railroads. It was one more barrier between the people and the corporations, and it made effective regulation more difficult. Farmers' conventions, although far from consistent in this matter, tended to support bills that provided for schedules without reference to the board of commissioners. The commission, on the other hand, was the basis of the legislation proposed by the house committee on railroads. Immediately following the decision in the *McLean County* case, Jesse Hildrup introduced a bill empowering the Railroad and Warehouse Commission to fix schedules of maximum rates and fares, which were to be prima facie reasonable in all state courts. According to his own report, Hildrup was concerned about the reaction of eastern capital to the farmers' revolt. The value of western railway stocks was declining, and a new embargo upon risk capital seemed likely unless some authority which the railroads could trust was found. He thought that the commission might be converted into just such an authority, and so he placed in its hands the power of determining prima facie reasonable rates.[87]

For two months the general assembly struggled with the problem of drafting a law acceptable to a majority of both houses, the chief point of contention being section eight of the Hildrup bill which gave rate-fixing powers to the commission. In April the Illinois State Farmers' Association added to the tension by holding a mass meeting in Springfield for the avowed purpose of securing a control law acceptable to the farmers. Although the convention did not endorse any particular bill, the Legislative Farmers' Club opposed the Hildrup measure and the more militant farmers called it a sell-out to the railroads. In the end, however, it was essentially the Hildrup bill, with its provision for a commission, which passed the legislature. The most significant of all the Granger railroad laws was enacted in spite of the efforts of leaders of the farmers' movement to prevent its passage.[88]

The act of May 2, 1873, provided that any railroad corporation charging more than a fair and reasonable rate of toll would be deemed guilty of extortion. If any railroad charged higher rates for a long haul than for a short haul, it would be "deemed and taken against such railroad corporation" as prima facie evidence of unjust discrimination. Similar provisions were added to cover personal discrimination and unequal terminal charges. In addition the act stated that it was not to be deemed a sufficient excuse or justification for any of the above discriminations that the station at which the lower charge was imposed was a point at which there existed competition with another railroad or some other means of transportation. The Railroad and Warehouse Commission was to investigate the enforcement of this provision and prosecute for violations. The commission was also directed to prepare for each railroad operating within the state a schedule of prima facie reasonable maximum rates. The schedules were to be revised as often as required and published whenever changes were made. This particular provision was to go into effect the following January.[89]

The long-and-short-haul provision and its specification with regard to competition came directly from Chief Justice Lawrence's opinion in the *McLean County* case. The section directing the commission to prepare schedules of rates that could be presented as prima facie evidence of reasonableness was an adaptation of the same doctrine to the problem of rate levels. Constitutionally, the act of 1873 indicated legislative approval of the *Dartmouth Col-*

lege decision with regard to the sanctity of charters and acceptance of the related contention that reasonableness in the case of railroad rates was purely a judicial matter. The legislature by an exercise of the police power could not impose maximum rates upon a railroad corporation if its charter protected it against legislative restriction, but it could assist the courts in enforcing the common law notion of reasonableness by providing new rules of evidence and shifting the burden of proof. Procedurally, the act recognized the inability of an individual shipper to challenge successfully in a court of law a giant corporation whose favor he could not afford to lose. It also gave recognition to the inability of the shipper as a plaintiff to prove unjust discrimination or unreasonableness when all the necessary evidence was in the possession of the defendant. The burden of proof was placed upon the corporation. The railroad managers had either to refute the facts of the charge or to establish justification for them on some grounds other than competition. Politically and economically, the law of 1873 recognized the impracticability of legislative regulation for a complex and constantly changing industry such as railroading. To a certain extent it may have reflected the popular reaction against legislative corruption that was receiving widespread attention at the time; it may also have reflected the even broader trend away from excessive legislative power. But even the purest and most carefully limited assembly was not capable, by itself, of supervising and controlling the railroads of a single state; a permanent, expert body was essential.[90]

The so-called strong commission established by the Illinois act of 1873 seems to have had no direct precedent, but commissioners and boards of various types were quite common in the nineteenth century. In many states there were boards of county commissioners who, among their other duties, were frequently empowered to fix tolls on privately operated roads, bridges, and ferries. Numerous public works commissions had supervised, regulated, and operated the internal improvement systems of the 1820s, 1830s, and 1840s, and a third type of commission had been developed to serve the legislatures in an advisory capacity on questions concerning banks, insurance companies, and railroads. But a state board that could fix standards of rates for private companies and actually take legal action to enforce these rates was something new.[91]

The origins of the Illinois commission are suggested by the purpose it was designed to serve. From the beginning of the intensive movement for governmental rate controls in Illinois, moderate reformers had been searching for a system that would be sufficiently flexible to allow for varying traffic conditions, while at the same time permitting the carriers to justify alleged abuses on grounds of economic necessity or advantage to the state. Obviously the legislature was not capable of exercising such flexible control because of its transitory character. Furthermore, the notion that reasonableness was purely a judicial matter had gained widespread support. The moderates saw a possible solution in more positive control by the courts, and to this end, they had suggested different means of bringing allegedly discriminatory or excessive rates to the attention of the courts. The Mack bill of 1867 provided for a board composed of executive officials who might secure changes in existing rate schedules through resort to the state supreme court. The Underwood plan of 1871 envisioned a special tribunal before which corporations as well as the public could state their cases. Others had suggested administrative boards to fix schedules of legal maximum rates as in Europe, but subject to judicial review on appeal by the carriers.[92] What was wanted, in other words, was an expert body authorized to determine standards of reasonableness from the point of view of individual and local interests. The carriers in turn were to be accorded due process of law and protection against arbitrary restrictions that might injure private interests.

Thus the act of 1873 was the embodiment of the conservative principles held by the moderates from the beginning of the movement for reform. The advisory commission of 1871 was transformed into a strong commission with power to fix and alter schedules of reasonable maximum rates. After taking testimony from both shippers and carriers, the board could arrive at a just standard of tolls for each class of railroad. It could then ask the roads to conform to these schedules, and if they refused, compel them to go to court to show cause. The railroads were still free to levy their freight and passenger charges exempt from all legislative interference, but the shipper had obtained a means of securing his right to fair treatment from the carrier through appeal to the commission or to the courts.

The commission of 1873, while distasteful to the more radical antimonopolists, was not particularly obnoxious to the railroads. They had given their consent to a similar principle in the Mack bill, and although they undoubtedly would have preferred no legislation at all, they considered the act of 1873 a great improvement over its predecessors. Consequently, no concerted effort was made to fight its adoption in the legislature and no attempt was made, as in the case of some of the Granger laws, to have it declared unconstitutional by the federal courts.[93]

The Illinois law of 1873 represented an intelligent compromise between the railroads and the commercial interests of the state. The carriers made their point that reasonableness was a judicial question and that a prorata tariff was incompatible with railroad economics, while the shippers gained acceptance of a new definition of unreasonable discrimination and established the principle that fairness in rate making was relative as well as absolute. The public had been compelled to abandon its assault upon the doctrine of vested rights, but the railroads had been forced to recognize an overriding obligation to the general welfare.

five   IOWA:

THE REVOLT OF
THE RIVER TOWNS

It was during the expansive 1850s, when the spirit of promotion was in the ascendancy, that railroad building was begun in Iowa. From the outset the policy of the Iowa legislature was generous to a fault. Construction was encouraged by a favorable program of taxation and local aid, as well as by an open-handed distribution of public lands. Although the Railroad Land Grant Act of 1856 reserved the traditional right of regulation for all roads deriving benefits under the act, and although the state constitution of 1857 provided for the amendment of all corporate charters subsequently granted, there was no attempt to impose statutory regulations upon rates and fares. There was, in fact, overwhelming popular sentiment against such restrictions. The reservation of the right of control over railway franchises was impelled more by a general distrust of corporate power, than by an immediate demand for controls over rates. The reluctance of outside capitalists to invest their money in western enterprises subject to such legislative interference was too well known, and Iowa, because she lacked adequate financial resources of her own, was courting the favor of outside capitalists. The state offered ample guarantees of operational freedom in the form of an insatiable demand for the benefits of railroad transportation.[1]

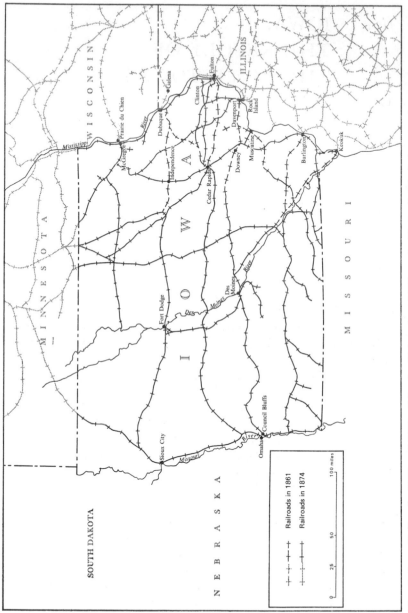

Map 2. Iowa Railroads, 1861 and 1874. (Map by University of Wisconsin Cartographic Laboratory.)

The first Iowa railroads were planned as feeder lines for the towns along the Mississippi River. They were conceived as connecting lines between the river and the interior, and as improved highways over which the grain of the prairies could be brought to the mills and landings at McGregor, Dubuque, Clinton, Davenport, Muscatine, Burlington, Fort Madison, Keokuk, and other ports along the banks of the great north-south waterway. Prior to 1860 the primary market for Iowa grain was St. Louis, and the Iowa river towns served as subsidiary collecting points. They served Iowa as Chicago served Illinois and as Milwaukee served Wisconsin; they were terminal collecting points, wholesale markets, banking centers, and mill towns, and the railroads had promised each one a wide and prosperous future.[2]

But the railroads soon proved a mixed blessing to the river towns of Iowa. Beginning in 1854 Chicago and Milwaukee-based rail lines reached the river at points opposite the Iowa terminals. The Milwaukee, the Illinois Central, the North Western, the Rock Island, and the Burlington railroads all laid their tracks to the river's edge and established running connections with roads on the other side. The impact of this Chicago–Milwaukee invasion upon the commercial life of Iowa was tremendous. The easygoing collection and distribution system established by merchants serving the older river trade was no match for the aggressive, highly competitive organization serving the Great Lakes ports. Ignoring the existing terminals, eastern grain buyers and wholesale merchants moved into the interior, going straight to the rural markets. Lumber for prairie farmhouses began to roll westward from Chicago to interior Iowa communities without using the facilities of the river-town markets. In like manner, grain and hogs were billed through directly to the lakes from local Iowa collecting points. Virtually overnight, the Mississippi ports had become mere way points on trunk lines serving the lake cities. Dubuque, Davenport, and Burlington were forced into direct competition with Chicago for the business of their own state.[3]

The market price of grain at each step in the chain of sale was that offered at the next terminal minus freight charges and the dealer's commission. Dubuque merchants, in other words, paid either St. Louis or Chicago prices less the cost of transportation to these markets; the grain buyers of Waterloo, Iowa, now paid either Dubuque or Chicago prices less the cost of shipment to one of these points. If Dubuque were to compete with Chicago for the grain of Waterloo and realize the profits of a primary grain market, it obviously had to pay a price equal to that offered by Chicago. However, its ability to do so depended in large measure upon the structure of rates on the Illinois Central and its Iowa trunk line.

During the late 1850s Chicago was replacing St. Louis as the principal market for Iowa grain. Under these circumstances the river-port grain buyers and wholesale merchants were bound to have trouble maintaining their position, and their difficulties were compounded after 1858 by railroad ratemaking policy. Freight charges between rural collecting points and the Mississippi, when added to the charges between the river and Chicago, totaled considerably more than the through charges for the same shipment between interior points and the lake. At times the aggregate rate between an interior town and the river exceeded the aggregate rate between the same town and Chicago. An expanding system of preferential long-haul rail rates was depriving the Iowa commercial centers of their former economic importance, and the state was in danger of becoming a mere agricultural province of Chicago.[4]

At the 1860 session of the Iowa General Assembly a number of petitions and resolutions were presented inquiring into the propriety of compelling Iowa railroads to charge the same rate per mile for transportation within the state as they did for passengers and freight destined beyond the state line. The representative from Jefferson County introduced a rate-control measure with additional provisions designed to correct the abuses of absentee ownership; the representative from Des Moines County presented a prorata bill requiring that all rates be fixed in strict accordance with the distance covered; and the mayor and aldermen of Burlington submitted a measure to regulate freight and passenger tariffs in the interest of Iowa commerce. The beginnings of the movement to impose statutory limitations upon Iowa railroads clearly stemmed from the discrimination practiced against local trading interests. However, the reaction of the state assembly to the introduction of the railroad rate problem into Iowa politics was decidedly hostile. The majority felt strongly that it would be "state suicide" to legislate against railroads at that time. Since Iowa was unable to supply sufficient capital to build her own roads, and since no eastern capitalist would invest money in a railroad over which he and his associates could not exercise control, rate restrictions were considered inimical to the best interests of the state. The need of the day was for more railroads. Accordingly, each of the rate-control measures was rejected.[5]

Instead, attention was turned to other means of restoring Iowa's economic independence. Although Iowa shared in the prosperity of the Civil War years, the native commercial interests of the state did not lose sight of their growing dependence upon Chicago and Milwaukee. They worked out a program which included demands for improved water routes to and from the East, thus permitting boats from the Great Lakes to come through to the river ports. When the war ended, this plan was enlarged to include the rejuvenation of the southern market with its promise of trade with the eastern seaboard and Europe by way of New Orleans. Plans were made for the improvement of the Mississippi north of Keokuk where the Des Moines and Rock Island rapids hindered river traffic and added greatly to the cost of water shipment. Enthusiastic support was given to such projects as the improvement of the Illinois and Michigan Canal and the construction of a Wisconsin-Fox River waterway. In fact, any improvement that promised to open direct water routes between Iowa and her eastern markets was sure to win the favor of the river communities.[6]

The plan for establishing a flourishing commerce by natural and artificial waterways, however, presupposed a system of railroad rates which would give favorable treatment to the river towns. Dubuque would still be hard put to compete with Chicago as a primary market if the Illinois Central asked a greater total charge for freight carried between interior points and Dubuque than it did for that shipped over the longer distance to Chicago. Produce would not stop at a river port if it could go at lower cost to a lake port. In order to make the river towns competitive it was necessary to level the rate structures on the various trunk lines leading to the lakes. Because this was a problem involving interstate commerce Iowa was in the vanguard of the campaign for federal regulation of railroad rates,[7] but national control did not seem probable in the near future. A system of state regulation capable of producing the same results was necessary.

It was impossible, of course, to raise the rates between interior towns and Chicago, because Iowa had no control over the Illinois segments of the trunk lines involved. For the same reason, a simple prorata law or a long-and-short-haul measure would have been of no benefit to the river ports. The base rate in either case would have to be an intrastate rate not necessarily affected by the Chicago rate. The only available solution was to lower charges between interior points and the Mississippi by imposing mandatory schedules of fixed maximum rates on all intrastate traffic. Such a program was prepared and presented to the general assembly of 1866.

Governor William Stone's message to the same legislature warned the senators and representatives that the people were still clamoring for more railroads. He claimed to speak for the farmers of the state when he advised the construction of additional competing transportation routes in place of hostile legislation as the best solution to the transportation problem. Nevertheless, the river interests, led by W. T. Barker of Dubuque and Samuel McNutt of Muscatine, put forward a plan for the statutory control of the rate levels of all Iowa railroads. Thomas Wilson of Dubuque sponsored a second reform bill placing the regulatory power in the hands of an independent commission. Wilson hoped to prevent the alienation of eastern capital, but the more radical element was extremely suspicious of halfway measures of this sort.[8]

The first significant vote on the rate question came with the introduction, by the house committee on commerce, of a bill designed to place a legal maximum upon Iowa rail rates and thereby to prevent discrimination against the river towns in favor of Chicago. When Wilson tried to amend the bill to give the rate-fixing authority to a commission, Barker asked if this idea had not originated with a railroad official. Wilson admitted that it had. The upshot of the debate was that Wilson's amendment was decisively defeated and the commerce committee bill was adopted by the house. The representatives of the western counties—the have-nots as far as railroads were concerned—supported the more radical committee bill only because it had even less chance than Wilson's amendment of passing the senate. There was neither surprise nor alarm when the measure died in the files of a senate committee. It is interesting to note that those representatives who had voted for the Wilson amendment voted against the committee bill; the opponents of commission control, on the other hand, proved to be supporters of the statutory maximum. In Iowa, as in all of the Granger states, commission control bore the stigma of railroad support and consequently was not acceptable to the radical proponents of regulation.[9]

During the debates on the railroad bill of 1866, Attorney General F. E. Bissell was asked for an opinion on the constitutionality of legislative rate control. Bissell took the position that railroads were private corporations, and that their charters could not be altered without their consent. Because the general act of incorporation under which all railroad charters had been granted contained no restrictions as to profits or charges and no specific reservations with respect to such matters, the essential franchise of the roads— their right to carry freight and passengers and their right to receive payment for these services—could not be impaired by legislative restrictions. He embellished his opinion with references to the prevailing doctrine of laissez faire. It had been the wise policy of Iowa, said Bissell, to leave the regulation of railroad charges to the laws of trade and competition "which extend over all civilized communities." Legislation, he was convinced, could never regulate such matters effectively. Bissell also attempted to argue against the force of the land grant act under which four of the major lines of the state were operating. He insisted that the provisions of the act which held the four roads "subject to such rules and regulations as may from time to time be enacted" did not refer to rate-making powers but only to the companies' use of the land grants.[10]

Representative Barker of Dubuque attempted to counter Bissell's opinion. He argued that railroad corporations were quasi-public, and that they had always been subject to legislative control. With words roughly prophetic of Reuben Benjamin's doctrine of inalienable sovereignty, he asserted that all grants must be construed strictly in favor of the state. The presumption must always be against the state's disarming itself of its sovereign powers.[11] But the Iowa legislature of 1866 was not basing its decision upon fine points of constitutional law; the debates turned primarily upon the effect of regulation on new construction.

The session of 1866 revealed the pattern of conflicting economic interests that would determine the course of the movement to reform railroad rate law in Iowa. The Mississippi River towns intended to reestablish their positions as terminal markets, and to this end they sought to revitalize the commerce of the river and to prevent rate discrimination against themselves in favor of Chicago. They placed themselves at the head of the postwar antimonopoly revolt. The promise of cheaper water routes to the seaboard combined with lower rail rates to the river made the program of the river towns acceptable to many communities in the interior. Furthermore, the plan appealed to the growing distrust of absentee ownership and the potent spirit of interstate rivalry. Iowa railroads, it was widely proclaimed, should be made to serve Iowa interests and not those of New York or Chicago. But the have-not areas, particularly in the western and northern parts of the state, had sectional interests of their own, and because they lacked transportation facilities, were understandably leary of unfriendly legislation. Side by side with reports of antimonopoly meetings, the Iowa press carried reports of conventions held to stimulate support for new construction. The latter, in fact, were far more numerous. Since the have-nots held a commanding majority in 1866, the postwar revolt against monopoly in Iowa was effectively smothered.[12]

When the general assembly next convened in January 1868 Governor Stone, who was retiring from office, delivered a farewell address full of references to the prosperity of the state. The railroads, he reported, were doing a splendid job of opening vacant areas to settlement and were giving rise to numerous towns and cities. By all means, the legislature should continue to encourage new construction and should avoid measures hostile to railroad development. Stone recognized, of course, that there were abuses in the management of railroads that ought to be prevented. Injudicious and discriminatory tariffs had become a subject of almost universal complaint, and there was undeniably a need for cheaper means of transportation to the eastern seaboard. But in his opinion the solution best calculated to solve both problems was the opening of rival water routes. Remove the obstructions from the Mississippi between Rock Island and Keokuk, and the northwest would no longer be at the mercy of the railroad corporations.[13]

Governor Stone's successor was Samuel Merrill, a Republican merchant and banker from the river town of McGregor. Merrill's ideas on the railroad problem were set forth in a special message to the assembly on January 24, 1868. Assuring his audience that he was fully aware of the dangers of discouraging construction, he recommended the insertion of a clause in every future railway charter that would prohibit discrimination in the arrangement of freight tariffs and passenger fares. It seemed only reasonable to the governor that transportation charges should be made prorata according to distance. He explained in a subsequent message that he was not in favor of absolute legal maxima since these could easily deter new enterprise, but he was in favor of enforcing equal charges—just how he did not say—and of reserving the right to regulate.[14] Merrill's views were vigorously supported by his attorney general, Henry O'Connor. In an opinion upholding the constitutionality of proposed legislation to regulate the rates of railroads already chartered, O'Connor urged the prohibition of rate-making abuses and punishment of the guilty parties. Unjust discrimination that builds up one city and destroys the trade of another, he declared, "shocks the most elementary notions of law. It is wholly inconsistent with the plainest notions of our institutions, and at war with the whole theory of our government." By virtue of the reservation clause in the state constitution, he said, the general assembly had full power to prevent such discrimination.[15]

The general assembly of 1868 considered a number of bills to prevent railways from discriminating "against the trade and commerce of the state." Proposals for investigatory commissions that would examine the nature and scope of discrimination were also discussed. But once again immediate regulation was defeated by the representatives of the western counties. In Iowa the early part of 1868 was "a season of Railroad Conventions" designed to encourage construction, not to restrict rates. The railroad fever of the postwar era was at its peak and would not tolerate legislation hostile to its purpose. The most that could be obtained from the assembly of 1868 was a series of reservation clauses known as the Doud amendments. Inserted in several private acts dealing with the extension and transfer of land grants, they provided that each railroad accepting a land grant would become subject "to such rules, regulations and rates of tariff for the transportation of freight and passengers as may from time to time be enacted and provided for by the General Assembly." Under the leadership of Representatives McNutt of Muscatine and James Wilson of Tama, and of Senators Eliab Doud of Van Buren and B. B. Richards of Dubuque, the amendments were pushed through the general assembly without much difficulty.[16] As measures designed to limit individual trunk lines, each of which had acquired the backing of important eastern interests, the Doud amendments did not have to buck the unified hostility of the have-not areas.

Following the adjournment of the assembly, however, two of the affected roads announced that all construction would cease until the obnoxious amendments were repealed. Indeed, work on the Dubuque and Sioux City Railroad was halted. The people of northwestern Iowa, faced with the loss of their long-awaited connection with the eastern market, were startled into action. The worst fears of the have-nots had suddenly become shocking realities; the irresponsible action of the legislature was driving capital out of the state and blocking the completion of much needed rail facilities. In the weeks following, Governor Merrill was swamped with appeals for an immediate extra session of the legislature. The president of the McGregor and Sioux City Railroad made a similar request on behalf of the stockholders of that road. A broad base of support for the movement could not be denied. But Merrill was in a good position to call the railroads' bluff. In the summer of 1868 five railroad lines based in either Chicago or Milwaukee stretched across Iowa in the direction of the new Union Pacific terminal at Omaha. One of the lines, the Cedar Rapids and Missouri River, operated by the Chicago and North Western, had completed its connection with Council Bluffs, Iowa, opposite Omaha, in 1867. The remaining four, three of them hindered by the Doud Amendments, were racing for the same objective with all possible speed. Was it likely that the uncompleted roads would forfeit all of the Omaha traffic when three of them were nearing their objective and the fourth was the sole representative of the Milwaukee interest? Merrill held his ground under the well-organized onslaught and waited. For all their threats the railroads continued to build, and the movement for repeal melted away.[17]

By 1870 Iowa was well integrated into the national railway net and was more than ever tributary to the Chicago market. The railroads, through their rate-making policies and their political strength in the state assembly, continued to defeat the commercial ambitions of the river towns. By steadily reducing their rates from interior points to Lake Michigan they had virtually neutralized the competitive possibilities of the river, and by playing upon the promotional aims of the have-not areas they had helped to prevent the adoption of active control laws and charter provisions. The rapid development of the railroad system, however, gave rise to other forms of rate inequality as well.[18] Centers served by a single line were beginning to complain of local discrimination. The grain buyers, retail merchants, bankers, lawyers, and other businessmen at the prairie way points were adding their voices to the protests of the river towns. The wave of discontent was moving westward across the state in the wake of railroad construction.[19]

Through vigorous political action and a continuous propaganda campaign, however, the merchants of the river towns, especially those of Dubuque, maintained their position of leadership in the movement for railroad rate restrictions.[20] The general assembly of 1870 was the recipient of scores of petitions demanding regulation of railroad rates and fares. The petitions poured in from every part of the state, but the legislative debates revealed that the bulk of them had been printed by the merchants of Dubuque and distributed along the rights-of-way of the major trunk lines. By January 1870 thousands of signatures had been obtained from the merchants and shippers of the collecting points. In the same month Dubuque further demonstrated her intention of leading the rate-control movement by calling a convention to protest local and terminal rate discrimination.[21]

The 1870 session of the legislature witnessed a determined bid to obtain a maximum-rate law. William Mills, a Dubuque lawyer, introduced a bill which became the focal point of debate in the house. The measure was frankly designed to prevent the diversion of trade from the river to Chicago, and according to the *Iowa City State Press,* was prepared by former Senator B. B. Richards, also of Dubuque. Early in February Richards appeared before the house committee on railroads. He cited examples of discrimination against the river towns and indicated the effect of current rate-making practices upon the commercial and industrial interests of the state. Flour mills along the Mississippi, he claimed, were forced out of business; farmers in the interior were deprived of their natural outlets down the river; grain buyers were compelled to move to Chicago in order to make a living; and the river ports were losing their natural advantage as lumber markets, all because of unequal freight rates. He asked for immediate adoption of the Mills bill as the only means of saving Iowa trade from complete destruction.[22]

The committee then took testimony from representatives of the railroad companies. The railroads took the position that their schedules were prepared in the interests of the farmers, and they pointed to the fact that low through rates to Chicago were the only means whereby the inland farmer could compete in the eastern market. As far as discrimination against trade within the state was concerned, they insisted that long experience had shown these distinctions to be both necessary and just. The differences in rates were simply the result of variations in traffic and costs. The proposed legislation, they concluded, would be extremely burdensome and would probably necessitate the abandonment of through-freight service.[23]

After hearing both sides, a majority of the house committee reported in favor of the Mills bill. A minority, to be sure, thought that such matters should be left to the workings of natural law, and they challenged the expediency of the measure for the usual have-not reason that it might deter capital from coming into Iowa.

But the house adopted the bill by a solid majority of 62 to 28, and with even greater ease, passed companion measures dealing with passenger fares and a supervisory commission similar to that of Connecticut. The senate, however, was less willing to follow the lead of the river interests. Although a number of control measures, including the Mills bill, were vigorously defended by Frank T. Campbell of Jasper County, John P. Irish of Iowa City, Samuel McNutt of Muscatine, Samuel H. Fairall of Iowa City, and M. B. Mulkern of Dubuque, all were doomed to failure. In the course of the debates members from several inland counties became bitter in their denunciation of the selfishness displayed by the river communities. They accused them of deliberately trying to prevent the construction of north-south lines and insisted that there was no popular demand in the interior for control legislation. The petitions, they asserted, meant nothing since they originated, for the most part, from a single source. The people of Iowa wanted railroads; they did not want regulation.[24]

There were other critics of both the house and senate control bills who based their opposition upon the intricacies of the rate problem. Senator Homer Newell, with slight exaggeration, called attention to the fact that every state in the Union from Maine to Iowa had considered the prorata principle and pronounced it unworkable. Senator William Larrabee pointed to the impossibility of fixing a just maximum rate for all the railroads in the state, raising the strong-road–weak-road problem, a continuing factor in the determination of rate-control legislation. This point, in fact, was growing in political consequence. The disparity in earning power among the different roads within the state made the imposition of a single effective maximum rate completely impossible. Obviously a rate that would be fair and just for a strong east-west line would be entirely unremunerative for a new north-south road. And since the river-town interests were concerned primarily with the trunk lines, the stringency of their maximum-rate proposals brought forward a weak-road faction willing to accept anti-discrimination laws, but hostile to rigid statutory limitations that might bankrupt the smaller lines. In 1870 the combined have-not and weak-road interests in the upper house prevailed. By very close margins the house measures were tabled, and a senate rate-control bill, introduced by Dubuque's Senator Mulkern, was defeated on its third reading.[25]

The state election of 1871, in which the railroad issue was not a major concern, produced a Republican landslide and brought to the governorship Cyrus C. Carpenter of Fort Dodge. Carpenter's views on the railroad question were moderate, well informed, and geared to the best interests of the interior collecting points. He did not doubt for a moment the right of the assembly to impose restrictions upon rates, and he recognized competition as the source, rather than the cure, for prevailing ills. Nevertheless, he was not prepared to endorse arbitrary fixed maxima. His own solution was to abolish all discrimination between individuals and localities without reference to the rate level and to open up improved water routes to the seaboard.[26]

Not satisfied with this, the Dubuque legislative delegation returned to Des Moines in 1872 with renewed intentions of securing their maximum rate law. Representative Frederick O'Donnell, acting as spokesman, reintroduced the so-called Dubuque bill which had been sponsored by Mills at the previous session, and proceeded to steer it through the house. An effort to have rate-fixing powers vested in a commission was easily brushed aside; a similar fate awaited a weak-road amendment exempting roads with annual gross earnings of less than $3,000 per mile. But the Dubuque bill did not get through completely unscathed. A group claiming to represent the interior collecting points succeeded in inserting a long-and-short-haul clause that would prevent a railroad from charging more for any short haul than it did for a longer haul on the same line. The chief complaint of the inland counties, they maintained, was discrimination against way points, not excessive rates. O'Donnell and his supporters hastened to assure the house that the original bill would accomplish the same purpose, and he voiced the hope that the chances of obtaining a rate-control measure at this session would not be jeopardized by the inclusion of a measure distasteful to the competitive centers. O'Donnell's fears proved unfounded, for the amended bill passed the house by a vote of 80 to 13.[27]

The Dubuque bill then went to the senate where it once again came under attack from the more moderate exponents of control. Senator John Y. Stone of Mills County proposed an amendment that would provide for a popularly elected commission. According to his plan the legislature would fix rates, but the commissioners would be authorized to modify them from time to time as they saw fit. The friends of the Dubuque measure rallied to the defense of untrammeled statutory control, claiming first that the legislature could not delegate its police powers and second that the remedy demanded by all the petitions presented at that session was fixed uniform rates. Stone countered with an appeal to the have-nots and finally succeeded in gaining his point. The senate concurred in the Dubuque bill as amended by Stone and sent it back to the house.[28]

The house immediately rejected the Stone amendment as a complete emasculation of the original measure. The radicals were convinced that a commission would be little more than an agency of the railroad companies, and they implied that the amendment was dictated by the corporations themselves. In the weeks that followed, three separate efforts were made to find a satisfactory compromise, but the deadlock remained unbroken. Toward the end of April the general assembly adjourned without reaching any agreement whatsoever. Although a large majority of both houses had recognized the need for some form of immediate regulation, the unwillingness of the fixed-maximum-rate group to withdraw from its original position made compromise impossible. Similarly, the have-not and weak-road elements flatly refused to yield.[29]

The general assembly of 1872, however, was to have another chance at solving the problem of railroad rates. In January 1873 it reassembled for the purpose of recodifying the laws of the state, a process that permitted amendments and additions equivalent to new legislation. During the winter of 1872–73, it should be noted, the state of Iowa had been shaken by the first rumblings of the coming farmers' revolt. The Iowa State Grange, more frankly political than its Illinois counterpart, was already a force to be reckoned with. It demonstrated its intention of influencing political opinion by holding a convention at Des Moines during the special session of the assembly. The grangers put forward a comprehensive program of reform. They asked for a government-built, double-track, all-freight railroad to the seaboard; state-owned, narrow-gauge feeder routes in Iowa; an end to railway land grants; and legislative regulation of intrastate rates.[30] But they took no definite stand on the dispute which had prevented the legislature from adopting a rate law at its previous session. It was not until the following year that the grange actually committed itself to a precise program. The session of 1873, meanwhile, seems to have been little affected by the emergence of the militant farmer.

The squabble between the house and senate of the previous year was repeated with only slightly improved results. The lower chamber, led once again by Representative O'Donnell of Dubuque, tried to insert a schedule of maximum rates into the section of the code dealing with internal improvements. The addition of a long-and-short-haul clause, distasteful to competitive centers, was forestalled by an agreement, made in caucus by the advocates of control, to exempt roads whose gross annual earnings did not exceed $4,000 per mile. With the weak-road faction pacified in this manner, the hopes of the radicals soared. But once again the senate proved adamant. McNutt's efforts to place a similar schedule of rates in the senate's version of the internal improvement section were frustrated by a tie vote. He succeeded in inserting a three and one-half cent maximum passenger-fare law, and he added a section protecting the Doud amendments, but these features were the only innovations in the railroad rate law of 1873. Once again the senate rejected the house proposal and refused to allow any changes in its bill.[31]

Because of divisions of opinion among the proponents of rate regulation, the legislature of 1872–73 had accomplished very little in the way of rate-law reform. Generally speaking, the representatives of eastern and southern areas, where strong railroads existed, supported direct legislative control, while members from the unserved and weak-road districts of the west and north held out for the more flexible commission system. However, the more numerous proponents of direct control were divided in turn between the river interests, who were determined to have fixed legal maxima, and the men from way-station areas who were more concerned with obtaining a long-and-short-haul measure. The river towns had succeeded thus far in retaining the initiative, and because of the regional appeal of their program with its insistence that Iowa railroads must serve Iowa interests, plus their promise that maximum charges would level the structure of rail rates in much the same way as would a prorata law, they had won the largest body of supporters. A shift of one vote in the senate of 1873 might have resulted in victory for the Dubuque schedule. But the maximum-rate group had yet to find a satisfactory means of pacifying the have-not and weak-road areas. The fear that rigid schedules would ruin the newer lines, halt construction, and drive capital from the state was sufficiently strong in 1873 to merit the attention of the most rabid advocate of legislative control.

The state elections in the fall of 1873 saw the appearance on Iowa ballots of a new party label. In an effort to capitalize on defections from the Republican ranks during the Grant administration and the current rumblings of rural discontent, a new opposition party known as the Anti-Monopolists was founded on the apparent ruins of the old Democratic party. The new party made notable gains in the general assembly, and although failing to win the governorship, cut deep into Carpenter's 1871 majority. But the railroad question can hardly be considered a decisive factor in the campaign, because since 1870 both Republican and opposition platforms had contained planks endorsing some form of state regulation.[32] Moreover, in the state legislature from 1860 on, party affiliation had not been a factor in the voting on control measures. It would appear that the railroad problem remained fundamentally sectional and did not become a party issue.

Governor Carpenter's message to the new general assembly, together with his second inaugural delivered four days later, included a careful analysis of the railroad problem as of January 1874. He pointed out that railway construction had fallen off sharply in the past two years, destroying the hopes of many that competition from new roads would be an adequate remedy. It was claimed, of course, that the fear of hostile legislation was the cause of the cessation of construction, and no doubt this was partly true, but this, said the Governor, was all the more reason to pass a rate law. A sensible, conservative measure would remove the fears of capitalists and encourage whatever new development was needed. The law should prevent railroads from unjustly discriminating against places and individuals, and it should prevent them from discouraging local trade and manufacturing. Freight should not be deterred from reaping the advantages of water transportation. The most effective form of control, he now thought, would be a maximum-rate law based on a system of classification that would provide a fair return on the actual paid-in capital of each road.[33]

The principle of classification suggested by Carpenter had helped secure the adoption of the Illinois Granger laws of 1871 and 1873. It was now to prove helpful in breaking the deadlock that existed in the Iowa assembly. Although the moderate reformers still pressed for commission control with the new Illinois system as their model, and although a small group continued to work for a simple antidiscrimination law, the great majority of the representatives in the legislature of 1874 were ready to accept the Dubuque formula as soon as it had been modified by a system of classification based on earnings. This was not the measure being advocated by the Iowa State Grange. The farmers' organization favored the more moderate system of regulation adopted by Illinois, and in this stand they had the enthusiastic support of the railroad lobby. Delegations of businessmen, on the other hand, appeared at Des Moines to urge the enactment of a maximum-rate law.[34]

Agreement on the principle of classification settled the differences between the strong-road–weak-road factions, and a report by the Illinois Railroad and Warehouse Commission provided a model upon which to base statutory limits. The chief obstacles of the previous session were thus overcome, and the final statute, adopted on March 19, 1874, was hammered out in the railroad committees of the two houses. In contrast with previous sessions there was relatively little debate on the floor, and no conference committee was necessary to settle the differences between senate and house. The bill's adoption by overwhelming majorities in both houses was almost anticlimactic. The heart of the law of 1874 was a detailed schedule of maximum rates graduated according to distance for all classes of freight. Its authorship was credited to Senator Frank T. Campbell, a Republican merchant and journalist from Jasper County who had been a staunch supporter of the

Dubuque bills. The schedule was based on the table of maximum rates issued by the Illinois Railroad and Warehouse Commission for the year 1874. On the basis of annual earnings, Iowa railroads were divided into three classes and were limited to 90 percent, 105 percent, and 120 percent of the established legal tariff according to their classification. Passenger fares were restricted to three, three and one-half, and four cents per mile, depending on the earning power of the road.[35] The schedule was obviously prepared in the interest of local Iowa commerce, and to a limited extent it seems to have had the desired effect. On some classes of freight it brought about a reduction of rates between interior points and the river amounting to as much as 50 percent. Nevertheless, Peter Dey, an Iowa railroad man, stated that the schedules were "the production of a mind familiar with the cost of railroad service and disposed to act justly." [36] William Larrabee, a member of the senate of 1874 who had voted against fixed rates, concluded that the schedules were both moderate and just.[37]

The Iowa Granger law, like its Illinois predecessors, was designed to protect the commercial interests of the state, but because of special economic and geographical circumstances it imposed fixed maximum rates without reference to discrimination against localities. Although designed to correct the evils of discrimination, it sought its goal indirectly rather than by statutory prohibition. The interests of the river towns, which came to be accepted as the interests of the entire state, could only be served in this way. As a contribution to the substantive law of the state, the act outlawed discrimination against persons in the form of rebates, drawbacks, and preferential rates. The initiative for the enforcement of the law, however, was left in the hands of individual shippers and travelers.

The Iowa law remained in force for a period of four years, but the continuing decline of through rates after 1873 made the schedule of maximum rates obsolete soon after it was prepared. Furthermore, the hoped-for development of water routes to the seaboard—the essential complement of rate restriction according to the original river-town program—had failed to materialize. The course of western trade in 1874 was running irresistibly eastward over rails that extended clear to the Atlantic ports. The percentage of trade stopping at the river remained relatively small.[38] Thus the primary goal of the first proponents of rate restriction was not realized. Beyond this, the Iowa Granger law of 1874 was entirely too rigid and too inadequate with respect to procedural guarantees to prevent discrimination against way points.

The railroads, meanwhile, made every effort to have the law set aside. They tried first to have it declared unconstitutional by the federal courts. Failing this, they applied pressure to the legislatures of 1876 and 1878, and by a well-managed program of propaganda, they were able to revive the old opposition to the principle of legislative control. The fear of alarming capital returned during the depression that followed the panic of 1873 and was used to the advantage of the railroads once again. In the interest of new economic development, the Iowa Granger law was repealed in 1878; it was replaced by a supervisory commission of the Massachusetts type.[39]

six

MINNESOTA: ROCHESTER VERSUS THE WINONA AND ST. PETER RAILROAD

THE DIFFICULTY of balancing promotional and regulatory needs is best illustrated by the experience of Minnesota.
The Granger laws of Minnesota evolved in much the same way
as those of Illinois, the conflict of mercantile interests within the
state was similar to that in Iowa, but the whole was seriously
complicated by Minnesota's tardiness in obtaining adequate railroad
facilities. When the movement for rate law reform began in the
upper Mississippi Valley, Minnesota was still waiting for its first
mile of track. Construction did not get under way until 1862,
and as a result, the state was caught up in the antimonopoly revolt in the midst of her first railway boom. The character and
early demise of rate regulation in the state were conditioned by
this fact.

The beginnings of railroad policy in Minnesota date from the
early 1850s. As the various lines of railroad pushed west from
Lake Michigan toward the Mississippi River, the fever of speculation and promotion spread to the farthest corners of settlement
in the upper valley. The pioneer citizens of the Minnesota Territory dreamt of a far-flung pattern of railroads connecting the
trading post of St. Paul with Duluth, St. Louis, and the valley
of the Red River of the North. They also contemplated feeder

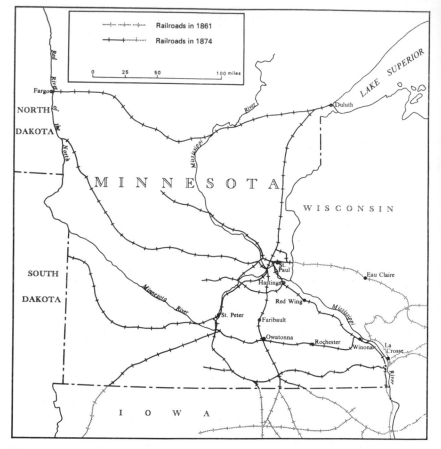

Map 3. Minnesota Railroads, 1874. (Map by University of Wisconsin Cartographic Laboratory.)

lines for the river trade running westward from Red Wing, Winona, and LaCrosse.[1] The territorial legislature granted charters for these projects, and in order to stimulate investment, made generous offers of corporate privilege and public aid.

The territorial charters were patterned after those of Illinois and Wisconsin, and with two exceptions, they gave the directors of the roads full power to establish and collect such rates as they deemed reasonable. Although fourteen of these charters provided for amendment at the discretion of the legislature, it was stipulated in all those granted after 1855 that such amendments were not to destroy any vested rights. In a great majority of cases, the legislature bargained away its police power over rates in order to obtain the necessary risk capital for the construction and operation of a railroad system.[2]

In addition to a free and liberal charter policy, the territorial assembly also inaugurated a program of land grants, loans, and exemptions from taxation. With the aid of these lavish inducements, preliminary construction was actually begun on four roads in 1857, but the panic of that same year put a quick end to these premature efforts. Eastern capital would not move, and without its support the western enterprises were virtually helpless. Despite her gallant efforts, Minnesota embarked upon statehood in 1857 without a single mile of railroad and with very poor prospects of obtaining any in the immediate future.[3]

The economic problems faced by a frontier commonwealth in the 1850s were revealed in the debates of the two conventions called to draw up a constitution for the new state.[4] Typically, the early settlers of Minnesota were prospectors and speculators bent upon reaping the benefits of discovery, development, and social and economic growth in a new territory.[5] Consequently, it was important to have a constitution that would attract outside capital. It is not surprising that the delegates to the two conventions spent many hours discussing the requirements of a basic law of incorporation.

By 1857 the principle of the general act of incorporation was well established, and it was also considered prudent to provide for the alteration and repeal of all corporate charters. But, as already indicated, both general acts of incorporation and reservation clauses were thought by many to be repugnant to capitalists seeking long-term investments in western enterprise. The necessity of protecting the people against associations of wealth and power had to be weighed against the need for internal improvements.[6]

On these matters, the two conventions proved to be in substantial agreement. The new constitution provided for general acts of incorporation, but made no stipulation with regard to the altering or repealing of charters. A special section on railroads declared that "all corporations being common carriers" receiving the benefits of the power of eminent domain, "shall be bound to carry the mineral, agricultural and other productions or manufacturers on equal and reasonable terms."[7] The meaning of this last provision is not very precise, but evidently the framers of the Minnesota Constitution were attempting to reinforce the traditional common law concept of fair and equal treatment as between persons. A distrust among the delegates of corporate power and privilege was very apparent. The other constitutional provisions bearing on railroad policy show a continuing reaction against the public works failures of the 1830s and 1840s, and generally speaking, are typical of the period. They prohibited the state from going into debt for public improvements or from being a party to such improvements except as trustee where land grants or other grants had been made. The credit of the state was not to be given or loaned to any association or corporation.[8] Minnesota was to foster corporate development through grants of land and special immunities, but it was not to become involved in the financing or administration of these undertakings.

In compliance with these constitutional provisions, the first state legislature of Minnesota enacted a general law of incorporation for railways. The act of 1858 was copied almost verbatim from the Ohio law of 1852 and contained the usual limitations with respect to rate levels. Passenger fares were restricted to 3 cents per mile and freight rates to 5 cents per ton per mile for all distances over thirty miles. For distances under thirty miles the companies could charge such reasonable rates as their directors saw fit to impose or as were prescribed by future legislation. Despite the desire of the pioneer settlers to encourage railway development, they did not consider it necessary to abandon all the traditional safeguards. The maximum freight rate imposed by the act was high by eastern standards, and it was well above the average that most western roads were charging at that time. Nevertheless, it proved to be lower than what the traffic would bear on some Minnesota roads.[9] The law of 1858 was not designed purely as an inducement for the railroads.

In spite of the constitutional and legislative restrictions imposed by the legislature, capitalists were not entirely barred from obtaining privileged corporate franchises in Minnesota. Following the panic of 1857 the four land-grant roads formed during the territorial period were acquired by the state through foreclosure and purchase. In a desperate effort to stimulate construction, the state proceeded to sell these charters in 1861 and 1862 to newly organized companies, or in one case out of four, back to the original owners. No effort was made to bring the charters within the terms of the law of 1858. The land-grant provisions were not only retained, but were greatly enlarged in order to assure completion of the lines. Furthermore, a number of special charters were granted by the legislature in defiance of the constitution in order to satisfy the demands of other railroad interests. In the final analysis, the early experience of Minnesota was similar to that of Illinois.[10]

Encouraged by special favors and grants in aid, the railroad system of Minnesota began to expand. Local subscriptions were added to state benefits, and by 1873, a respectable 1,950 miles of road were in operation. As the network spread, new settlers poured into the state turning their hands to the growing and marketing of wheat for the eastern market. For several years the lines of trade ran by rail to one of the river ports, then down the river to the rail heads at La Crosse, Prairie du Chien, Dunlieth, and Fulton, and across Wisconsin or Illinois by rail to Milwaukee or Chicago. In 1867, however, through rail connections were established with Chicago by way of the McGregor Western Railroad of Iowa, and in 1871 a bridge at La Crosse united the Southern Minnesota with the Milwaukee and St. Paul. By 1874 the railroads of Minnesota were tightly linked with systems radiating from Milwaukee and Chicago, and the transfer from rail to river and river to rail was a thing of the past. Meanwhile, an additional outlet to the East had been provided by way of Duluth. With the advantages of cheap overland transportation, Minnesota wheat was selling in England at prices below that at which most British farmers could produce it.[11]

But the blessings of Minnesota's cheap transportation were partially obscured by the concurrent rise of antimonopoly sentiment in the West. As early as March 1864 the businessmen of western Wisconsin and southeastern Minnesota gathered at Red Wing to protest wartime rate schedules on the combined rail and water routes to the lakes. In 1865 the St. Paul Board of Trade sought to gain the cooperation of the collecting points on the Minnesota and Mississippi rivers in an effort to have rail rates reduced, but they failed because of the mutual distrust and jealousy of the river towns.[12] In January and February 1866, however, an audible cry of protest came from the commercial centers of the state.

In January the merchants of St. Paul in company with members of the state legislature decided to call a convention of the people of the upper Mississippi Valley. The purpose of the meeting was to protest abuses existing in the grain trade and to form a league of merchants, shippers, and farmers interested in securing more favorable transportation rates for the shipment of their produce. In February 1866 several hundred delegates convened in St. Paul. Although the farming interests of the state were actively involved in the convention, the organization and leadership of the meeting remained in the hands of the merchants and businessmen of the principal river towns. It was primarily a commercial convention, not a meeting interested in the problem of rate discrimination. To this extent it differed from the antimonopoly gatherings of Illinois and Iowa where unequal rates were likely to be discussed in conjunction with the need for cheap transportation. Minnesota in 1866 had yet to acquire a highly competitive railroad system. Her problem was not the existence of local and personal discrimination, but rather rail and water rate levels that failed to decline along with postwar grain prices. The resolutions adopted by the convention called for improvement of the Mississippi River, revival of the river route to New Orleans, construction of a railroad from the Mississippi to Lake Superior, formation of a cooperative steamboat line on the upper river, and regulation of railway rates in Wisconsin.[13] There is no indication of a prorata movement in Minnesota politics much before 1870.[14]

Regardless of the aims of the antimonopoly revolt in Minnesota, however, the principle of legislative control received a setback during the 1867 meeting of the legislature. At that session the Southern Minnesota Railroad was given a grant of land subject to the provision that the assembly might fix and regulate the rates for freight and passengers on all the company's lines. The bill was duly passed in this form, but its constitutionality was questioned, and an opinion was requested from the state's attorney general. The opinion was given too late to affect the vote on the original grant, but not too late to prevent its amendment by the same legislature.[15]

Attorney General Colville took the position that all railroad corporations, regardless of constitutional provisions, were bound to carry goods and passengers at equal and reasonable rates. Failure to do so would amount to a violation of the franchise and would render the charter liable to recall by the legislature. But whereas the legislature might punish the grantee for misuse of the franchise, it could not interfere with the management of the road. The reasonableness of rates was a matter for judicial consideration only, unless the company's charter compelled it to submit to legislative control.[16] The effect of Colville's opinion was strong enough to tip the balance of legislative opinion away from further reservation clauses, and it resulted in the immediate repeal of that portion of the Southern Minnesota's land grant that provided for future rate restrictions.

The antimonopoly revolt, however, had left its mark upon the basic railroad law of the state, and it had prevented the wholesale abdication of legislative authority during the early promotion period. Charters and charter amendments granted between 1865 and 1867 were apt to include stipulations with regard to the reasonableness of rates and even reservations of the right of legislative control. As in Iowa, the state was able to use land grants and local subscriptions as inducements for private investment. Although grants of immunity from legislative control were resorted to in some cases, the practice was not universal. Renewed demands for reform found the state legislature in control of part, if not all, of Minnesota's railway system.

During the remainder of the 1860s, the railroads of the state were allowed a period of relative quiet and security. A steady reduction of freight rates accompanied by the return of prosperity, the rapid construction of supposedly competing lines, and the demand for still more of them all contributed to this period of calm. The only evidence of dissatisfaction with railroad rates between 1867 and 1870 was a scattering of petitions asking for legislation to reduce the level of rates and to prevent consolidation and the introduction of two unsuccessful bills providing for the appointment of a supervisory commission.[17]

During this same period, however, a highly competitive network of railroads was being built. In the southeastern corner of the state, the Southern Minnesota, the Winona and St. Peter, and the Hastings and Dakota were running parallel lines westward from their terminals on the Mississippi River. Farther to the north, the St. Paul and Pacific Railroad was building across the central part of the state toward the Red River Valley. Cutting across these east-west roads was the Minnesota Central and the St. Paul and Sioux City, and to the north, the Lake Superior and Mississippi had all but finished the important rail connection between the river and Duluth. At the same time a number of consolidations and agreements brought the competitive lines of the southeast under the control of Milwaukee and Chicago railroad interests. In 1867 the Winona and St. Peter was acquired by the Chicago and North Western, and shortly thereafter the remaining southern lines were partially consolidated with the Milwaukee and St. Paul. A greatly intensified contest for the trade of Minnesota between the great rival collecting points of the West was inaugurated with its customary effect upon the rate structures of the various roads. The period of quiet soon came to an end.[18]

In January 1870 the Minnesota lumber interests issued a complaint against rate discrimination in favor of the Chicago dealers, and Governor Austin spoke of rebates and drawbacks that made competition among wheat buyers, lumber dealers, and businessmen all but impossible. In the state assembly, Representative Cool of Winona County referred to the frequent and urgent complaints of railroad rate discrimination, and he asked that the railroad committee draw up a bill if it found that such complaints were well founded. Both the governor and the senate judiciary committee advised the appointment of a commission to make further studies of the problem, and the senate willingly complied with their suggestion. The house, however, did not see the need for a commission, and it let the bill die in committee. The senate, meanwhile, refused to consider a more positive rate-control measure introduced by J. A. Leonard of Rochester. The legislature of 1870 adjourned without having taken any definite steps toward a solution of its new railway problem.[19]

During the summer of 1870 the counties of southeastern Minnesota broke forth in bitter revolt against the arbitrary rate policies of the railroads in that area. The Republican party of the First Congressional District condemned the consolidation of parallel roads and protested the extortionate rates charged by the companies at noncompetitive points. Between endorsements of General Grant and resolutions in favor of a lower tariff, the party demanded that the railroads be restrained by state and federal authority from disrupting the commerce and industry of the country by the arbitrary and unequal arrangement of rates. In Olmstead County, the center of agitation, the Democrats likewise condemned the railroads for oppressing the farmers, merchants, and tradesmen of the state.[20] In September 1870 a nonpartisan indignation meeting was called at Rochester, Minnesota, to protest the abuses practiced by the Winona and St. Peter, and subsequent action stemming directly from this gathering led to the enactment of the first Minnesota Granger law. The role of Rochester in leading the movement for rate-law reform provides an interesting case study in the organization of antimonopoly sentiment.

Almost from the beginning, the grain trade of Minnesota had been handled by specialized dealers acting as agents for larger buyers in the primary markets, mills, railroads, or packet lines. In an important collecting point such as Rochester there were many of these dealers representing the interests of various companies and various cities. They banded together, for their own interest and for that of the community, into a board of trade which policed the market and served as an information center for its members. Although the Rochester market was unquestionably competitive, the merchants of the town had definite common interests and were not above trying to stabilize and control the prices of their principal commodities.[21]

The sole railroad serving Rochester was the Winona and St. Peter, owned since 1867 by the Chicago and North Western. The policy of the road, as might be expected, was to originate as much traffic as possible at Rochester and to encourage shipment from that point over the longest possible part of its line. This meant keeping its rates low enough to prevent the diversion of farm products to the Southern Minnesota, the Minnesota Central, or the river collecting point of Red Wing. But the company also kept its rates high enough to realize the greatest possible benefit from its monopoly of business. The principal problem at Rochester, according to testimony taken in 1871, was to prevent the loss of traffic to the Southern Minnesota.[22]

In the summer of 1870 the Winona and St. Peter put its own grain buyers in Rochester. According to the company's testimony, the resident merchants had combined to keep the local price of grain down and had forced farmers to take their grain to collecting points on the Southern Minnesota. To prevent further loss of business, the railroad made an agreement with a grain company whereby preferential rates would be given if the company would guarantee to pay all farmers full Milwaukee prices less transportation charges. In order to make possible a remunerative preferential rate, the road raised its common tariff for the shipment of wheat to Winona by 4 cents per bushel. The Rochester merchants, supported by the local press, accused the railroad of trying to drive all the regular buyers from the market. They insisted that the real reason behind the granting of preferential rates was to get the business of privileged buyers at competitive points and to encourage through billing to Chicago instead of Milwaukee. They hoped that such unfair tactics would not fool the Olmstead County farmers who would always get a better price in a truly competitive market. The explanations offered by either side were plausible and, of course, were not mutually exclusive. The fact that the

Southern Minnesota would soon complain of loss of traffic to the Winona and St. Peter and would adopt the very same tactics as a means of restoring its position gives credence to the railroad's claims.[23]

Personal discrimination, however, was not the only complaint of the Rochester merchants. As a way point on a competitive railroad, Rochester was the victim of local discrimination as well. The first report of the Minnesota railroad commissioner shows that during 1871 the average rate for wheat on the Winona and St. Peter was 3.8 cents per ton per mile. The average charge for this service at the town of Owatonna, where competition from another railroad existed, was 2.6 cents, while at Rochester it was a full 6 cents. Such evidence does not necessarily indicate unfair discrimination, but if we assume that all the traffic considered in computing the averages was carried between the two points mentioned and Winona, then Rochester was paying more to get its wheat to the river than its rival collecting point some forty miles farther west. That such was actually the case is indicated by testimony taken in a legislative investigation in 1871.[24]

The Rochester merchants had no doubts as to the injustice of the treatment accorded them by the Winona and St. Peter. In September 1870 they called the first of three conventions held to consider a line of political action to meet the emergency. The first meeting was attended by local businessmen and is significant only for its resolution to press for legislative reform of railroad-rate law. The second held in December 1870 included delegates from all of southeastern Minnesota and proved to be an effective sounding board for the growing feeling of discontent. Although the largest number of delegates came from Olmstead County, the entire district was well represented. Many of the future leaders of the legislative movement to impose rate restrictions, including Amos Coggswell and Ignatius Donnelly, were on hand to express their views and those of their respective communities. The sentiment of the convention, to be sure, was not entirely one sided. There were some who spoke of rival transportation routes as the only sure means of obtaining relief, but for the most part, the delegates were convinced of the need for immediate legislative action. Accordingly, a number of steps were taken to impress the next legislature with the urgency of the railroad problem. A memorial outlining grievances and stating demands was prepared and distributed throughout the district for signatures, a permanent committee of Rochester citizens was appointed to keep the issue before the public, and a lobby composed of representatives from the First Congressional District was appointed to press the matter before the legislature itself. The delegates also decided, at the suggestion of Dr. William Mayo of Rochester, to hold a mass meeting in St. Paul during the coming legislative session.[25]

The demands of the second convention as outlined in its memorial included a law that would compel the railroads to carry freight and passengers at fair, equitable, and reasonable rates. The delegates wanted a measure outlawing perferential rates, drawbacks, and rebates and another law preventing the railroad companies from owning and operating their own elevators and from purchasing grain for speculation. State Representative R. A. Jones of Rochester promised to work for suitable regulatory measures when the legislature convened the following month.[26]

The third convention growing out of the Rochester movement assembled in St. Paul during the first week of January 1871. Unfortunately for the cause, Dr. Mayo's high hopes for a mass meeting failed to materialize. On the first day of the convention the turnout was so small that Ignatius Donnelly refused to speak, and the meeting had to be postponed. On the following day, however, a "crowd of 150," according to the unsympathetic *St. Paul Press,* assembled and carried through the work of the convention.[27] A committee of St. Paul merchants and lawyers was designated to frame a bill for the regulation of railroad rates and the correction of abuses in railway management, and an executive committee was appointed to direct activities following adjournment.[28] As a display of popular feeling, the meeting was unquestionably a failure; as a gathering of important commercial interests capable of exerting pressure on the legislature, it probably achieved results far beyond the weight of its numbers.

Other influences as well were brought to bear on the legislature of 1871. Governor Horace Austin, a Republican backed by solid Republican majorities in both houses, was a strong supporter of rate-law reform. His annual address of 1871 demonstrated a thorough understanding of the railroad problem and a close familiarity with the debates and proceedings of the Illinois Constitutional Convention of the previous year. In the course of his address, he counseled moderation so as not to discourage new construction, but he suggested a program of action taken almost word for word from article 12 of the Illinois Constitution. He warned that some communities in the state were outraged almost to the point of violence as the result of the railroads' discriminatory practices. Some measure of control would have to be adopted.[29]

The legislature of 1871 set up a joint committee to investigate the railroad problem. The committee did not have time to make a thorough study, and in some respects the report is a disappointment, but it provided the legislature with a clear understanding of the type of grievance that had produced the cry for reform. The recommendations of the committee called for the appointment of a commissioner of railroads and for the passage of a law regulating all freight and passenger tariffs. The recommendation for the appointment of a commissioner was carried out by the legislature with little debate. By an act of March 4, 1871, the office of railroad commissioner was established. As in the case of the Illinois board created in the same year, the commissioner's duties were largely investigatory, and apparently were copied from the Vermont law of 1855. The possibility of obtaining a rate-control law looked less promising. The halls of the legislature were filled with lobbyists representing the railroad interests, who in order to promote further construction, were making an effort to secure additional land grants for new roads. The chances of obtaining a severely restrictive measure seemed rather remote.[30]

Of the several control bills referred to the railroad committees, the one receiving most careful consideration was the Jones bill, introduced by the representative from Rochester and probably prepared with the aid of the committee of St. Paul lawyers and merchants. It was a maximum-rate measure including a detailed classification of freights and a schedule of fixed tariffs graduated according to distance. The schedules were arranged so as to give special protection to persons shipping over short distances. The bill also guarded against preferential rates and rebates by stipulating that any rate charged below the legal maximum would have to be offered as the common rate for all like services at the same station.[31]

In the lower house the Jones bill received the endorsement of the judiciary committee which reported, on the basis of the principle of inalienable sovereignty, that charter rights would not impede the legislature's efforts to control rates. The committee on railroads then advised adoption in slightly amended form, and with very little debate, the house adopted the measure by the surprising vote of 43 to 4. The senate proved equally agreeable. After making one minor change to which the house consented by a unanimous vote, the senate gave its approval by a convincing majority of 18 to 4.[32] With comparative ease, an arbitrary exercise of the legislative police power received the endorsement of a legislature in which the railway interests were strong enough to push through a notoriously bad land grab.

A possible explanation of the large favorable majorities in both houses is the reasonable level of rates fixed by the bill. Passenger fares were limited to 5 cents per mile instead of the customary 3 cents. The freight-rate maxima were correspondingly generous, being 5 cents per ton per mile, for example, on all kinds of grain transported from twenty to fifty miles, which included the distance from Rochester to Winona. There is, indeed, some evidence that railroad officials had a hand in preparing the schedules.[33] Furthermore, the law did not attempt to impose prorata or even long-and-short-haul restrictions on the companies' rate-making powers. It was not a particularly stringent measure. There is also the possibility that the railway corporations were convinced of the unconstitutionality of the measure and consequently made no effort to stir up the resistance of the have-nots. The fact that they were interested in the so-called land grab would explain their reluctance to arouse the hostility of the haves. In any event, the railroads did not attempt to block the adoption of the first Minnesota Granger law.

The origins of the act of 1871 can be traced in good part to the reaction of the mercantile community of Rochester to the discriminations practiced against it by the Winona and St. Peter Railroad. In the movement to correct these alleged abuses the Rochester merchants gained the support of towns with similar grievances and of the producing population whose fortunes were tied to the less favored collecting points. Because of the relevancy of railroad rate-making practices to every aspect of the local economy, the unequal practices of the various corporations aroused the ire of all classes and all parties. The effective centers of protest, however, were the collecting points where the results of discrimination were most immediately apparent.[34]

Between 1871 and 1874 there was little agitation for further legislation on railroad rates in Minnesota. The legislature returned to its earlier policy of inserting reservation clauses in all new charters and charter amendments, but no significant movement to pass additional general controls developed. The law of 1871, to be sure, was subjected to a certain amount of well-deserved criticism. The new railroad commissioner, with the support of Governor Austin, suggested that certain changes be made in order to make the law more flexible and more directly applicable to the principle abuse of discrimination. Among his suggestions were a long-and-short-haul measure patterned after that of Massachusetts and authority for the commissioner to prosecute violations of the law as had been provided for in the Illinois act of 1871. In the legislature of 1872 an unsuccessful attempt was made to secure adoption of a long-and-short-haul law, and some effort was made to secure amendments to the existing law in 1873. But by and large, the period from 1871 to 1874 was one of reserved judgments.[35]

For one thing, the people of Minnesota were waiting for the outcome of two lawsuits involving the constitutionality of the act of 1871. Shortly after the law went into effect, the Rochester firm of John D. Blake and Company brought action against the Winona and St. Peter for refusal to deliver certain goods upon the tender of legal rates as prescribed by the law of 1871. The district court of Olmstead County decided against Blake and Company, declaring that the legislature had no power to fix maximum rates. The case was immediately taken on appeal to the state supreme court. At about the same time, the state took action against the Winona and St. Peter for collecting rates in excess of the legal limit and for demanding unreasonable and extortionate charges. The railroad demurred on the first count, holding that the act of 1871 was unconstitutional; the second charge was denied. As in the Blake case, the district court declared in favor of the railroad company and the fight was carried to the state supreme court. The court heard both cases concurrently during the October term of 1872.[36]

In the case of *Blake v. Winona & St. Peter Railroad,* state's attorney W. P. Clough took the position that the right to demand tolls on a public highway was an extraordinary power partaking of the quality of sovereignty, and that it could not pass by implication to a corporate franchise. Since the charter of the Winona and St. Peter did not specifically grant the company the authority to collect whatever tolls it might choose to establish, the state was not barred from placing reasonable limits upon the company's rates through subsequent legislative enactment. Counsel for the railroad rested its reply upon the sanctity of the corporate franchise and the implied power to collect such tolls as the company saw fit to impose. It also maintained that reasonableness was purely a judicial question, and that consequently, the act of 1871 was an unconstitutional exercise of legislative power. In the case of the state against the railroad, identical arguments were presented, but counsel for the people added Reuben Benjamin's doctrine of inalienable police power.[37] Decisions in each of the cases were filed in the last week of May 1873. The opinion of the court in *Blake v. Winona & St. Peter Railroad* proved to be the controlling one and was rendered in favor of the appellant. The court denied that there had been any usurpation of judicial power and recognized the right of the legislature to regulate tolls in the absence of a specific grant of immunity. The charter of the Winona and St. Peter contained no such grant. The right of legislative control, said the court, was "one of those plain and simple propositions . . . upon which, because it is so indisputably true, there can be no accumulation of authorities." [38]

The long-awaited review of the law of 1871 settled the question of legislative authority with respect to all Minnesota railroads whose charters did not contain specific grants of immunity. The way was cleared for additional legislation whenever the demand should arise. But there was a second reason for the relative calm between 1871 and 1874. During these years a vigorous rate war was being waged between the Chicago and Milwaukee lines on the one hand and the newly completed Lake Superior and Mississippi line on the other. Duluth was now in a position to challenge the dominance of the Lake Michigan ports. As a general rule, rate wars contributed to local and personal discrimination, but because of the relatively decentralized marketing system of Minnesota and because the various railroads were fighting for traffic at the initial collecting points and not at the major terminals, the result of the Minnesota war was to give extremely favorable rates to large numbers of towns that might otherwise have suffered. The first report of the Minnesota railroad commissioner, covering the year 1871, remarked upon the great reduction in the price of transportation during that twelve-month period. It was during that summer that the Milwaukee and St. Paul reduced its rates in such a way as to make every station on its road as "close" to Chicago as to Duluth.[39]

The rate war continued for two years, creating unusual prosperity for large segments of the population, and despite the fact that intrastate trade was brought to a virtual standstill because of the greater attraction of the lake markets, the commercial interests of the state remained relatively content. In the fall of 1873, however, a truce was arranged between the warring parties. The Duluth road, now leased to the Northern Pacific, had been forced to reorganize and was in such a condition as to make continuation of the war unprofitable for the Lake Michigan roads. Normal competitive conditions returned to plague shippers, merchants, and producers at unfavored intermediate points. The law of 1871 proved unable to meet the challenge.[40]

During the state elections held in the fall of 1873, the railroad problem stood high on the list of campaign issues. As in Iowa, a new Anti-Monopoly party organized by a coalition of Democrats and dissident Republicans appeared on the ballot as a catch-all opposition party. It made the regulation of railroad rates one of the fundamental planks of its platform, and through the active campaigning of such men as Ignatius Donnelly, sought to capitalize on the growing discontent among the farming population. The

Republicans, in reply to this new challenge, pointed to their achievements embodied in the act of 1871 and promised additional reforms in railroad rate law. On the railroad question there was no real distinction between the promises of the two parties. In an unusually large vote for an off year election the Republican ticket scored a clear-cut victory.[41]

As a result of the campaign, the legislature of 1874 was committed to a general revision of the law of 1871. To aid them in their work, the legislators now had the able reports of A. J. Edgerton, state commissioner of railroads. In his annual report for 1873, the commissioner reviewed the weaknesses of the law of 1871 in the light of its three-year existence and the recent litigation concerning its constitutionality. The *Blake* case, he pointed out, had been decided by the state supreme court on the grounds that the charter of the Winona and St. Peter did not specifically authorize the company to collect whatever tolls it might see fit to impose. The legislature had a right to place reasonable limits upon the rate-making powers of the Winona road because that right had not been bargained away in the form of a charter contract. There were other Minnesota railroads, however, that did possess privileged franchises with respect to rates, and they were not subject to the act of 1871 or to any form of statutory control. To guard against these privileged companies, Edgerton suggested that the legislature supplement the existing law with the Illinois system of judicial control. The weaknesses of the act of 1871, according to Edgerton, were its failure to deal effectively with the problem of local discrimination, its reliance upon individual shippers for enforcement, and its inability to affect interstate rates. The first two problems could be solved by state legislation similar to that in force in Illinois; the third would require federal controls.[42] Minnesota, like Iowa, was much concerned with the regulation of interstate commerce because of her dependence upon Wisconsin and Illinois railroads to reach some of her principal markets.

The report of the commissioner was augmented by the valedictory address of Governor Austin in 1874. The law of 1871, he maintained, was "too arbitrary and unelastic" to provide an adequate system of control. It was too hard on the weak roads, too lenient on the strong, and took no account of varying conditions on individual lines. The departing governor was strongly in favor of adopting the Illinois commission system with its flexible schedules of prima facie reasonable rates for each road.[43]

A different approach to the problem was suggested by Austin's successor. The new governor was Cushman K. Davis, a young Republican lawyer from St. Paul with firm convictions on the subject of vested corporate rights. Although he accepted the sanctity of charter contracts as laid down by the *Dartmouth College* decision, he was in favor of taking vigorous steps to recapture the right of legislative control over all corporate franchises. This he proposed to do through constitutional amendment, by the inclusion of reservation clauses in all amendments to existing charters, and where necessary, through the use of the power of eminent domain. His solution to the railroad problem was to make all roads subject to the legislative police power and to exercise this power with suitable force. As a result of his well-known views on corporation control, Davis gained a wide following among the antimonopolists of the state, and for a while, had considered joining the new opposition party. His decision to remain within the Republican ranks may have accounted for the small number of independent voters who joined the new party.[44]

The 1874 legislature divided into two camps: the rate fixers, who followed the lead of Governor Davis, and the advocates of judicial control, who favored the more moderate course proposed by Austin. Despite the apparent concern with extortionate charges and cheap transportation, the leaders of both factions were agreed that discrimination was still the principal abuse.[45] Evidence of this fact was present in Commissioner Edgerton's report for 1873 which told of complaints of local discrimination by the lumber dealers, merchants, and millers of Faribault against the Milwaukee and St. Paul. In January 1874 the St. Paul Chamber of Commerce reported in favor of rate regulation on behalf of the commercial centers of the northwest and affirmed that unless something was done to prevent terminal discrimination, they would become "mere drivelling tributaries to the ruling cities of Lake Michigan." [46] With the completion of new lines across Wisconsin and the construction of new bridges across the Mississippi, the river towns of Minnesota were beginning to share the fate of their Iowa neighbors. Shortly thereafter the senate investigated personal discrimination along the Southern Minnesota Railroad and found conditions identical with those existing on the Winona and St. Peter in 1871. Each of the forms of discrimination hitherto mentioned contributed to the demand for more effective rate regulation in Minnesota.[47]

Hostility toward the rate-making practices of the railroads was by no means universal,[48] but it is remarkable in view of the relatively recent development of railroads in Minnesota that there was not a more outspoken have-not, weak-road faction in the legislature at this time. In explanation of this puzzling circumstance two hypotheses are suggested. The first recognizes the fact that railroads had preceded inland settlement in Minnesota to a greater extent than in any other Granger state. The fact that nearly one-quarter of the land area of Minnesota was granted to aid railroad construction demonstrates both the paucity of settlers in the state prior to construction and the importance of the railroads as colonizing agents. A population map of the state as of 1875 shows a particularly close affinity between rail and river routes and the pattern of occupied land. There undoubtedly were fewer have-nots in Minnesota than in either Iowa or Illinois at a comparable stage of development.[49]

The second hypothesis concerns the attraction of the Illinois method of control for those who tended to support the railroad interests. In both Illinois and Iowa, commission control with its flexible system of classification and its acceptance of judicial review in all cases of alleged discrimination or extortion had won the votes of the weak-road and have-not representatives. If such was the case in Minnesota, the debates of 1874 may indicate the strength rather than the weakness of have-not, weak-road interests even though these groups did not express the usual fears.

The moderate reformers, regardless of their motives, favored the adoption of the Illinois plan in toto; the extremists like Ignatius Donnelly wanted to retain the principle of the act of 1871, but also wanted to drastically reduce the legal maxima; a third faction, led by Amos Coggswell of Owatonna, wanted to enact the Illinois plan in its entirety, but also to limit the discretion of the commission with regard to rate levels by means of strict legislative maxima. The commission, in effect, would be permitted to lower rates but could never raise them above the point deemed reasonable by the legislature. The Minnesota House of Representatives tended to favor this last plan by a ratio of about two to one.[50]

The senate of 1874, however, was more conservative than the house. Its railroad committee was composed almost entirely of business and professional men who indicated a desire to curb discriminatory practices, but who showed no sign of wanting to punish the railroads unnecessarily.[51] The bill which they introduced was patterned on the Illinois law of 1873, as recommended by the railroad commissioner and by former Governor Austin. The senate beat down the efforts of such Anti-Monopolists as Donnelly and Wilkinson to fix limits upon the discretion of the commission, and they adopted the measure by a vote of 27 to 9.[52]

The house proceeded to amend the senate bill by imposing statutory limits upon the powers of the senate's commission, but the senate refused to accept the change and called for a conference committee. It failed to produce a satisfactory settlement and another was called. The second committee agreed to the senate bill in all its essential features, and in this form the measure was finally adopted by a vote of 83 to 3 in the house, and 34 to 2 in the senate.[53] The only two die-hards in the senate were President Drake of the St. Paul and Sioux City Railroad Company and the irrepressible Mr. Donnelly who later insisted that "if a majority of both branches had been railroad employees . . . they could not have acted more satisfactorily to the railroads." [54]

The Minnesota law of 1874 was identical in principle to the Illinois statute of the previous year. It declared certain acts of discrimination to be prima facie unjust, regardless of competitive factors. It also established a three-man commission with power to fix schedules of reasonable maximum rates, and it stipulated that these tariffs would be accepted as prima facie evidence of reasonableness in all state courts. The rate law of 1871 and parts of the commission law of the same year were summarily repealed.[55]

The law of 1874 was in effect for only one year, however. As a result of the panic and depression of 1873 the railroads of Minnesota found themselves in desperate financial straits. Before the beginning of 1875, the former monopolistic ogres had become objects of public sympathy, and a surge of latent have-not opinion rose up in the interest of repeal. The law of 1874 was compelled to bear the blame for the financial crisis and was accused of stopping the flow of investment capital into the state. Although a handful of the old antimonopolists, including Donnelly, rallied around the law because they felt it to be preferable to no legislation at all, the entire system was swept away in 1875 and replaced by a single advisory commissioner and a few simple prohibitions against personal discrimination. Interestingly enough, the law of 1874 did not come under heavy attack from the railroad interests as a whole. Like its predecessor in Illinois, it was considered a great improvement over direct legislative control and was not challenged on broad constitutional grounds. The railroads, in fact, gave public indication of their willingness to conform to the schedules established by the new board. However, the demand for controls vanished as quickly as it had appeared, largely due to the weak economic position of Minnesota and the fear of alarming capital during a depression. Even the moderate principle of the Illinois system could not withstand this sudden reaction against economic restrictions.[56]

The mercurial attitude of the people of Minnesota toward the railroad rate problem was a result of the immaturity of the state's major commercial and industrial interests. The van of the westward movement did not reach Minnesota until after the Civil War, and there were no well-established patterns of commerce associated with the grain trade prior to that time. Before 1859 the principal export of the state had been furs. The trade in wheat, which came to dominate the economy in the sixties, was largely a product of the railroads. Consequently, the introduction of a new form of transportation did not turn trade out of older channels as it had in Iowa. There were no suffering, river-town mercantile interests to give leadership and consistency to the movement for state regulation of rates.[57]

When transportation costs became a problem for the grain trade in Minnesota, the conflict of interests was much simpler than in any other of the Granger states. The antimonopoly revolt of the mid-sixties reflected the entire state's dependence upon favorable water and rail rates to the lake ports; the movement for rate-law reform after 1870 coincided with the beginnings of competitive all-rail service to these same ports. The state veered sharply toward controls in the mid-sixties and again in the early seventies, but the slightest suggestion of a hostile reaction by railroad capital was capable of reversing the trend. Although there were relatively few have-nots in Minnesota, there was an almost unanimous interest in the larger development of the state's economy. The most flexible system of rate regulation collapsed in 1875 in the face of financial stringency with very little encouragement from the railroads themselves. More than a decade would pass before the promotional and regulatory demands of the state could be brought into balance.

seven WISCONSIN:
POLITICS AND
THE POTTER LAW

O F ALL THE GRANGER railroad laws passed by the states of the upper Mississippi Valley, none attracted more attention at the time, and none has been subjected to more intensive study since, than the so-called Potter law of Wisconsin. The Potter law became the symbol of Granger radicalism and was characterized by Charles Francis Adams, Jr. as "the most ignorant, arbitrary and wholly unjustifiable law to be found in the history of railroad legislation." [1] As the Granger law most written about in the eastern press, it was accepted as typical of western legislation generally, and it accounted for much of the hostility toward the movement as a whole.

Although there is good reason to question the Potter law's reputation for radicalism, there is little doubt as to its inadequacy. The law was poorly drawn and contributed little if anything to the solution of the railway problem. For these reasons, it probably deserved much of the criticism leveled against it. But it is quite wrong to assume that the movement for rate-law reform in Wisconsin was typical; it was the least typical of all those included in this study.

Wisconsin, like Iowa, embarked upon statehood in the midst of the general reaction against the public works failures of the 1840s.

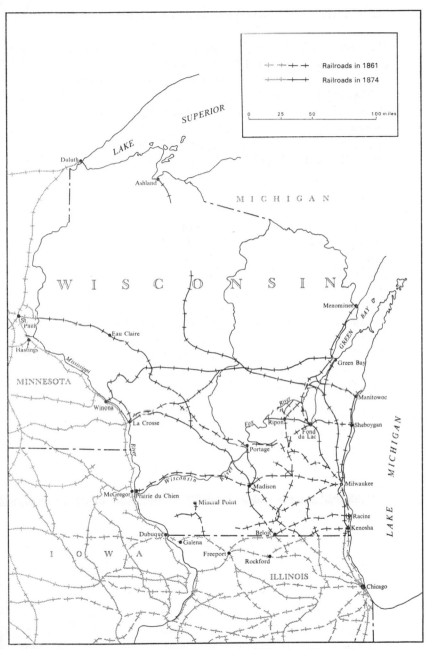

Map 4. Wisconsin Railroads, 1861 and 1874. (Map by University of Wisconsin Cartographic Laboratory.)

Her first constitution, ratified in 1848, stipulated that "the State shall never contract any debt for works of internal improvement, or be a party in carrying on such works" except insofar as might be required by a donation of public land. Further provisions declared that all corporations without banking privileges should be formed under general laws unless, in the judgment of the legislature, the objects of the corporation could not be attained in this way. The constitution also declared that all acts of incorporation, whether general or special, could be altered or repealed at any time after their adoption.[2] Because of this reservation of legislative power, the question of vested rights was never a major issue in the Wisconsin movement for government control.

Although no construction was carried out prior to 1848, the charter policy of Wisconsin, like that of Minnesota, had its beginnings in the territorial period. The grants of the late 1830s and early 1840s contained the usual restrictions and reservations with regard to rates found in eastern charters of the same period. During the late 1840s, however, the trend was to drop such provisions, and after 1850 specific restrictions upon rate-making practices disappeared altogether. A general power of revision was implied in all charters issued after the adoption of the constitution, but within its bounds, the legislature adopted a liberal attitude toward foreign investors in an effort to encourage railroad expansion. The lawmakers also served the interests of railroad development by refusing to adopt a general act of incorporation. Despite the apparent popularity of such measures, the legislature favored the free granting of special charters as the basis of its railroad policy.[3]

Public aid for the railroads of Wisconsin came in the form of land grants and local subscriptions. The former were not extensive and did not come until after the Civil War; the latter were permitted without limit until 1870 when the first of a series of statutory restrictions was imposed. An amendment to the state constitution, ratified in 1874, fixed a maximum on local indebtedness of five percent of the assessed value of taxable property in any town, village, county, or city. Additional local aid for the early railroad projects was provided by a reckless system of railway farm mortgages, a form of private subscription that led to financial ruin for many an innocent farmer, and in the process, created tremendous hostility toward railroad corporations. Between 1850 and 1857 some 6,000 farmers mortgaged their homesteads to the extent of $4.5 to $5 million in order to buy stock in local railroad enterprises. The farmers' interest in the various companies was wiped out by the panic of 1857, but the mortgages remained to plague the economic and political life of southern Wisconsin for many years to come.[4]

In 1860 Wisconsin could boast 905 miles of railroad; in 1870 she could claim 1,525. Although the totals are not very impressive, it must be realized that much of this was accomplished without the aid of outside capital. For a number of reasons, eastern investors had tended to bypass Wisconsin in favor of Illinois, Iowa, and Minnesota until 1865. The attraction of more liberal railway policies in Illinois and Minnesota, the favorable location of Iowa with respect to the transcontinental route, the decline of the wheat growing industry in southern Wisconsin, and the repudiation of debts growing out of the railway-farm mortgage plan were all factors in the diversion of eastern funds from Wisconsin enterprise. But the absence of railroad construction in Wisconsin, particularly between 1858 and 1868, does not detract from the strategic importance of those lines in operation. During the sixties Milwaukee, on the strength of her rail connections, alternated with Chicago as the largest primary wheat market in the world. With two roads tapping the Mississippi River and a closely knit pattern of rails covering the Rock River Valley, Wisconsin mercantile interests were in a good position to compete with their arch rival to the south. In the 1860s Milwaukee was the seat of one of the most aggressive railroad systems in the country.[5]

Local ownership and control, however, were no guarantee against arbitrary or piratical rate making. Complaints of extortion and unethical business methods became quite prevalent during the late 1850s, and there is clear evidence of local discrimination in rate schedules as early as 1857. Financial difficulties resulting from the panic of that year induced a rash of small rate wars with their accompanying tendency to unsettle commercial values. As in the other states of the upper valley, however, the beginnings of the movement to reform the rate law of the state are very obscure.

In the legislative sessions of 1859 and 1861 there were efforts to secure the establishment of a railroad commission and to obtain the enactment of a general law of incorporation for railroads. In 1861 and 1862 there was a demand for the regulation of rate levels. A desire to change the law on discrimination was first manifested during the 1861 legislative session when the citizens of Ripon introduced a petition and resolution asking for the adoption of a prorata law. Demands for a uniform rate law were heard again in the legislatures of 1862 and 1863, and they were mentioned by the press in 1863 in connection with the question of consolidating the east-west roads of the state. By 1864 the demand had become sufficiently loud to inspire the appointment of a special committee in the lower house of the state legislature.[6]

The reports submitted by the house committee give a clear picture of the Wisconsin railroad problem in 1864. The majority report did not question the right of regulation, but it expressed the fear that the results of such legislation might not be altogether beneficial. In the first place, the bills in question would be unfair to the railroads already in operation since they were just beginning to get back on their feet after the lean years of 1857–62. The only thing that had induced their construction and maintenance, said the report, was the promise of freedom to fix their own tolls. To withdraw this privilege without just cause would do severe damage to the credit of the state. In the second place, it would be extremely difficult to attract much needed outside capital if it were to become known that Wisconsin franchises were subject to change or withdrawal at the mere caprice of the legislature. The benefits of railroad transportation had reached only a small part of the state and could not be extended without foreign aid. The only way to attract capital was to give assurance of security. Third, the majority report felt that the prorata principle was entirely too rigid. If applied to interstate lines, it would be impossible for Wisconsin interests to compete with Illinois for the through traffic between the river and the lakes. Until it was shown that the railroads were violating their charters or that some great public necessity demanded reform, the legislature should refrain from playing freight agent. The majority recommended that all the regulatory measures under its consideration be indefinitely postponed.[7]

The minority of the select committee did not take issue with the majority on any major point. It agreed that a strict prorata law would be unwise and that the legislature was not competent to fix rates. Its purpose in presenting a separate report was merely to express an opinion with regard to certain related complaints. Although the *Wisconsin State Journal* insisted that no measure had ever been "so universally demanded by the people," and dozens of petitions were available to support this claim, the legislature was unable to produce even a minority report in favor of a prorata bill. The railroad lobby, with the willing support of the large have-not areas in the northern and western parts of the state, was simply too strong to be denied.[8]

The legislature of the following year paid much less attention to the railroad rate question, but in 1866 transportation charges were again the great topic of debate. The decline of grain prices after the war had depressed conditions in the West and had helped to bring about the antimonopoly revolt. "From various parts of the state," said Governor Fairchild in January 1866, "are heard great complaints of the unjust exactions of railroad companies in relation to prices charged for freight, and unjust discriminations against some localities in favor of others." Fairchild suggested that these complaints be investigated to see if the corporations really were abusing their privileges, "oppressing the people or seriously inconveniencing the business men and farmers of the state." [9]

During the 1866 session each house sponsored a rate-control measure designed to curb the principal abuses of railroad management. The senate committee on railroads favored a commission bill introduced by Senator Bentley of Sheboygan County. The measure called for a three-man board with power to fix mandatory freight and passenger tariffs for each railroad. Under the terms of the bill, the various railroad companies of the state were to submit twice each year their schedules of rates for the coming six-month period. The commission would review them and approve or modify as they saw fit, subject to certain restrictions in the law.

All rates would have to be the same in both directions, and no more than a twenty-five percent difference between rates for the same distance on different parts of the road was to be permitted. There was to be no discrimination of any sort between persons, and in cases of violation, the commission was to conduct all legal proceedings.[10]

During the debates in the senate, which sat as a committee of the whole, the bill was attacked largely because of its stringency. Representatives from northern and western counties feared its effect upon future construction, while others objected to the extent of the commission's regulatory powers, which amounted to little less than managerial authority. Certainly this was one of the strongest commission bills proposed by any of the Granger states during this period, the alternative being a simple uniform rate bill that would protect the interior collecting points against local discrimination. Senator Bentley defended his bill on the grounds that it met the complaints coming from "businessmen, manufacturers and farmers" and would provide a permanent tribunal to which the railroads, as well as the people, could look for protection. He pointed to New England precedents and declared that eastern capitalists were accustomed to commission control and would not be deterred by his proposed law from investing in Wisconsin enterprises.[11]

Failing to meet either with complete approval or disapproval, Bentley's bill was referred to a special committee for reconsideration and amendment. The special committee, which included Bentley, met with railroad officials, and apparently as a result, submitted a similar but less rigid substitute bill. The committee concluded that a definite, uniform policy was the first requisite of Wisconsin railroad supervision. The substitute bill called for a three-man commission clothed with judicial instead of administrative powers. All complaints about rates were to be brought before the board whose decision after hearing both sides was final. Discrimination against individuals was outlawed, but problems of rate structure were left to the commission. After further modification aiming toward even less strict control, the substitute bill was eventually passed by the senate by a vote of 18 to 6.[12]

The assembly, meanwhile, had settled upon "a bill to establish a uniform tariff" presented by Representative Robbins of Grant County. The bill was probably written by Cadwallader C. Washburn, a lawyer and businessman from Mineral Point, who was soon to be elected governor of the state. It included a detailed schedule of maximum rates graduated according to distance in such a way as to prevent local discrimination, and according to one member, so as to prevent the diversion of Wisconsin traffic to Chicago. With a few minor amendments the bill was adopted by the lower house by the decisive vote of 65 to 17.[13] The assembly vote on its own bill, however, is apt to be misleading. The have-nots were obviously stronger than the vote indicated, but they probably realized that the senate would reject a rigid measure whereas a more moderate law might get through.

Now a familiar pattern of events followed. The assembly bill was rejected by the senate because it was too rigid; the senate bill was amended by the lower house in such a way as to be unacceptable to its parent body.[14] Two houses, both willing to adopt some form of state control, failed to compromise their differences and adjourned without accomplishing a thing.

The failure of the 1866 session marked the climax of the anti-monopoly revolt and the beginning of a strange intermission in the movement to reform railroad rate law in Wisconsin. The anti-monopoly outcry of 1865–66 was silenced by the return of favorable conditions in the grain market and by renewed hope of obtaining additional railroad facilities. In the face of widespread agitation and the renewed competition of the St. Louis market, the railroads began to reduce their through rates from the abnormal high of the late war years. The continuing demands for cheap canal transportation and improved river routes also helped lower rates. In the more northerly settlements, railroad fever returned with a vengeance in the late sixties, and the disease was caught by southern commercial interests anxious to tap the new wheat lands of the western counties and by the lumber and iron regions of the north. Between 1867 and 1874 approximately 1,400 miles of road were added to the 1,030 miles in operation at the close of the Civil War. During this period of rapid expansion, the voices of protest against railroad rate policy were stilled.[15]

In 1867 Governor Fairchild reminded the legislature that "a

portion of our people are still complaining that unjust discriminations are made . . . and demanding the aid of legislative enactment
to reduce the tariffs of freight to a more equitable standard." [16]
The legislature responded with its last serious effort to enact a
control measure prior to the adoption of the famous Potter law
of 1874. Representative Robbins reintroduced the assembly bill of
the previous session, and after consenting to considerable modification, succeeded in getting it passed by the lower house. But again
the senate rejected the measure on the grounds that it was too
rigid. It was a threat to new and weak roads, according to its
critics, and it was contrary to the promises made to railway capitalists. If adopted, it would divert all the trade between the
Mississippi and the lakes to Illinois railroads. A strong minority
in the senate, however, insisted that the bill was necessary in order
to put a stop to unjust discrimination and to give shippers a choice
of markets. Under the existing system, they complained, the Chicago and North Western Railroad compelled its trade to go to
Chicago, while the Milwaukee and St. Paul Railroad forced its
business to Milwaukee. The shipper was unable to exercise any
discretion whatsoever. But the reform element was unable to
prevent indefinite postponement by a vote of 17 to 9.[17]

Between 1867 and 1874 no rate-reform bill was passed by either
house of the Wisconsin legislature. Although a handful of antidiscrimination measures were introduced during this period, only
one reached a third reading and only one received any attention
from the Madison press. Petitions and memorials on the subject
of railroad rates are almost entirely lacking. Between Fairchild's
address of 1867 and Governor Washburn's first message in January 1872, there was no recommendation for any control legislation from the chief executive of the state. Although the continual
appearance of one or two reform bills at each session indicated
that the problem of unequal rate structures was still present, and
although Governor Washburn's 1872 address spoke of complaints
of unjust discrimination in particular localities, the political impetus for reform was lacking.[18] At a time when neighboring states
were in the midst of heated debates over the vital railway issue,
the Wisconsin legislature was seemingly undisturbed.

The absence of agitation for rate controls between 1867 and

1874 is all the more surprising in view of the presence of a number of factors usually conducive to antirailroad sentiment. In the late sixties and early seventies there was a growing resentment in Wisconsin against absentee ownership and control, and the same period saw the growth of two giant, allied railroad monopolies. By 1870 practically the entire transportation business of the state was in the hands of the Chicago and North Western and the Milwaukee and St. Paul. This was also a time of serious depression in the Wisconsin wheat industry. Furthermore, it was during the latter part of this period that the Wisconsin railroads were waging their open and declared rate war with the Lake Superior and Mississippi Railroad for the lucrative grain trade of Minnesota. A situation more likely to produce complaints of local discrimination is difficult to imagine.[19]

A completely satisfactory explanation of this apparent lack of interest in rate-law reform has not been found in the available documents. A number of hypotheses, however, can be put forward as possible answers. It is possible that the more serious distortions in Wisconsin rate structures disappeared after 1867 because of the growth of monopolistic conditions. Following the panic of 1857 there was a period of intense competition among a relatively large number of independent lines which had produced the inevitable result. Widespread discrimination against persons and localities had become commonplace during the war years and had given rise to a vigorous movement for reform. In the immediate postwar period, however, the consolidation of independent and often competing lines was carried out by two groups of eastern capitalists, and an effective truce was arranged between the resulting systems. The Milwaukee and St. Paul and the Chicago and North Western inaugurated a policy of exchanging board members in 1868, and in the following year, they went so far as to elect the same president. The latter practice was abandoned almost immediately, but the days of cut-throat competition among Wisconsin railroads was obviously over. Henceforth there was less need for discriminatory rate making on the part of the major companies, and therefore, less need for rate regulation. There are no available figures to support this point, but the Milwaukee Chamber of Commerce Report for 1871 declared that steps had been taken to guard against unfavorable discrimination in spite of the rate war with the Duluth road.[20]

A second factor was the continuance of widespread railroad fever, strong enough to snuff out the antimonopoly revolt in 1867 and still sufficiently strong in 1871 to secure legislation for the purpose of encouraging the construction of new roads. If abuses in rate making actually did exist, the hope of obtaining additional competitive lines and the fear of repelling the necessary capital could have served as a deterrent to popular agitation.[21]

A final consideration is the unique relationship in Wisconsin between railroad management, the local mercantile community, and state politics. In most western states the purchase of controlling interests in state railroads by eastern capitalists resulted in a distinct separation between management on the one hand and local business and government on the other; the relationship became almost entirely a matter of contract. The natural tendency under these circumstances was for local commercial and political interests to combine forces against the outsider and to try to control him through legislative action. But this was not the case in Wisconsin. In spite of a trend toward absentee ownership, the transfer of control out of the hands of Wisconsin mercantile groups was not complete. The two great railroad systems of the state remained closely interwoven with the local business establishment and were actively involved in state political organizations.

The key figure in this relationship was Alexander Mitchell, a Scottish immigrant who settled in Milwaukee in 1839 and built a fortune in banking and insurance enterprises. By 1870 he was the unquestioned leader of the Milwaukee business community and a dominant power in state politics. His role in the development and consolidation of the Milwaukee and St. Paul had brought him to the presidency of that company in 1866, and it was Mitchell who served briefly as president of both that railroad and the North Western between 1869 and 1870. He was also the leader of the state Democratic party and the representative of his district in Congress from 1871 to 1875. It is likely that Mitchell's influence and his dedication to the economic well being of Milwaukee prevented the growth of the usual tensions associated with absentee ownership. Mitchell dominated the Milwaukee and St. Paul in spite of the preponderance of New Yorkers on its board, and his maintenance of harmonious relations with the Chicago and North Western undoubtedly helped prevent the worst abuses of railway competition. His active involvement in Wisconsin politics, moreover, prevented the relationship between the government and the railroads from becoming purely contractual. The Milwaukee and St. Paul Railroad was an important part of the Democratic party in Wisconsin; the North Western, to a lesser degree, was tied to the Republican party. When one considers the close cooperation between the two companies after 1867, it is apparent that railway politics in Wisconsin had a special character.[22]

It is quite possible that the overpowering monopoly of interests represented by Alexander Mitchell served to mollify the conflicts that had troubled the commercial and political life of the other Granger states. This is not to say that there was no resentment against Mitchell or his company. The hostility toward railroads and their monopolistic practices may well have been greater in Wisconsin than in any of the other states of the upper Mississippi Valley,[23] but the unity of economic and political interests made it exceptionally difficult to assault the system with any hope of success. As long as the worst abuses of rate making were kept in check by the system itself, there was little chance of the railroad problem becoming a significant political issue in Wisconsin. The feeble attempts at reform between 1867 and 1874 were all stifled in their infancy, and the sudden reemergence of the problem in the latter year was largely due to a series of new political and economic circumstances.

The Republican party had controlled the governorship and both houses of the state legislature without interruption since 1856, but the party faced the election of 1873 with its forces in serious disarray. The Liberal Republican rift of the previous year had not healed, and the party had lost considerable support in the cities because of its stand on the temperance issue. The Republican legislature, with strong support from the Republican governor, Cadwallader C. Washburn, passed a tough antisaloon measure much to the alarm of the brewery and liquor interests and to the dismay of the large German population. The party's problems were further compounded by Governor Washburn's futile but forthright stand on the railroad question. The governor had been a leader of the antimonopoly revolt in the postwar years and he continued to press for antidiscrimination laws despite the decline in popular agitation for reform. He warned repeatedly against careless grants of power and privilege to railroad corporations, and he twice recommended the creation of an advisory commission to supervise railway operations within the state. The legislature, to be sure, had not responded to his appeals, but the companies were anxious to have him replaced. Still another cause for alarm was the rapid growth of the movement for rural organization during the winter of 1872–73. The political significance of the Grange was difficult to gauge, but the Republicans had carried the rural districts in the past and would have to hold their vote in order to win in the future. While the governor's stand on the railroad question was apt to help the party in depressed farm areas, the evidence of widespread unrest was disquieting to the party in power.[24]

With their best chance for victory in over a decade, the Democrats set out to exploit every weak point in the Republican ranks. Abandoning their traditional party label, they attempted to form a coalition of dissident forces under the reform banner. With skillful leadership from Democratic party chairman George Paul and with the enthusiastic backing of Alexander Mitchell, they sought to combine regular Democrats, Liberal Republicans, urban opponents of the temperance law, and rural supporters of railroad regulation into a single party. To oppose Washburn in the gubernatorial election they nominated William R. Taylor, a prosperous Dane County farmer and Granger, who was a moderate on railroad regulation.[25]

With both parties out to capture the support of the Grangers, the candidates placed considerable emphasis on transportation and marketing problems. Although it was clear that Governor Washburn was the more radical of the two on these issues, Taylor made a sincere effort to identify his party with the cause of reform in spite of his obvious debt to Mitchell and the St. Paul railroad. Taylor's desire to work for an effective system of state railway control was beyond question. Presumably the Reform party leaders intended to absorb a part of the movement for rate regulation within their own ranks and to channel it in a direction acceptable to the railroad companies. The move was politically astute, but in a sense, their strategy let loose the forces of popular discontent at a time when the railroads were particularly vulnerable to attack. In the end they were not able to control the course of events.[26]

The Reform party, nevertheless, won a decisive victory in 1873. Taylor was elected governor by a comfortable margin of 15,000 votes, the Reformers took the lower house of the legislature with seats to spare, and they came within one seat of winning the senate. The decisive factors were the defection of Liberal Republicans and the shift in urban votes because of the temperance question.[27] Since both parties advocated railroad reforms it is impossible to measure the impact of the railroad problem on the outcome, but the margin of Reform victory indicated nothing about the possibility of legislative action. The temper of the new legislature, however, soon showed that both parties took the problem seriously. Partisan politics, on the other hand, was to play a larger role in the enactment of control laws in Wisconsin than in any other Granger state.

The stated goal of the Reformers was a "conservative yet a strong anti-monopoly document to fulfill the expectations of the people. . . ."[28] During the campaign the party had taken a stand in favor of regulation, and Governor Taylor, in his first address to the legislature, had recommended that appropriate legislation be passed. His suggestions were moderate and undoubtedly indicated the restraining hand of his backers. Railroads, he cautioned, were entitled to a fair return on their investment, but discrimination among shippers should be prevented and punished. Holding that rates of freight and passenger fares were subject to revision by state authority, he urged the establishment of an advisory commission, and for the particular benefit of the farmer, he requested that Congress be petitioned to provide further internal improvements for the western states.[29]

Equally moderate were the demands of the Wisconsin State Grange, an organization that the Reformers claimed to represent. The Grangers asked for the appointment of "commissioners with full power to regulate and prevent unjust discriminations or excessive tariff rates . . . and to report facts on which to base future and judicious legislation." [30] The Reformers appeared to be in a good position to enact mild control measures reasonably satisfactory to all their constituents.

But by the beginning of 1874, the demand for rate-law reform had swelled to more than moderate proportions. The sudden reawakening of the people of Wisconsin to the threat of arbitrary rate making was due in the first place to a change in policy on the part of the railroads themselves. As the election campaign of the previous year got under way, the two major roads announced an increase in rates that would go into effect on September 15. The timing of the announcement suggests that it was related to the companies' cessation of hostilities with the Lake Superior and Mississippi Railroad of Minnesota. The unrestrained rate war between the Wisconsin railroads and the Duluth road had entered a new phase in the fall of 1873. The reorganization of the latter company under the auspices of the Northern Pacific had put the line in a much stronger financial condition and had enabled it to substantially reduce rates. As a result, the rate-cutting practices of the Milwaukee and St. Paul, and to a lesser extent those of the North Western, designed to hold the Minnesota grain trade for Milwaukee and Chicago, were no longer profitable for the two Wisconsin companies. Normal competitive relations with the Duluth road were now in effect. The upward adjustment of rates in Wisconsin was one of the consequences of the truce, but it gave the commercial and industrial interests of the state a new cause for complaint at a most inopportune time.[31]

A second factor in the regeneration of the movement for rate-law reform was the growth of antimonopoly feeling within the Milwaukee business community. By virtue of his banking and railroad interests, Alexander Mitchell was a powerful influence in the Milwaukee Chamber of Commerce, but his hold on the trade of the city was as disturbing as it was pervasive. Mitchell's Wisconsin Fire and Marine Insurance Company Bank was the largest financial institution in the state, and its influence was felt in all the city's credit operations. For the most part, the wheat trade of Milwaukee was brought into the city over the tracks of

Mitchell's Milwaukee and St. Paul Railroad, and virtually all of the city's grain elevators were owned by this railroad. While the larger grain merchants operated with the blessing and cooperation of the Mitchell monopoly and kept a steady flow of grain coming into the city, the system did not work to the advantage of all concerned.[32]

In 1870 the smaller commission merchants of Milwaukee, under the leadership of Francis H. West, began to push for reforms in the local grain market. Working within the chamber of commerce, they tried to curb the monopolistic influence of the Milwaukee and St. Paul and to reduce the cost of storage in Milwaukee grain elevators. West's election to the presidency of the chamber in 1871 and 1872 indicated that the rebellion had reached sizeable proportions, and that there were issues involved that affected the prosperity of the entire city. The newspapers of Milwaukee, with one exception, supported the antimonopoly faction and warned of the detrimental effect that monopoly was having on the city's trade. They blamed the Milwaukee and St. Paul for recent large-scale diversions of wheat to Chicago.[33] But in spite of its broad base, the revolt failed to attain its objectives. By 1873 West had given up all hope of bringing about reforms within the chamber itself and had decided to seek his objectives through political action. He had come to believe, as had one of the city's newspapers, that the remedy for Milwaukee's problems lay in Madison, and that the solution was to send to the next legislature "able, thinking business men—be they farmers or merchants—who comprehended the wants and rights of the business community, who cannot be bought or cheated."[34] In the fall of 1873 West presented himself as a Reform party candidate for the state assembly, but he ran on a radical antimonopoly platform all his own. He carried his district with little difficulty, and when the legislature convened the following winter, it was West who came forward as the leader of the more radical forces working for railroad and warehouse regulation.[35]

With the appearance of new problems and new leadership, the railroad question emerged suddenly, if briefly, as a major public issue in Wisconsin politics. The disintegration of traditional party alignments together with the rise of an effective farmers' organization had facilitated its resurgence, and the old alliance of railroads, the mercantile community, and state party organizations proved unable to control it. In the midst of a confused struggle for partisan advantage, the railroad problem became one of the first objects of legislative action.

When the legislative session of 1874 got under way, a joint committee on railroad tariffs and taxation was appointed to carry out the wishes of the Reform coalition. After due deliberation, the committee reported a bill modeled after the Illinois law of 1873. The bill was reported simultaneously in both houses of the legislature.[36]

Assemblyman Francis West, however, was not satisfied with halfway measures. Irritated by the fact that he had not been appointed to the joint committee on railroad tariffs, he introduced two bills of his own: one dealt with warehousing, the other with rail rates. Counting on the support of the Milwaukee business community, he proposed to limit the charges of warehousemen to one cent per bushel, roughly half of the prevailing rate, for each of the first fifteen days of storage and to limit rail charges by a detailed schedule of fixed maxima graduated according to distance. Although the proposed rail rates were not thought to be confiscatory, the governor was authorized to raise the legal maxima by as much as ten percent if he considered such a move advisable.[37]

West's stringent warehouse bill passed the lower house with the support of the Republican minority, but it failed in the senate in spite of a Republican majority. The support of the Milwaukee delegation melted away in the face of threats from the railroad monopoly. The city was in need of additional elevators, and Mitchell assured the business leaders of the community that there could be no further construction if the warehouse bill were to pass. Although there is good reason to believe that a majority of the members of the chamber of commerce originally favored the bill, they refuse to defend it for fear of reprisals. The opponents of regulation, meanwhile, were encouraged to speak in the name of the mercantile interests and to promote the measure's defeat. A similar fate awaited West's railroad bill. In the first major floor fight on the issue of railway control, his strict schedules of maximum rates were set aside in favor of the milder committee bill.

The house adopted the latter by a decisive vote of 69 to 14 and sent it off to the senate. The Reform coalition seemed to be in full control.[38]

The Republican senate, however, had no intention of conceding an easy victory to the upstart Reformers. Realizing that their opponents would have to hedge on the railroad question if really tested, the Republican high command decided to outreform the Reformers. It is probable that there was more genuine reform sentiment in the Republican party than among the Reformers, but the desire for partisan advantage was clearly evident in the bill introduced by the Republican leaders. The bill had been written by Senator R. L. D. Potter of Waushara County, a lawyer with no particular experience in railway matters from a county without a single mile of track. The opposition maintained that the real purpose of the bill was to defeat regulation.[39]

The Potter bill divided the railways of the state into three classes based on earnings and imposed maximum fares of three, three-and-one-half, and four cents per mile upon each of them. Freights were classified in detail, and on certain specified classes, absolute maximum rates, graduated according to distance, were imposed. For non-specified categories of freight the roads were to ask no more than they had charged on June 1, 1873. To give a limited flexibility to the schedules, the bill called for the creation of a three-man commission that could reduce, but not raise, the legal rates if it felt that the roads in question would not be injured thereby. The decisions of the commission in such cases were to be binding. On balance the Potter bill was less severe than the West bill even though it imposed lower rates on the crucial trade in wheat and flour.[40] However, its provision for a commission that could lower the statutory rate limits gave the measure a punitive character that the West bill lacked. Furthermore, it contained no provision whatever to guard against either local or personal discrimination.

The strategy of the Republican leadership was to present a law that was sufficiently strict to satisfy the more radical advocates of control. If the legislature adopted it, their party would receive credit for its passage while all the headaches of enforcement would be piled on their opponents. If the legislature did not pass it, the blame for ineffective regulation would fall on the Reform party majority, and the subservience of the self-styled reformers to the corporate interests would be exposed for all to see.[41]

When the joint committee bill adopted by the assembly came up for consideration in the senate, the Republicans substituted the essential features of the Potter bill as an amendment and sent it back to the lower house. And so began the succession of plots and counterplots that marred the progress of rate-law reform in Wisconsin. The representatives of the railroad interests in the Reform party countered the Republican move with a plan of their own. Having failed in their first efforts to get a conservative commission bill through the senate, they attempted to bring about a stalemate that would block all further reform efforts. With this in mind the Reform party leaders moved to reconsider the more radical West bill in place of the Potter schedules, and they succeeded in getting it passed by the assembly by a lopsided vote of 56 to 13.[42] The Reform party, it appeared, had now thrown its support to a measure just as severe as the Potter bill which it sent off to the Republican senate for further action.

As anticipated, the senate again substituted the Potter bill for the assembly bill, and the railroad strategy of deadlock based on partisan rivalry seemed about to succeed. But they had not counted on the independence of Assemblyman West. Faced with the possibility of losing all chance to have a regulatory measure passed by the 1874 session, the Milwaukee commission merchant swallowed his pride and threw his support to the Republican bill. His action swung most of the Reform votes in the lower house and assured the measure's passage by a decisive vote of 69 to 14. To compensate for the bill's failure to deal with the problem of discrimination, a second statute was hastily adopted outlawing rebates, drawbacks, and other forms of personal preference.[43] Governor Taylor added his signature to both measures and brought the movement for state regulation in Wisconsin to an unsatisfactory conclusion.

All students of the Potter law have agreed that partisan politics was a controlling influence in the shaping of the Wisconsin Granger laws. Although it is clear that there was substantial bipartisan support in the legislature of 1874 for some form of regulation, the stratagems of the party managers make it all but impossible to assess the contributions of the various interest groups to the final outcome. Apparently the railroads were willing to accept commission control, but they were equally prepared to obstruct all regulatory legislation. They were able at all times to count on the support of the have-nots in the northern part of the state and on a good share of the Milwaukee delegation. Leadership for the more radical supporters of state controls, however, came from this same Milwaukee delegation and reflected the growth of antimonopoly feeling among businessmen in the commercial centers of the state. Francis West, the leading Milwaukee reformer, on the other hand, received his most consistent support from the rural areas of southern Wisconsin.[44]

The railroad problem in Wisconsin was complicated by a depression in the state's wheat industry. Soil depletion made it increasingly difficult for farmers in the southern counties to compete with the newer settlements in Iowa and Minnesota. For a time this disadvantage was offset by the favored position of the Wisconsin farmer in the Milwaukee market. Largely through the efforts of Alexander Mitchell and the St. Paul Railroad, and by agreement with the Chicago and North Western, Milwaukee held its position as a primary wheat market in spite of the inroads of Chicago and Duluth. This was accomplished in a way that gave highly favourable rate structures to Wisconsin farmers. The bitter rate war of 1871–73 between the Milwaukee and St. Paul and the Lake Superior and Mississippi railroads prolonged this advantage, but the sudden termination of the contest in September 1873 brought farmers and local grain buyers in southern Wisconsin to the brink of ruin. Wisconsin wheat was unable to compete with Iowa and Minnesota wheat when forced to bear the higher transportation charge. Consequently, the embattled wheat farmer was a more prominent figure in the movement for state railway control in Wisconsin than he was in any other of the Granger states.[45]

The concern of the Wisconsin farmer, of course, was expressed in conjunction with, and not in opposition to, the complaints of businessmen in the rural collecting points. "The wrath of the rural communities . . . hot though it might be," wrote one contemporary observer, "could cause the railroad managers little trouble, unless backed by the more intelligent indignation of the cities and villages. . . ." [46] The comment was less than flattering to the struggling farmers of the state, but it indicated that the pattern of protest in Wisconsin was not too different from that of the other states in the upper Mississippi Valley. There is more evidence of effective agricultural participation in the movement for reform in Wisconsin, but this participation still depended on the political leadership of similarly outraged shippers and merchants.

The Potter law, for all its shortcomings, did conform to the special needs of the state. As in Iowa, the need was to bring intrastate rates back into line with interstate rates, and hopefully in the process, to restore the viability of the Wisconsin wheat industry. Whether the legal schedules were imposed by statute or by commission ruling, a ceiling had to be placed on all local rates, and a long-and-short-haul law would have been of little help since Wisconsin could not control the rates to Chicago or Duluth or those from Minnesota to Milwaukee.

The conditions that produced the Potter law, nevertheless, were as much political as they were economic, and a restoration of the old alliance between the railroads, the business community, and political organizations soon led to the law's demise. With an assist from the hard times that followed the financial panic of 1873, the railroads were able to rally the support of the have-not counties in the northern part of the state, the inadequacies of the law became evident in spite of a favorable ruling from the Wisconsin Supreme Court, and the not-so-subtle pressures of Alexander Mitchell and the St. Paul company brought the Milwaukee business interests into line. Reform, with its mixed connotation in Wisconsin, ceased to be an issue after 1874, and the politics of the state returned to more normal channels. The legislature of 1875 raised by eight percent the maxima imposed by the Potter law, and the legislature of the following year repealed the law. Statutory control was replaced by a general law requiring fair and equal treatment for all shippers and passengers and by the establishment of a single railroad commissioner with investigatory and advisory powers. [47]

eight THE GRANGERS AND
THE GRANGER LAWS

$\rm T$HE FARMERS' MOVEMENT became a recognizable force in western politics during the winter of 1872–73. Through the organization of clubs dedicated to the improvement of rural life, American farmers found a means of applying sustained political pressure on behalf of an agricultural program, and they began to make demands that were independent of other regional economic considerations. By 1873 an agrarian crusade with overtones of class consciousness was stirring the politics of the upper Mississippi Valley and adding its voice to the movement for railroad regulation.

The largest and best known of the farmers' organizations to emerge in the postwar period was the Order of Patrons of Husbandry, or Grange. Founded in 1867 by Oliver H. Kelley, an official of the United States Department of Agriculture, it assumed a position of leadership among rural fraternities in the early 1870s and gave its name to the broader movement of that period. Unlike earlier agricultural societies and clubs, the Grange was concerned less with the science of farming and more with the social and economic well-being of its members. It sought to restore and enhance the quality of rural life in America through programs of education and self-help.[1]

161

By 1873 there were over 3,000 granges in the United States, more than 2,000 of them in the four states of the upper Mississippi Valley, and they were becoming a definite factor in local politics. The Grange was not a political party; its state and national leaders vigorously and consistently resisted the tendency of local chapters to involve themselves in partisan activities. But during the winter of 1872–73, the local granges became focal points for rising agrarian discontent. In response to increasing economic pressures they assumed a role in public affairs that went far beyond the intent of their founders and made the name *Granger* synonymous with *antimonopoly* and *reform*. The Patrons of Husbandry suddenly found itself at the center of a movement over which it had very little control.[2]

The ensuing Granger movement was a confused mixture of political forces without clear definition and without a precise program. In large measure the demands of the grangers reflected the farmers' general distrust of business. The farmer was convinced that he was getting far less than a fair share of the market value of his produce, and he blamed this on the fact that carriers and middlemen were taking more than they were entitled to in the form of commissions and transportation and storage charges. The entire commercial system, he believed, was shot through with speculation and corrupt business practices that robbed the toiler of his just rewards. Railroad charges were an important aspect of this larger problem, but to the militant farmer the specific inadequacies of railroad rate law were less serious than the basic immorality of the system as a whole. The best solution to the transportation problem was to be found in more direct and presumably cheaper means of getting crops to market. Waterways, farmers' railroads, and cooperative grain elevators were more appropriate than the legal complexities of rate regulation. The farmer also retained his distrust of "soulless corporations" and was easily persuaded that railroads should be subordinated to public authority. At the same time, he showed little confidence in legislative control and continued to look to competition from waterways and more railways for a solution to some of his problems. The state and the law, the farmer believed, were too easily perverted into instruments of advantage for the commercial classes.[3]

On another level the demands of the Granger movement were indistinguishable from the sectional claims of the earlier anti-monopoly revolt. The plight of the western producer was often traced to absentee ownership of railroad and warehouse facilities and to the selfish unwillingness of eastern-owned corporations to serve western interests. The answer, it was maintained, lay in straightforward assertions of state legislative power. The leaders of the local granges were apt to be the more affluent farmers with mixed agricultural and commercial interests. Even though they spoke as producers, their business operations were entirely compatible with those of the local mercantile communities. Their grievances were sectional rather than agricultural, and for this reason they were concerned with the railroad problem in its basic form. Unjust discrimination rather than extortionate charges, they agreed, was the principal source of mischief and should be the first object of legislative action.[4]

Furthermore, there remained in western America a belief in the promise and integrity of the Mississippi Valley as a distinct region. There were many who believed that the valley, north and south, had become too dependent upon outside markets and that it should be allowed to develop its own economic destiny. The Mississippi River formed the natural axis of economic life in the West and should be made to serve as its principal highway once again. Oliver H. Kelley, the founder of the Grange, was among those who believed in the promise of a great western commercial empire. In March 1866 Kelley wrote in his diary:

The West and Northwest must take advantage of Southern markets —let the Mississippi river and the Southern rail roads be their outlet. Our interests are united & Minnesota is to derive more benefit from the South than from the East—because she will be a great manufacturing section. *If the West & South blend their interests we need never fear any further trouble [.] let us take the sensible view of the matter & cut aloof from the Radical Tariff interests of the East.*[5]

Kelley did not confine his organizational activities on behalf of the Grange to the Mississippi Valley; the Patrons of Husbandry was a national fraternity both in principle and in fact. However,

Kelley was a Minnesota resident and was sensitive to the needs of the valley. He shared the sectional views of many westerners—views that had been widely expressed in the early war years following the closing of the Mississippi and which continued to animate western feelings during the antimonopoly revolt. This spirit of regionalism remained and was an essential part of the Granger movement in the Middle West.[6]

The aims of the Granger movement were somewhat distorted by the efforts of the major political parties to capture the voting potential of the new farmers' organizations. The Democratic party in the West had been badly demoralized by the events of the Civil War and was desperate to find new strength on the basis of new issues. In spite of its domination by Bourbon mercantile interests, the western Democracy made strenuous efforts to identify itself with the cause of the farmer and to assume the leadership of antimonopoly forces. Its prewar association with western and river interests gave historical justification for its stand, and there was still a tradition within the party of hostility to eastern capitalists. The Republicans, meanwhile, were sufficiently shaken by the Liberal Republican revolt of 1872 to run scared in the local elections of 1873. They were compelled to counter Democratic efforts on behalf of the farmer in order to hold their share of the rural vote. The result was an exaggerated emphasis upon reform in the elections of 1873 and a tendency on the part of convention delegates and party candidates to castigate the railroads as the chief enemy of the farming class. In reality, the grangers were neither so radical nor so single-mindedly hostile to the railroad interests as their self-styled political leaders made them seem.[7]

The Granger movement, in other words, served a mixture of agricultural, sectional, and political interests, and to the extent that it adopted the struggle for rate-law reform, it did so because of the relevance of rate reform to these three interests. By the hundreds, farmers joined the cry for reform in the early seventies, throwing their weight behind one or another of the many proposals for government regulation. To disregard their active participation in the movement would be quite wrong. Granger literature was filled with commentary on the railroad problem and with claims that the Grange led in the drive for controls. But eastern journalists, led by E. L. Godkin of the *Nation,* were too quick to identify the movement for rural organization and the movement for rate regulation as one and the same and to characterize the legislation of 1874 as Granger legislation. It seems clear that they did so with some malice aforethought in order to affix the stigma of agrarian radicalism on all subsequent efforts to regulate rates.[8] Obviously, it is misleading to correlate the agitation for state railway control with farmer discontent. The movement for rate-law reform, like the railroad problem itself, was national in scope and free of class bias. If sectionalism was a major force in shaping particular provisions of various laws, agrarian radicalism certainly was not. Against the background of existing legislation and charter provisions, and after more than two decades of prorata agitation in the East, the agrarianism of the Granger laws all but disappears. No social upheaval was needed to make the legislatures of the upper Mississippi Valley think in terms of state regulation. Price controls, though no longer commonplace, were still a part of state and local government. They could be considered radical only if they conflicted with charter provisions, and even then there was ample eastern precedent for legislative attacks on corporate privilege.

The basic problem was rate discrimination, and this affected every part of the community. Merchants at way points and terminal markets, in fact, were more apt to be adversely affected by this abuse than were farmers who often had a choice of collecting points and a choice of buyers. The early complaints of unfair rate making represented the grievances of specific districts and localities rather than the plight of any particular class. In most cases, initiative and leadership were provided by shippers and businessmen working through their boards of trade, mercantile associations, commercial conventions, and the regular political machinery of the state. Farmers were often in enthusiastic attendance at the antimonopoly conventions, particularly when cheap transportation was the subject of discussion, but prior to 1872 the leadership of the business centers was not challenged.

Similarly, the opposition to rate restrictions was a regional or local matter and showed no evidence of class struggle. The inhabitants of undeveloped rural areas, the have-nots, were always the railroad's best defense against regulatory legislation. The railroad companies, on the other hand, were almost always at odds with local business communities and rarely could count on their political support.

The situation was changed somewhat by the agrarian resurgence after 1872, but except for Wisconsin, there is little evidence of a strong agrarian influence on the movement for rate regulation. The local granges tended to be a moderate force. For example, the Illinois Grange approved Chief Justice Lawrence's decision calling for judicial review; in Iowa they supported the same commission bill that the railroad lobby was working for; in Wisconsin they also recommended commission control; and in Minnesota the grange split, with the leaders fighting vigorously against all political involvement.[9]

The Antimonopoly and Reform parties of Iowa, Minnesota, and Wisconsin attracted a number of leaders of the farmers' movement, but the controlling group in all three states was the regular Democratic organization joined by some Liberal Republicans. The enthusiasm of these groups for railway reform was questionable to say the least. Donnelly in Minnesota, West in Wisconsin, and McNutt in Iowa were not typical of the antimonopoly leaders. In the elections of 1873 it was the Republican party that took the stronger stand on rate control, and it was the Republican party that carried the rural counties.[10]

The Illinois State Farmers' Association, under the leadership of Willard Flagg, one of the wealthiest commercial farmers in the state, was the most radical of the politically oriented farm groups, but it emerged too late to affect the elections of 1872 in Illinois. Its attempt to influence the general assembly of 1873 by holding a convention in Springfield during the legislative session was one of the clearest expressions of rural militancy in the whole Granger movement, but its influence was largely negative. The conservatism of the Illinois law of 1873 can be attributed in part to the fears of assembly leaders like Jesse Hildrup that radicalism would alarm the capitalists.

The political activities of the more aggressive reformers of the Granger movement reached their peak during 1873 and 1874, and yet it was during these years that both Illinois and Minnesota backed away from strict legislative control and adopted systems of commission control more acceptable to the railroad companies. In Iowa a more stringent system of statutory regulation was adopted in 1874, but it followed a pattern long advocated by the representatives of the river towns.

Only in Wisconsin does the farmers' movement seem to have played an important part in the actual shaping of a Granger law. The severe depression of the wheat industry in that state—a local depression that was not shared by other agricultural areas in the upper Mississippi Valley—gave the rural counties of southern Wisconsin a special interest in rate restriction. The more radical advocates of reform were members of the Milwaukee business community, but the greatest political support came from farming communities in the southern part of the state. The sudden reappearance of the railroad problem in 1873 meant that the movement for reform had no immediate political background and no well-established leadership in the Wisconsin state government. Governor Washburn was in the best position to provide that leadership, but he was soundly defeated by the Reformers just when his recommendations were beginning to attract political support. The confusion of the legislative session of 1874 and its failure to pass a satisfactory rate law can be blamed, to a great extent, on these circumstances. Since farmers were the largest group advocating controls in 1874, the legislative leaders made every effort to satisfy their demands, but Wisconsin was a special case.

The awakening of the western farmer to the need for political action undoubtedly broadened the base of support for railroad regulation in the Granger states. It is possible that this development was decisive in Wisconsin. But the influence of the larger farm vote was not a radical influence. The evidence suggests that it was a moderating force which worked through the Republican party rather than through the antimonopoly coalitions. The leadership in the actual framing of legislative policy, however, remained in the hands of established political leaders who spoke for the traditional mercantile and industrial interests of the separate states. The Granger laws were prepared by lawyers, usually with the help of merchants and shippers, and sometimes with the aid of railroad officials. Their agrarianism was an invention of their enemies.

The same might be said of the Granger legislation's reputation for radicalism. The movement to reform railroad rate law in the upper Mississippi Valley was a regional manifestation of a nation-wide development. It had few local peculiarities not found else-where in the broader fight against rate inequalities, and it con-tributed few original substantive rules to American law. Its major innovations were either procedural or belonged to that twilight zone where substance and procedure are hard to distinguish. All the important Granger innovations—the strong commission, judi-cial review, and the classification of roads based on earnings—were concessions to the railroad interests.

In the upper Mississippi Valley, the evolution of legal and ad-ministrative ideas followed the pattern of the nation as a whole. Crude prorata bills and rigid schedules of maximum rates gave way to long-and-short-haul clauses and legal tariffs graduated ac-cording to distance and differentiated on the basis of financial clas-sification. In the West as in the East, the opposition to state con-trols was based upon economic and political considerations and not upon constitutional or philosophical ideas. The have-not, weak-road areas fought legislation that endangered the development of new lines or threatened the existence of weak roads. They blocked measures that seemed calculated to "alarm capital and crush enter-prise." The ultimate success of the reform movement depended upon the extension of railroad facilities to unserved areas and upon the modification of regulatory principles in line with corporate demands. The trend between 1860 and 1874 was everywhere to-ward a recognition of the peculiarities of railroad economics and an acceptance of the need for flexibility in the administration of controls. From the standpoint of both law and economics, the Granger laws of 1871 were far more stringent than those of 1873 and 1874.

In dealing with discrimination, the Granger states varied their approach to adjust to local economic and political considerations. Personal discrimination was attacked directly; local discrimination was treated in accordance with the particular sectional interests of the different states. The desire to control the flow of trade for the benefit of the state was as important to the lawmakers as was the protection of individual interests. The schedules of the Minnesota law of 1871 and the Iowa law of 1874 gave definite preference to intrastate trade, especially that stopping at the river. The legislation of Illinois and Wisconsin reflected the rivalry of Chicago, St. Louis, Milwaukee, Duluth, and other primary collecting points for the trade of the trans-Mississippi West. By 1874, however, the general principle of the long-and-short-haul clause had triumphed in Illinois and Minnesota.

Since the problem of discrimination could never be divorced entirely from the problem of rate levels, each state provided in some way for the establishment of legal maxima. At first, Illinois arbitrarily restricted each companies' charges to those actually in force during the year 1870. When combined with provisions against local discrimination, this compelled each company to base its entire schedule of tolls on rates previously charged at competitive points. This highly restrictive measure was a temporary expedient; Illinois ultimately placed the problem in the hands of a commission, a solution copied by Minnesota. Wisconsin, like Iowa, designated legal maxima by statute, but gave a limited power of modification to her commission.

From the standpoint of substantive and procedural law, the chief contribution of the Granger railroad legislation can be traced to the judicial opinion of Chief Justice Charles Lawrence of the Illinois Supreme Court. Lawrence, in recommending legislation that took the final say in all matters of rate control out of the hands of the Illinois legislature and placed it in the hands of the courts, laid the foundation for modern American rate law. Using the spirit rather than the letter of the common law against unjust discrimination, the chief justice applied it to railroad practice, and there emerged an interesting reversal of terms. The common law, developed in an age of competitive carriers and noncompetitive highways, had concerned itself with personal discrimination only. It declared that unjust discrimination consisted of charging one individual more than the common rate for a given service under similar conditions. It held that a rate above the usual level at a particular station was prima facie evidence of unjust treatment, and the common law did not accept monopolistic conditions as a valid excuse for discrimination. Lawrence, in dealing with local discrimination, established a rule suited to the age of monopolistic carriers and competitive highways. He declared that a charge below the common rate—in this case a lesser charge for a greater distance—was prima facie evidence of unjust treatment, and that competition was not a valid excuse. In the Illinois act of 1873, this principle was logically extended to cover all cases of personal discrimination involving preferential rates. But it was the court and not the legislature that passed on the injustice of the rate. The law merely provided rules of evidence, procedure, and punishments.

The other important legal contributions of the Granger laws, also found for the first time in Illinois legislation, were even more distinctly procedural. A board of commissioners was established and endowed with power to institute legal proceedings against those railroads that failed to comply with state law. To assist individual shippers in future judicial struggles with giant railroad corporations, the commission was also authorized to prepare schedules of charges that could be presented in all state courts as prima facie evidence of what reasonable maximum rates might be in each instance. The burden of proof in all cases involving claims of unreasonable rail rates was thereby shifted to the carrier.

The Illinois system of judicial control was copied by Minnesota and by several other states. It remained on the statute books of Illinois after many of the other experiments had been swept away, and in 1887 it was used as a model for the first Interstate Commerce Act.[11] Of all the Granger railroad laws the Illinois act of 1873 was the most moderate and the one most satisfactory to the railroad interests. It not only included the concessions made by all the states of the upper Mississippi Valley to the requirements of railroad economics and the strong-and-weak-road problem, but it also incorporated the doctrine maintained by railroad attorneys that reasonableness, or more correctly, unreasonableness, was purely a judicial matter. It is hard to find any radicalism in the Illinois act of 1873.

The Illinois and Minnesota laws of 1871 and the Iowa and Wisconsin statutes of 1874, on the other hand, imposed fixed maximum rates upon all traffic carried within their states. The level of charges imposed by legislative authority in each case was below that in force at the time and put binding restrictions on the companies' freedom of operation. Price fixing of this sort was not new, of course, but if the legislatures of the various states persisted in applying the principle, it would seriously impair the value of railroad shares. The companies were willing to concede the appropriateness of antidiscrimination measures as long as the laws permitted them an opportunity to defend their action in court. But rigid rate maxima were a different matter entirely.

On this point the railroad leaders took the strongest possible stand, even to the extent of supporting other forms of regulation in the hope of warding off the greater evil of fixed maxima. They had relied on the "alarmed capital" argument as their principal defense, and this argument had served them well through the 1850s and 1860s. It was the rallying point for the have-not and weak-road interests, and it successfully blocked most hostile legislation during the construction of each state's railroad network. The increasing failure of this argument after 1870, however, compelled the companies to fall back on the courts, which had not been particularly friendly to railroad interests. The state legislatures, for the most part, had proven far more willing to shape the law in favor of railroad construction and operation. When it became necessary for the railroads to resort to the courts for protection against these same legislatures, the possibilities for favorable action were severely limited. Defense against hostile statutes could sometimes be found in the contract clauses of state and federal constitutions, but there was no established body of law upon which the companies could stand in opposition to rate regulation. Somewhat reluctantly, therefore, the larger railroad companies in the upper Mississippi Valley set out in 1874 to prove that legislative rate restrictions were not only unwise and detrimental to the economic progress of the state, but were also contrary to American principles of constitutional law and subversive of fundamental rights of property. For the first time in American history, a group of business corporations challenged the sovereign power of the states to regulate rates and prices.

nine **PUBLIC POLICY**
AND PRIVATE RIGHTS

J UDICIAL REVIEW of the Granger laws began with
the indictment of various railroad and warehouse companies for
failure to observe the Illinois and Minnesota statutes of 1871. It
ended with two obscure opinions by the United States Supreme
Court in 1883.[1] The climax of this long history of litigation came
in March 1877 when the Supreme Court gave its opinion in a
series of eight cases known collectively as the Granger cases.[2] By
that time a good part of the legislation had been substantially
altered, if not actually repealed. Nevertheless, the railroad and
warehouse interests pressed their appeals, hoping to find sanctuary
in the federal courts against all further attempts at legislative
control.

The eight Granger cases, decided in 1877, contained the entire
substance of the companies' plea. The laws under attack were the
Illinois Warehouse Act of 1871, the Minnesota Railroad Act of
the same year, and the Iowa and Wisconsin laws of 1874. The
Illinois and Minnesota statutes of 1873 and 1874 were not being
challenged. The only issue was the right of state legislatures to fix
maximum rates and to make those rates binding on railroads and
warehouses in their respective states. The commission system of
control was never seriously questioned on constitutional grounds.[3]

From the outset, the major railroad and grain elevator companies had refused to be bound by the obnoxious laws, and whenever private or public suits had been brought against them, they fought in the state courts as best they could. By 1874 they had won their battle against the Illinois Railroad Act of 1871, they had lost in the Minnesota Supreme Court, and a case involving the Illinois Warehouse Act of 1871 was still pending.[4] But with the adoption of the Iowa and Wisconsin laws of 1874, the companies decided to change their tactics; they now took the initiative and transferred the contest to the federal courts. To this end, they undertook to block all further state action by federal injunction. They were not wholly successful in their efforts, but their actions did help to bring the offending laws before the United States Supreme Court with a minimum of delay.

The decision to invoke federal authority and to remove the dispute from state jurisdiction was made by the owners of the larger railroad companies: the Chicago and North Western; the Chicago, Milwaukee, and St. Paul (until 1874 the Milwaukee and St. Paul); and the Chicago, Burlington, and Quincy. The Chicago and North Western or its subsidiaries and affiliates were involved in five of the eight Granger cases, while the Milwaukee Road was a party to two of the suits, and the Burlington was the plaintiff in one.[5] Although there was much consultation among all the major companies prior to this action, the main burden of litigation was carried by these three railroads. This was entirely appropriate. The North Western, the Milwaukee, and the Burlington railroads were among the largest combinations of industrial capital in the country. All were owned largely by eastern capitalists, and all were ably led. The North Western and the Milwaukee owned properties in all four Granger states, while the Burlington operated in three of them. Each had recently consolidated its interstate holdings, and each had ambitious plans for further expansion. The three companies agreed that the rates imposed in Iowa and Wisconsin would reduce their net earnings by at least one quarter. If this proved to be true, it would be impossible for them to meet their obligations to their bondholders and stockholders.[6] Furthermore, the various laws denied them the opportunity to operate freely as interstate systems, since they were compelled to conform to different rules and standards of management in each of the four states. For all these reasons the value of their properties was seriously impaired, and the need to escape state legislative jurisdiction was compelling.

As might be expected, the North Western and the Milwaukee roads acted as virtually one company in all the legal action that followed. Before taking any measures with respect to the Potter law, they asked for advisory opinions on the validity of the law from three of the country's leading attorneys: namely, E. Rockwood Hoar, attorney general under President Grant; William M. Evarts, attorney general under President Johnson and soon to be secretary of state under President Hayes; and former Supreme Court Justice Benjamin R. Curtis. These three distinguished constitutional lawyers all agreed that the Potter law was invalid and recommended that it be challenged in the federal courts.[7] The companies eagerly complied. Presidents Albert Keep of the North Western and Alexander Mitchell of the Milwaukee informed Wisconsin Governor Taylor of their decision. "Being fully conscious that the enforcement of this law will ruin the property of the company," wrote Mitchell, "and feeling assured of the correctness of the opinions of the eminent counsel who have examined the question, the directors feel compelled to disregard the provisions of the law so far as it fixes a tariff of rates for the company until the courts have finally passed upon the question of validity." [8] The North Western then invoked federal jurisdiction by filing parallel suits on behalf of its bondholders and stockholders in the federal court of the Western District of Wisconsin. The plea asked for an injunction restraining both the company and the state from complying with the provisions of the Potter law on the grounds that the act was unconstitutional.[9]

Meanwhile, the Burlington had reached a similar decision. Faced with a large number of suits for charges in excess of the legal rates in Iowa, the company attempted to block all further state judicial action. It sought an injunction in the Circuit Court of the United States for Iowa, asking that the state's attorney general be stopped from prosecuting any suit involving the law of 1874. The plea maintained that the law was in violation of both the United States and Iowa constitutions.[10]

The railroads preferred to make their stand in the federal courts for a number of reasons. In the first place, the companies seriously doubted the impartiality of the state courts, and it is true that these courts were highly responsive to popular political pressures. In Illinois, Iowa, and Minnesota the judges were elected, and the candidates' views on current issues were often decisive in their selection. Thus the defeat of Chief Justice Charles Lawrence of the Illinois Supreme Court in his bid for reelection in 1873 was commonly attributed to his ruling against the Illinois railroad law of 1871. Similar circumstances obtained even where judges were appointed. In Wisconsin, for example, Governor Taylor appointed the highly respected but somewhat controversial Edward G. Ryan of Milwaukee to fill the vacancy created by Chief Justice Luther Dixon's resignation early in 1874. Taylor's choice was quite frankly influenced by his desire to have the Potter law upheld, and Ryan was known to favor it.[11] Politics was always a factor in the selection of state judges, and in 1874 feelings against the railroads were running high.

The rulings of the various state courts on the issues relevant to the Granger cases, moreover, did not promise much relief for railroad and elevator interests. The railway corporations intended to show that their charter rights had been impaired. Along with their warehouse allies they intended to prove that legislative rate restrictions violated fundamental rights of property. Carrying this argument to its logical conclusion, they were prepared to claim, in the words of former Justice Curtis, that "it is not within the field of legislation under any American constitution, to fix and prescribe for the future what price shall be demanded either for commodities or for personal service, or *for a union of both.*"[12] In other words, the reasonableness of rates was a matter for judicial determination. State court opinions were not in sympathy with any of these claims, arguing that a charter offered protection against legislative regulation only where specific grants of immunity had been made. In matters of this kind a corporation had no more rights against the state than an ordinary businessman, and both were subject to the same police regulations, including price regulations. State, and for that matter, federal rulings provided little room for argument on this score.[13]

With regard to property rights, the state courts had been no more encouraging. During the 1850s and 1860s a number of cases involving state prohibition laws had come up for adjudication. Many of these laws severely restricted the sale of intoxicating beverages, and in some cases, the business of liquor dealers had been completely destroyed. In a series of court actions, the dealers claimed that the laws deprived them of property without just compensation or due process of law, and they held that this was a violation of the state constitutions. With one exception, however, the courts ruled that there had been no deprivation of property. The value of property, according to state court rulings, was not measured in commercial terms; liquor was valuable because it could be consumed, not because it could be sold for a profit. Since in most cases the dealers retained full title to all the beverages in question, and since the owners had no legal claim to the anticipated return or profit that the sale of the liquor might bring, they could not claim any loss of property.[14]

There had been one exception to this general rule. In *Wynehamer v. The People* the New York Court of Appeals held that a prohibition law was unconstitutional, but because the actual confiscation of liquor was involved in this case, it was more than a matter of anticipated profits. One of the judges in the majority, Judge George Franklin Comstock, insisted that legislative action by itself did not constitute due process of law in cases involving private rights. Judicial review of the legislative decision was required. In his opinion the New York prohibition law was invalid because it failed to adequately compensate the dealers for their losses. Since this was the opinion of only one of the judges, it was not the basis of the majority decision, but Comstock's opinion was to have a considerable influence. It meant, in effect, that the courts should have the final say in all matters involving rights of life, liberty, and property.[15]

Comstock's view of due process was not widely held in 1856, the year of the *Wynehamer* decision, and it was not widely held by state judges in the 1870s. Although its influence was growing, the doctrine still offered little protection against legislative police power. Decisions affecting the use of property were still thought to be well within the province of the legislatures. The courts intervened only when a person was actually deprived of possession or personal use of tangible property.

On broad questions concerning the role of government in the economy, the state courts were ambiguous. The legislative power to fix reasonable standards of rates and prices had never been denied, but at the same time, the courts had begun to acknowledge the existence of so-called private businesses. In popular usage the term *private business* originally meant individual, as opposed to corporate, enterprise. The classical economists had favored private enterprise in this sense. But in the United States during the debates over public works, the term had acquired a different meaning. After 1837, the demonstrated superiority of privately owned business was attributed to the private initiative of the owners, even though they were stockholders in large corporations. The reaction against public works blurred the distinction between individual and corporate enterprise and combined them both under the heading of private business as opposed to state operations. The states withdrew from business enterprises after 1837, and their withdrawal had often been accompanied by constitutional amendments limiting any future participation. As a result of their unfortunate experiences with internal improvements, the people had demanded a clear separation of government and business amounting to a denial of all public interest in commercial and industrial undertakings.[16] At the same time, the correlative assumption had been made that business enterprise did not serve a public purpose, and this idea had also begun to find its way into the law of the land.

Two different editions of Angell and Ames' treatise, *Private Corporations Aggregate,* illustrate the change in attitude following the debacles of the late 1830s. The first edition, published in 1832, declared that the purpose of a business corporation was "to gain the union, contribution, and assistance of several persons for the successful promotions of some design of general utility, though the corporation may, at the same time be established for the advantage of those who are members of it. . . . The design of a corporation is to provide for some good that is useful to the public." [17] The sixth edition, published in 1858, declared that "acts done by business corporations are done with a view to their own interest, and if thereby they incidentally promote that of the public, it cannot reasonably be supposed they do it from any spirit of liberality they have beyond that of their fellow citizens. Both the property and the sole object of every such corporation are essentially private, and from them the individuals composing the company corporate are to derive profit." [18]

If the sole purpose of a business was "essentially private," certain limitations on the powers of state legislatures logically followed. During the 1850s and 1860s the courts began to impose tight restrictions on the powers of local governments to subsidize business enterprises. Taxation for this purpose, it was now said, would not serve a public need and would therefore be void. A justice of the Maine Supreme Court commented in 1870 that "there is nothing of a public nature any more entitling the manufacturer to public gifts than the sailor, the mechanic, the lumberman, or the farmer." [19] The judge then proceeded to explain how public and private purposes could be distinguished. "Is the object one of those which government was instituted to provide for—or is it one which by long-settled usage has been left to be fostered by private enterprise, industry, and liberality, because its profits flow directly into the pockets of private individuals or corporations, and the benefit which it confers on the community is only incidental and secondary." [20] Purpose, in other words, was a matter of interest or ownership. In a subsequent ruling the Maine court went on to state that "it is beyond the legislative power by force of an enactment to make that public which is essentially private." [21] Other courts took the same position at this time. [22]

Local subsidies for railroads, it is true, were permitted to continue, but this was only because railroads served a commonly recognized public purpose. A Pennsylvania court noted that a railroad was not "a mere private enterprise, like the building of a tavern, store, mill, or blacksmith's shop." [23] But even in the case of railroads there were indications of a changing view. Following a series of unhappy experiences with local railroad subsidies in the 1850s, efforts were made to block this last remnant of public aid. A number of state courts took the position that railroad enterprise should also be considered entirely private. Expressing surprise "that the voluntary use of private capital, for the exclusive advantage and profit of those who contribute it is a *public use* of it, justifying compulsory taxation in favor of this private enterprise," Judge John F. Dillon's court declared the Iowa aid law of 1868 unconstitutional.[24] In 1870 Judge Thomas M. Cooley declared that railroads "cannot be aided by the public funds any more than can any other private undertaking. . . ." [25] The Wisconsin Supreme Court ruled similarly that same year.[26]

In the case of railroads, the state courts were overruled by the United States Supreme Court in 1873. Railroads were indeed a matter of public concern, according to the Court, and local governments could not escape their obligations on the grounds of private purpose.[27] Consequently, the idea that business might serve a public purpose was not wiped out altogether. A few common callings remained among a growing number of private enterprises, but even before the federal court ruling, the railroad corporations saw little benefit in the new legal concept of private business. They were more than willing to admit their public character in order to obtain local subsidies, and insofar as the idea of private business had been advanced in railroad cases, it had been used to the disadvantage of the companies. Furthermore, there was no reason to assume that privateness in business granted immunity from legislative control. This might be a logical inference, consistent with the principles of laissez faire that had helped to shape the idea of private enterprise, but it was no more than that. The state courts had not suggested that the principle placed any limitation on the police power.

For good reasons, therefore, the railroads did not look to the state courts for protection. Evidence of judicial hostility to corporate interests together with the weight of legal precedent dictated a different course of action. Hence the decision to go immediately into the federal courts. As it turned out, the companies were not able to avoid further state litigation. The federal district and circuit courts in Wisconsin and Iowa refused to grant the necessary injunctions, and the many state suits against the railroads were allowed to continue toward their almost inevitable conclusion. The federal courts, at the same time, readily acknowledged the need for further review of the state statutes and immediately granted appeals to the United States Supreme Court in all the injunction cases. But the first battle in the companies' new judicial offensive clearly went to the states. Faced with the necessity of waiting for the Supreme Court's ruling, the corporations decided that it would be both politic and expedient to obey the provisions of the restrictive laws in the interim.[28]

When the Wisconsin and Illinois state courts completed their deliberations on the Granger laws, the companies' expectations were fully confirmed. The power of the legislature to regulate rail-road rates in Wisconsin had been reserved to the satisfaction of Chief Justice Ryan and the state supreme court. The Illinois court ruled that Munn and Scott's grain elevator company in Chicago had not been deprived of any property rights by the Warehouse Act of 1871 because anticipated profits were not a part of those rights.[29] In both cases, the Granger laws were held to be proper exercises of the legislative police power.

In due course, however, the pleas of the railroad and warehouse companies were placed before the United States Supreme Court in a series of eight cases. One came on appeal from the state courts of Minnesota, two from the courts of Wisconsin, and one from the courts of Illinois. Four came up from the lower federal courts in Wisconsin, Iowa, and Minnesota.[30] It was not possible for the Court to hear them consecutively, but it treated them from the beginning as parts of a whole. As early as 1874 the cases were being referred to collectively as the Granger cases.[31]

In their advisory opinions on the Potter law, attorneys Evarts, Curtis, and Hoar had all asserted with confidence that the law was in violation of the United States Constitution, and that the federal courts would find it so even if the state courts would not. It can be assumed that these men were fully aware of the body of precedent on all the relevant issues—the pertinent cases were too numerous and too recent to be overlooked—but they obviously had reason to expect that the federal courts would give a different interpretation to the law. Their confidence was due in part to the fact that the Supreme Court had only recently been called upon to review cases of this nature. Prior to the adoption of the Fourteenth Amendment in 1868, the Court did not have jurisdiction in such matters. Although the Court would not ignore state precedents, it would be free to give them fresh consideration in light of new trends in American legal and constitutional thought. The weight of precedent, the lawyers anticipated, would not lie so heavily upon the federal judges.

The Granger cases involved a conflict between public policy and private rights. The power of the community to regulate business in the common interest was pitted against the right of the citizen to enjoy the rewards of his enterprise. The law had always been concerned with both, but traditionally the balance between the two had been a matter for legislative deliberation.[32] The courts might intervene in the absence of statute in order to assure reasonable and equal charges, but once the legislatures acted, the courts deferred to their judgment. If the legislatures abused their authority, the remedy was at the polls and not in the courts.[33] This had been the essence of the state court rulings in the prohibition cases, and more recently, in the Granger cases.

In the absence of specific constitutional limitations the state assemblies had always enjoyed broad freedom of action. In the whole area of private rights their jurisdiction had been virtually unchallenged. The state courts had rarely intervened, and the federal courts had resolutely denied their own authority to do so. This did not mean that private rights were ignored, but it did mean that they were often compelled to give way to the demands of public policy.[34] A reaction against legislative authority, however, began to appear in the middle decades of the nineteenth century. There is need for much further study of this change in attitude, but it is apparent that the debates over slavery and the economic breakdown of the late 1830s were major contributory factors. The slavery controversy revived faith in natural rights principles, and the severe panics of 1837 and 1839 encouraged a greater reliance on natural laws of trade. The wisdom of state legislatures was being questioned on a broad front. The slavery debates in particular provoked a reevaluation of constitutional liberties. It seemed obvious to many lawyers that legislative decisions did not give full weight to the rights of the individual citizen, and that too often these rights were sacrificed in the name of public policy. The trend in legal thinking, therefore, was toward a substantive interpretation of due process that placed the final determination of private rights in the hands of the courts.[35] The newer view had had little impact on state court rulings prior to 1870—Judge Comstock's opinion in the New York temperance case was one of the few exceptions—but when Thomas M. Cooley expounded the new view in 1868 a large segment of the American bar was ready to accept it.[36]

The Fourteenth Amendment, adopted in 1868, was influenced in part by the new concern for private rights, and in the eyes of many leading lawyers it provided an excellent opportunity for the implementation of the new principles of constitutional liberty under the leadership of the federal government.[37] The new amendment greatly enlarged the jurisdiction of the federal courts, and although its provisions had been designed primarily to protect the civil rights of Negroes, they necessarily entailed review by the federal courts of a great mass of state legislation. Thus the whole area of private rights could now come under federal supervision.

In the *Slaughterhouse Cases* of 1873 the Supreme Court indicated that it did not intend to revolutionize the law of the land with one blow because, in the opinion of the majority, this was not the intent of the Fourteenth Amendment.[38] But a second opinion in the same year, *Bartemeyer v. Iowa,* showed the Court's willingness to assume some jurisdiction over private rights under certain circumstances. In this case the Court agreed to review one of the state prohibition laws on the grounds that it violated the property and due process guarantees of the Fourteenth Amendment. The case was a poor one, strained out of all proportion to test a constitutional principle, but the Court accepted it nevertheless. The plea of the liquor dealer was finally denied, but Justice Samuel Freeman Miller, presenting the opinion of the Court, declared that a restriction on the sale of liquor could conceivably be so rigid that it would deprive a dealer of property without due process of law. Justice Joseph Bradley, in a concurring opinion, agreed that a dealer might be entitled to compensation. The Court thus indicated a willingness to review regulatory statutes and to scrutinize their effect on individual rights. *Bartemeyer v. Iowa* was a major victory for private interests.[39]

Against this background Attorneys Curtis, Evarts, and Hoar recommended a review of the Granger laws in the federal courts.

If the Supreme Court accepted the new concepts of private rights and due process of law, the state court decisions might well be overruled. Three of the best legal minds in the country were confident that this would be the result, and their opinion was confirmed by other prominent lawyers in the press and in the law journals.[40] With this assurance the railroad companies were prepared to wage a major legal battle.

It is doubtful if a more formidable array of legal talent was ever assembled. The North Western and Milwaukee roads employed the services of Evarts, Curtis, and Hoar as well as those of John W. Cary, a distinguished Milwaukee attorney, Charles B. Lawrence, the recently defeated chief justice of the Illinois Supreme Court, Burton C. Cook of Chicago, and E. W. Stoughton of New York. Munn and Scott, the North Western's warehouse affiliate, employed William C. Goudy and John N. Jewett, leaders of the Chicago bar. The Burlington called upon their own corporation counsel, David Rorer, along with Orville H. Browning of Illinois, a former secretary of the interior, and Senator Frederick T. Frelinghuysen of New Jersey, a future secretary of state. The eminent legal reformer, David Dudley Field, filed a written argument on behalf of the Western Union Railroad, a part of the Chicago, Milwaukee, and St. Paul. And finally, with the permission of the Court, briefs and arguments were presented by counsel for the Central Pacific Railroad of California.[41] In the words of C. Peter Magrath it was a veritable "Who's Who of the post-Civil War American bar." [42]

Oral arguments in seven of the eight cases were heard over a period of four months. *Winona & St. Peter Railroad v. Blake* came first, followed by the four Wisconsin cases: *Peik v. Chicago & North Western Railway, Lawrence v. Chicago & North Western Railway, Chicago, Milwaukee & St. Paul Railway v. Ackley,* and *Stone v. Wisconsin.* Then came *Chicago, Burlington & Quincy Railroad v. Iowa* and *Munn v. Illinois.* Little known but very able states' attorneys presented solid briefs and arguments based on massive statutory and judicial precedent. The factual evidence in support of legislative regulation of rates and prices was overwhelming. "From time immemorial," said Minnesota Attorney General William P. Clough, "the right to regulate both the price and the manner of particular classes of service has been exercised by the state, both in the mother country, and in this one. . . ." [43] The burden of proof was clearly on plaintiffs in error. The arguments of railway and elevator counsel, in contrast, were necessarily thin on precedent but filled with references to fundamental principles of law and justice. Legislative regulation of rail rates, Frederick Frelinghuysen contended, "is not so much doing violence to any one particular principle of law, as it is doing violence to the whole system of jurisprudence." [44]

The strategy of the railroad and warehouse attorneys is revealed in their briefs and arguments. They maintained that the Granger laws interfered with interstate commerce and violated certain charter rights. They also argued that the laws impaired obligations of contracts between the railroads and their creditors because the reduction in earnings would prevent the companies from making interest payments on their bonded debts. But these were not the central issues. The crux of their arguments turned on the nature of property rights, the threat of legislative infringement upon these rights, and the necessity for judicial intervention and control. Counsel made strenuous efforts to establish a concept of property consistent with modern business needs. The repeated refusal of the state courts to consider anticipated income as a part of the property right was held to be quite unrealistic. John Cary insisted that "property is chiefly valuable to the owner on account of the income it yields." He urged the Court, in effect, to look upon property as a business asset and to judge its value accordingly.[45] Orville Browning made essentially the same plea: "Income is property, as well as that out of which it proceeds, and by the same authority that the owner is deprived of the one, he may be deprived of the other." [46] John Jewett was less restrained. "Is there any man on earth," he asked, "mean enough to say, or of comprehension so warped and twisted as to believe, that if services and the use of property of the market value of $10, in the absence of legislation, is, by legislation reduced to one cent, property is not taken, or the owner is not deprived of property?" [47] Railroad counsel also stressed the fact that ownership in a railway corporation was synonymous with investment. "The only purpose of investing in [a railroad] is to obtain a fair profit . . . ," E. W. Stoughton declared. "Whenever, therefore, its income is taken, or so controlled by the State that none, or less than a just compensation is derivable from its property, the latter is in a most substantial sense taken without due process of law and without compensation." Millions of dollars had been invested in railway enterprise for the sole purpose of realizing a fair return. These properties could be rendered virtually worthless as investments if the rights of this special form of property were not respected. "The right of stockholders to a fair return for their investment," Stoughton concluded, "was as sacred as that of any other owner of private property to its proceeds. . . ." [48]

The Court was repeatedly urged to recognize the needs of an expanding industrial capitalism. "Capitalists," Browning argued, "will not adventure money in railroads which are under the absolute domination of legislatures." [49] Dire consequences were predicted if the rights of property were not expanded to cover the rights of venture capital. "It is the beginning of the operation of the commune in the legislation of this country," cried Cary, "and if not checked at the threshold, will ultimately overthrow not only the rights of property, but personal liberty and independence as well." [50]

Having asserted and defined the rights of business property, counsel attacked the powers of the state legislatures. Legislative regulation of prices, they contended, was not consistent with principles of constitutional liberty. "The idea that the legislature has a general power [to fix prices]," C. B. Lawrence contended, "is at war with every principle of free government, and with all those provisions of our American Constitution which were designed to protect the natural rights of man against legislative aggression." [51] Counsel took issue with the states' claims that railroads and grain elevators could be subjected to regulation because of their special public character. "The right to build and operate a warehouse," said William Goudy, "was at common law, and always has been a private and individual right. The business is in its nature a private business." [52] Cary insisted that the railroad business "is no more of a public character than a hundred other kinds of business which are admitted to be private and the compensation fixed by those engaged therein, without interference of the State." [53]

Jewett brushed aside as relics of a by-gone age the many examples of price fixing cited by the states' attorneys. They were out of step with "the new theory and ideas of protection to private rights upon which this government was founded." He urged the Court to strike down these "implements of a former system" and to restrain "the pretensions of legislative power in the States." [54] Urging protection for private rights, he called for a new *Dartmouth College* decision which would "hold in check all the efforts of radical politicians and crazy communists, who have from time to time, sought to make capital for themselves by the overthrow of the financial interests and credit of the country." [55]

Coming finally to a specific point of constitutional law, counsel argued that legislative regulation of rates and prices was not constitutional because it failed to provide adequate safeguards for rights of property and consequently was not due process of law. Citing Judge Comstock's opinion in *Wynehamer v. The People,* Frelinghuysen asserted that "that due process of law without which the citizen may not be deprived of property is not committed to the legislature." He did not maintain that railroad and warehouse companies had a right to exact any price they wished for their services—they could exact no more than a reasonable price—but reasonableness was not to be determined by arbitrary legislative fiat.[56] Lawrence held that "its determination belongs to the courts, where the company can justify its charges by proper evidence, and be heard in its own defense." He pointed to the complexity of the problems involved in judgments of this nature. Clearly such matters were beyond the competence of a legislative body.[57] Browning agreed. He could not imagine "a less suitable depository of the power to fix and regulate railroad fares . . . than the General Assembly. . . ." [58]

In one sense the arguments of railroad and warehouse counsel were all-or-nothing arguments offering no compromise with the legislative authority. On the other hand, they did not posit absolute freedom from public control. Judicial review of rates was found to be entirely acceptable and even desirable. The problem was to establish standards of reasonableness sufficiently flexible to protect both the public and the companies' property. That the companies wanted these standards based primarily on the needs of the companies rather than on those of their customers is quite obvious.[59] But here was the limit of their claim. Here was the tacit acceptance of the kind of regulation imposed by the Illinois act of 1873, an act for which lawyer Charles Lawrence could claim a good deal of responsibility.

The Court delivered its opinions in the eight Granger cases on March 1, 1877, more than a year after hearing oral arguments. "We have kept the cases long under advisement," explained Chief Justice Morrison R. Waite, "in order that their decision might be the result of our mature deliberation." In presenting its findings the Court placed the warehouse case first. Munn and Scott was a partnership rather than a corporation, and consequently its suit, free of all the complications resulting from corporate charter provisions, permitted a more direct confrontation with the basic issues raised by plaintiff's counsel.[60] The powers of the state legislatures, the extent of the property right, and the meaning of due process of law were all considered at some length in this context. The railroad cases were then dealt with briefly in accordance with the *Munn* ruling. Questions of interstate commerce and contract rights were disposed of at appropriate points along the way.

The Court rejected the railroad and warehouse plea on all counts. "It has been customary in England from time immemorial, and in this country from its first colonization," Waite declared, "to regulate ferries, common carriers, hackmen, bakers, millers, wharfingers, innkeepers, etc., and in so doing to fix a maximum of charge to be made for services rendered, accommodations furnished, and articles sold." The exercise of this police power by the Granger state legislatures had been entirely consistent with this practice. "We think it has never yet been successfully contended that such legislation came within any of the constitutional prohibitions against interference with private property." The reasonableness of rates and prices was not a judicial question alone. In the absence of statutory regulations the courts might intervene in the interest of fair and equal treatment, but once the legislature had taken control, the courts had to abide by its decisions. "We know this is a power which may be abused; but that is no argument against its existence. For protection against abuses by the legislature the people must resort to the polls, not to the courts." [61]

The remaining issues were dealt with very quickly. There had been no infringement upon the federal government's authority to regulate interstate commerce. If Congress had assumed jurisdiction over the commerce in question its control would be exclusive, but it had not done so. The states had a right to regulate as much of that commerce as took place within their own borders.[62] Similarly, the Court found no impairment of contract obligations as Iowa, Minnesota, and Wisconsin had all reserved the right to alter or amend the charters they granted.[63] The argument that it was the duty of the railroad companies to pay interest on their bonded debt had little force, since obligations to creditors did not take precedence over obligations to the public.[64]

Reduced to their simplest terms, the decisions in the Granger cases seem to be straightforward reaffirmations of state court rulings. This restricted view of the matter, however, is misleading and robs the cases of much of their historical significance. In *Munn v. Illinois* the Court was not satisfied simply to state the law as it applied to the cases at hand. Rather, it felt compelled to give an elaborate rationale of the legislative power over prices. In the process, the Court placed the Granger cases in a constitutional framework that departed considerably from established constitutional tradition. The new ideas of private rights and due process were very much a part of its ruling.

The Court did not concede an unlimited power over prices to the state legislatures, but confined this power to a particular category of businesses, those in which the use of property was "clothed with a public interest." "When . . . one devotes his property to a use in which the public has an interest," said Waite, "he in effect grants to the public an interest in that use, and must submit to be controlled by the public for the common good, to the extent of the interest he has created." The principle was vague and could have justified public regulation of any business, but the Court made it clear that the real test of the need for public control was the existence of monopoly.[65]

A monopoly, in the eyes of the Court, did not necessarily mean exclusive privilege. It meant that the public was somehow compelled to make use of the services involved, and that the business stood in a special relationship to the community at large. In an earlier time this had been true of bakers and innkeepers; it was now true of Chicago grain elevators and western railroads. "They stand in the very 'gateway of commerce, and take toll from all who pass.' " [66] Property, in the case of elevators and railroads, was clearly affected with a public interest which gave the community the right to legislatively regulate prices.[67]

The Court justified this principle on the basis of ancient common law usage. Lord Chief Justice Matthew Hale, in a seventeenth-century treatise on the law governing the ports of England, had said that if a man sets up a wharf or crane he "may take what rates he and his customers can agree [on] . . . for he doth no more than is lawful." If, however, "the king or subject have a public wharf, into which all persons . . . must come," then "the duties must be reasonable and moderate, though settled by the king's license or charter. For now the wharf and crane . . . are affected with a public interest, and they cease to be *juris privati* only." [68] In 1810 Lord Ellenborough ruled that "there is no doubt . . . that every man may fix which price he pleases upon his own property or the use of it, but if . . . the public have a right to resort to his premises . . . and he have a monopoly in them for that purpose, if he will take the benefit of that monopoly he must . . . perform the duty attached to it on reasonable terms." [69] In each case the existence of a monopoly established the need for control.

Charles Fairman has shown that Supreme Court Justice Joseph Bradley was largely responsible for the inclusion of these English texts. Bradley had prepared a memorandum on the Granger cases for Chief Justice Waite, who had relied very heavily on it in preparing the majority opinion. Bradley reviewed the common law precedents for public regulation and included all the texts that bolstered the final decision. He made it clear that the citations were all statements of judicial policy, that they were applicable

only in the absence of statute, and that they had nothing whatsoever to do with legislative power. Nevertheless, he was whole-
heartedly in accord with the principles expressed, and he thought
them applicable to the Granger cases.[70]

Prior to his appointment to the Supreme Court, Bradley had
been general counsel for the Camden and Amboy Railroad, the
most notorious of all the antebellum railway monopolies. His experience had convinced him of the dangers of unchecked monopolies, and in his memorandum to Waite he expressed his views with
considerable feeling: "Unrestricted monopolies as to those things
which the people must have and use, are a canker in any society,
and have ever been the occasion of civil convulsions and revolu-
tions. A people disposed for freedom will not tolerate this kind
of oppression at the hands of private corporations or private citizens." [71]

But there were two sides to the principle that Bradley adduced.
Lord Hale had also asserted a man's lawful right to make the
most of his own, and Lord Ellenborough had referred to "a general principle favored both in law and justice, that every man may
fix which price he pleases upon his own property or the use of
it." [72] Again, these were statements of judicial policy, and they
posed no limitation upon the power of Parliament, but they were
very much a part of the principle that Bradley urged in support
of public control of monopolies. Bradley did not suggest that this
common law principle be accepted as a rule of American constitutional law. He advanced the principle merely as partial justification for legislative regulation of railroads and warehouses. In the
Court's final opinion in the *Munn* case, however, the principle did
appear as a rule of constitutional law. The whole public interest
doctrine was drawn from Lord Hale's dicta. On Hale's supposed
authority, businesses were separated once again into two categories:
those in which property was affected with a public interest and
those in which it was not. The Court did not refer to the earlier
distinction, made by both state and federal courts, for the purpose
of allowing or disallowing public subsidies, but the division was
substantially the same. Public utilities served a special public
purpose or use, and it was this attribute that permitted regulation
as well as public subsidy. Private businesses did not serve such a

purpose or use, and consequently, they were free from public influence and control. Bradley's original use of the principle had not been so prescriptive, but he nevertheless gave his wholehearted approval to Waite's opinion.[73]

From the standpoint of constitutional law the significant point is not that a further distinction had been made between public and private business, but rather that this distinction was to be made by the courts and not by the legislatures. The text of *Munn v. Illinois* clearly implies the point, and it is confirmed by Waite's private correspondence. In a letter written shortly after the decision, the chief justice commented on the difficulty the Court would have in drawing the line in certain cases.[74] Subsequent Supreme Court decisions took it for granted that the Court was expected to make the decision.

An important result of the Court's decision in the Granger cases, therefore, was the placing of a broad class of private rights beyond the reach of the state legislatures. These were rights of economic liberty identified with the new concept of private business. The Court does not appear to have regarded them as rights of property since it rejected the railroad and warehouse argument concerning the right to a "fair return," but rights of liberty were at stake—rights resulting from a proper separation of business and government.[75] The conduct of trade was no longer a matter for legislative direction, and a man was now free to enjoy the fruits of his labors subject only to the salutary restraints of the laws of trade and to standards of fair practice required by the common law. In law, as in prevailing economic theory, there was justification for government intervention only in cases of monopoly where natural market forces were unable to protect the public interest. And it was the courts, not the legislatures, who were to be the final judges of the need for government involvement. In the last analysis, then, the Granger decisions incorporated all the constitutional implications of the trend toward laissez faire.

The Court's implied limitation of the police power in the interest of private economic freedom reflected its acceptance of the newer concept of due process of law. Without any clear constitutional sanction, the Court grafted its own ideas of private rights upon the law of the land and sharply curtailed the powers of the state legislatures. There is little discussion of the meaning of due process in the *Munn* decision, but the Court's judgment was so in tune with prevailing economic and constitutional ideas that there was no apparent protest over its assumption of jurisdiction. The only objections stemmed from the exceptions that had been made in the case of railroads and warehouses.[76]

It is apparent, then, that the Supreme Court accepted the new concept of private rights and due process, but not in such a way as to benefit the railway interests. Counsel had failed completely in their efforts to win judicial protection for their companies' property, and in view of the requirements of the new industrial order, their claims were not outrageous. They had ample cause to question the competence of state assemblies to act as modern regulatory agencies, and they had dutifully suggested a viable alternative to legislative control. But it was all to no avail.

It is significant that a group of lawyers worthy of appointment to the highest court in the land should have had so little sympathy for the needs of venture capital in 1877. Although several of the justices had worked for railroad corporations, they looked upon the demands of industrial capitalism with suspicion. Justice Miller commented privately, "I have met with but few things of a character affecting the public good of the whole country that has shaken my faith in human nature as much as the united, vigorous, and selfish effort of the capitalists . . . a class whose only interest or stake in the country is the ownership of these bonds and stocks. They engage in no commerce, no trade, no manufactures, no agriculture. They *produce nothing*." [77] The members of the Waite court were products of the antebellum era, and the fact that two of the justices dissented from the Court's ruling in all eight of the Granger cases must have been small consolation to the railway and elevator companies. Justice Stephen Field, supported by Justice Strong, gave one of his most memorable minority opinions in the *Munn* case. Field's dissent was little more than a critical commentary on the majority opinion, and apparently was written sometime after the Court's announcement of its findings.[78] He gave appellant's counsel every point and called the majority opinion "subversive of the rights of private property." [79] In his dissenting opinion, Field took counsel's position that the unreasonableness of a charge was a matter for judicial consideration only. He scolded the Court for missing an opportunity to define the limits of state power in such a way as to safeguard the private interests of stockholders and at the same time to protect the public against arbitrary and extortionate charges.[80] Indicating that he saw eye to eye with railroad counsel, he stated: "The questions presented are of the gravest importance and their solution must materially affect the value of property invested in railroads to the amount of many hundreds of millions, and will have great influence in encouraging or repelling future investment in such property." [81]

This was a minority opinion in 1877, but it was an accurate forecast of things to come. In time, the Court responded more favorably to the needs of the new industrial order, and by the 1890s Field's view was that of the majority. In 1890 the Court ruled that the reasonableness of a railroad rate was quite properly a matter for judicial determination.[82] In 1898 it declared that owners of business property were indeed entitled to a fair return on a fair evaluation of their property, and that to deny them this by legislative action was to deprive them of property without due process of law.[83] Thus the contention of the railroad owners, first asserted in the struggle over the Granger laws, was finally vindicated. After twenty years, the radicalism of the more stringent Granger laws was judicially confirmed.

ten SUMMARY

I N 1877 THE UNITED STATES Supreme Court upheld
the power of the states to regulate intrastate commerce in spite
of the claims of private industrial capital. Although this power
might be limited by the contract clause of the Constitution and
by the new doctrine of public interest, it extended to the control
of all essential commercial facilities and included the right to fix
rates and prices by statute. The Court made it clear that in the
future the judiciary would have to be consulted more frequently
on matters of this kind, but the right of the legislatures to pursue
traditional economic policies was affirmed.

The economy of the United States from the time of independence had been structured within state lines and in accordance with
principles that reflected the dominance of mercantile and agricultural interests. Whereas a considerable degree of freedom was
accorded to all industrial undertakings, the states had attempted
to monopolize and control the commerce within their borders for
the benefit of their own trading interests. In this process the
larger marketing centers had exercised a political influence far in
excess of their proportionate strength in the electorate, and they
generally determined the legislative policies of the states in col-
laboration with the more important landed interests. Through

elaborate policies of promotion and public works, including rail-roads, these interests attempted to shape their economies in accord-ance with local, rather than regional or national, goals.

Following the financial disasters of the late 1830s and early 1840s, the states withdrew from their involvement with commer-cial and industrial activities and placed greater reliance on private initiative and competitive market forces for the stimulation and regulation of economic activity. They did so with the expectation that these natural forces would serve traditional economic goals, but they soon discovered that a new breed of railway capitalists was taking advantage of new economic opportunities to develop regional systems that seriously threatened the prosperity of the established order. Having divested themselves of the responsibility of directing and even operating railway enterprise, the states found that they had acquired an equally troublesome railroad problem.

Competitive interstate railroad operations produced rate-making practices that conflicted not only with local business interests, but also with basic standards of law and equity. Common law rules and procedures proved incapable of dealing with the many forms of railroad rate discrimination that resulted from competition among privately owned highways, and it became necessary to take the issue before the state legislatures. There, the new owners of interstate properties, with millions of dollars of accumulated capital at stake, came into conflict with the older mercantile and industrial establishments. The state assemblies found it all but impossible to reconcile the two interests and with increasing regu-larity fell back upon arbitrary legislative restrictions in order to satisfy local demands. Antidiscrimination laws and schedules of fixed maximum rates became more and more common during the 1860s and 1870s.

The power to pass such laws was really beyond question;[1] the wisdom of doing so was another matter. From the outset rail rates had been subjected to various forms of legislative regulation, but railway economics was poorly understood in the middle decades of the nineteenth century. The size of the industry, moreover, had introduced problems that were entirely without precedent. The capitalist—the investor in railroad shares—whether he was a local taxpayer or an absentee owner, was an indispensable part of the new order of private enterprise, and his interests could not be ignored without imperiling the whole system. Legislative trial and error produced numerous attempts at compromise during the sixties and seventies, and along with the many short-lived failures there emerged the beginnings of a workable system of public regulation. In time, flexible antidiscrimination laws and commission-controlled rates subject to judicial review became the basis of much legislation.

The Granger laws of the 1870s were part of this process of trial and error. Because of the unusually competitive nature of railroad enterprise in the upper Mississippi Valley and because of the high concentration of absentee control in that area, the Granger states became major centers of political experiment with the railroad question. The great distance between these states and their eastern markets, the rawness of their burgeoning economies, and the immaturity of their political life undoubtedly intensified the difficulties they experienced. The strong sense of sectionalism in the West was another factor that gave a distinctive character to the movement for reform in the Mississippi Valley, but the Farmers' Movement of the 1870s was not a major force in the shaping of this regulatory legislation. The so-called Granger laws dealt with issues that were national in scope, and in most every case the leaders of the movement for reform were merchants and businessmen rather than farmers.

In response to the aggressive attacks by western state legislatures, the great railroad systems of the upper Mississippi Valley retaliated with the first major judicial blow on behalf of the rights of industrial capital. By the mid-seventies the need for court action in defense of investors' rights coincided with the feasibility of such action, thus enabling the railroads to assume the judicial offensive. Before 1870 even the strongest of the railroad builders had depended to a considerable degree upon the financial aid of local communities through which they intended to run their trains. To entrepreneurs like John Murray Forbes, local subscriptions were the measure of a railroad's promise, and few were willing to undertake operations without such evidence of local support. The opportunities for land grants prior to 1873 were a second consideration which kept the corporations under obligation to the states and discouraged any inclination to break with their authority. By the mid-seventies, however, the possibilities for public aid in the form of local subscriptions and land grants were rapidly diminishing, and the ability of private capital to carry the burden of new development had been adequately demonstrated.[2] Faced with a rash of legislative restrictions, the larger systems decided in 1874 to defy the legislatures and to demand the protection of the federal courts.

From the standpoint of the railroad leaders the first judicial offensive was an unqualified failure. Even though their action provoked a redefinition of business rights that augured well for their future, they failed to win court approval for any of their claims regarding the rights of industrial property. The courts left them at the mercy of the state legislatures. These same legislatures, to be sure, were even then in the process of granting the rights of property and due process that the courts had withheld. Through the Illinois system of regulation, which became the model for future state legislation regarding rates and which provided the substance of the Interstate Commerce Act of 1887, the railroads were winning recognition of the principle that the determination of reasonableness—or rather unreasonableness—was a matter for judicial action.

In the final analysis, however, the Supreme Court's ruling in 1877 was a victory for traditional mercantile interests working through traditional legislative channels. The Granger laws and the Granger cases reaffirmed established state policy and public law. Although they made important concessions to the new industrialists on matters of economics and broad principles of private rights, they were rooted in the mercantile order of the antebellum period. They differed according to the special needs of local collecting points and terminal markets, the relative maturity of the railroad system in each state, and the climate of local politics, but they are best understood as part of the national reaction of the mercantile community to the rise of interstate railway systems.

NOTES
TABLE OF CASES
BIBLIOGRAPHICAL ESSAY
INDEX

NOTES

1 The progress of valley settlement was determined in large
measure by Indian removal policies. Among the works consulted
on the early settlement of the upper Mississippi Valley are Harlan
H. Barrows, *Geography of the Middle Illinois Valley,* Illinois
State Geological Survey Bulletin no. 15 (Urbana, Ill., 1910);
William V. Pooley, *The Settlement of Illinois from 1830–1850*
(Madison, Wis., 1908); Judson Fisk Lee, "Transportation—A
Factor in the Development of Northern Illinois Previous to 1860,"
Journal of the Illinois State Historical Society 10 (April 1917):
17–85; William J. Petersen, *Steamboating on the Upper Missis-
sippi: The Water Way to Iowa* (Iowa City, 1937), esp. pp. 296–
390; Cardinal Goodwin, "The American Occupation of Iowa,
1833–1860," *Iowa Journal of History and Politics* 17 (January
1919): 83–102; Orin Grant Libby, *Significance of the Lead and
Shot Trade in Early Wisconsin History,* State Historical Society
of Wisconsin Collections 13 (Madison, 1895), pp. 293–334; John
G. Thompson, *The Rise and Decline of the Wheat Growing
Industry in Wisconsin,* University of Wisconsin Bulletins, Economics and Political Science Series 5, no. 3 (Madison, 1908),
pp. 295–544; Wilson P. Shortridge, *The Transition of a Typical
Frontier with Illustrations from the Life of Henry Hastings
Sibley* (Menasha, Wis., 1919).

2 For the development of the agricultural economy, see Allan G. Bogue, *From Prairie to Corn Belt: Farming on the Illinois and Iowa Prairies in the Nineteenth Century* (Chicago, 1963); Richard Bardolph, "Illinois Agriculture in Transition, 1820–1870," pt. 1, *Journal of the Illinois State Historical Society* 41 (September 1948): 244–64; Joseph Schafer, *A History of Agriculture in Wisconsin* (Madison, Wis., 1922); and Henrietta M. Larson, *The Wheat Market and the Farmer in Minnesota, 1858–1900,* Faculty of Political Science, Columbia University Studies in History, Economics and Public Law 122, no. 2 (New York, 1926).

3 There is an extensive literature on the two commercial systems and their rivalry. Louis Hunter, *Steamboats on the Western Rivers* (Cambridge, Mass., 1949), provides an exhaustive treatment of river commerce. Thomas D. Odle, "The American Grain Trade of the Great Lakes, 1825–1873," *Inland Seas* 7 (1951): 237–45; 8 (1952): 23–28, 99–104, 177–92, 248–54; 9 (1953): 52–58, 105–9, 162–68, 256–62, describes the lake trade. John G. Clark, *The Grain Trade of the Old Northwest* (Urbana, Ill., 1966), provides a full and careful treatment of both systems before the Civil War. All of the above are concerned to some degree with the diversion of trade from one system to the other; Clark deals with it extensively. Wyatt Winton Belcher, *The Economic Rivalry Between St. Louis and Chicago, 1850–1880* (New York, 1947) places the problem of rivalry in broad perspective. Older treatments of the subject are John B. Appleton, *The Declining Significance of the Mississippi as a Commercial Highway in the Middle of the Nineteenth Century,* Geographical Society of Philadelphia Bulletin 28 (October 1930): 267–84; Louis Bernard Schmidt, "The Internal Grain Trade of the United States, 1860–1890," *Iowa Journal of History and Politics* 18 (January 1920): 94–124; 19 (April, July 1921): 196–245, 414–55; 20 (January 1922): 70–131; G. W. Stephens, *Some Aspects of Early Intersectional Rivalry for the Commerce of the Upper Mississippi Valley,* Washington University Studies, Humanistics Series 10 (April 1923): 277–300; and R. B. Way, *The Commerce of the Lower Mississippi in the Period 1830–1860,* Mississippi Valley Historical Association Proceedings 10 (1918–1919): 57–68.

4 During the pioneer period most of the grain was fed to cattle or hogs or was processed in some form before final shipment. References to the grain trade include the trade in grain-fed animals as

well as that in bulk grains. For a description of the river trade, see Hunter, *Steamboats on the Western Rivers,* pp. 53–54, and chap. 7; Clark, *Grain Trade,* pp. 27–28, 41–42.

5 The importance of the western trade to the plantation economy has been seriously questioned. There was, however, a reasonably stable market for produce and provisions in the Mississippi River towns. Morton Rothstein, "Antebellum Wheat and Cotton Exports: A Contrast in Marketing Organization and Economic Development," *Agricultural History* 40 (April 1966): 91–92, and n. 3. See also Clark, *Grain Trade,* pp. 27–28, 41–42, 145–46.

6 Clark, *Grain Trade,* pp. 156–63; Belcher, *Economic Rivalry Between St. Louis and Chicago,* pp. 29–31.

7 Belcher, *Economic Rivalry Between St. Louis and Chicago,* pp. 92–93, 112–13, 169; Hunter, *Steamboats on the Western Rivers,* pp. 188–205; Clark, *Grain Trade,* pp. 43, 51, 167; John G. Clark, "The Antebellum Grain Trade of New Orleans: Changing Patterns in the Relation of New Orleans with the Old Northwest," *Agricultural History* 38 (July 1964): 137.

8 Clark deals with New Orleans as an export depot for western grain in the article last cited and in his *Grain Trade,* chap. 2, and pp. 167–69, 270. On the attitude of southwestern mercantile interests, see Merle E. Reed, *New Orleans and the Railroads: The Struggle for Commercial Empire, 1830–1860* (Baton Rouge, La., 1966), pp. 62–67, 107, and Hunter, *Steamboats on the Western Rivers,* p. 192. There was almost no expenditure on river improvements between 1846 and 1866. For the complacency of the river merchants and their lack of attention to railroads, see Clark, *Grain Trade,* p. 270; Belcher, *Economic Rivalry Between St. Louis and Chicago,* pp. 12–17, 112–13; and Reed, *New Orleans and the Railroads,* pp. 21, 60–61.

9 For a description of the steamboat business, see Hunter, *Steamboats on the Western Rivers,* chap. 7. Trade and transportation on the river were so intimately connected that they were really a single interest (ibid., pp. 359–61).

10 The relationship of this wave of settlement to railroad construction is discussed in Albert Fishlow, *American Railroads and the Transformation of the Antebellum Economy* (Cambridge, Mass., 1965), pp. 163–204, and in Arthur M. Johnson and Barry E. Supple, *Boston Capitalists and Western Railroads* (Cambridge, Mass., 1967), pp. 190–91.

11 Clark discusses the rise of the Lake Michigan ports and the early rivalry among these ports in *Grain Trade,* chap. 4, esp. pp. 81–82, 84–91, 95, 98–101.

12 For the transportation problem at the lake ports, see Appleton, *Declining Significance of the Mississippi as a Commercial Highway,* pp. 269–84; Barrows, "Geography of the Middle Illinois Valley," pp. 82–83; Pooley, *Settlement of Illinois,* pp. 98, 135–46, 548, 569–70; Bessie Louise Pierce, *A History of Chicago,* 3 vols. (Chicago, 1937–57), 1: 61–74, 96–134; Thompson, *Rise and Decline of Wheat Growing in Wisconsin,* pp. 16, 139 n. 1; Libby, *Significance of the Lead and Shot Trade in Early Wisconsin History,* pp. 293–334; Schafer, *History of Agriculture in Wisconsin,* pp. 30–33, 41; Balthasar H. Meyer, *A History of Early Railroad Legislation in Wisconsin,* State Historical Society of Wisconsin Collections 14 (Madison, 1898), pp. 206–23; Caroline E. MacGill and others, *History of Transportation in the United States before 1860* (Washington, 1917), pp. 515–18. For the growth of railroads, see Pierce, *History of Chicago,* 1: 118–19; Pooley, *Settlement of Illinois,* pp. 571–72; Carl Ortwin Sauer, *Geography of the Upper Illinois Valley and History of Its Development,* Illinois State Geological Survey Bulletin no. 27, pp. 174–75; Lee, "Transportation— A Factor in the Development of Northern Illinois Previous to 1860," p. 39; *Merchants' Magazine and Commercial Review* 21 (1849): 560.

All railroad mileage figures are taken from Henry V. Poor, *A Manual of the Railroads of the United States for 1875–76* (New York, 1875) (hereafter cited as Poor's *Manual*).

13 Thompson, *Rise and Decline of Wheat Growing in Wisconsin,* pp. 35–36, 42, 140 n. 5, 200; Clark, *Grain Trade,* pp. 95–99.

14 Lester B. Shippee, "The First Railroad Between the Mississippi and Lake Superior," *Mississippi Valley Historical Review* 5 (September 1918): 121–42.

15 William J. Petersen, "Railroads Come to Iowa," *Palimpsest* 41 (April 1960). See histories of the major roads: August Derleth, *The Milwaukee Road: Its First Hundred Years* (New York, 1948); Robert J. Casey and W. A. S. Douglas, *Pioneer Railroad: The Story of the Chicago and North Western System* (New York, 1948); Carlton J. Corliss, *Main Line of Mid-America: The Story of the Illinois Central* (New York, 1950); William Edward Hayes, *Iron Road to Empire: The History of 100 Years of the Progress and Achievements of the Rock Island Lines* (New

York, 1953); and Richard C. Overton, *Burlington Route: A History of the Burlington Lines* (New York, 1965).

16 Odle, "American Grain Trade of the Great Lakes," 8: 177–88.

17 Ibid., 189–91; Clark, *Grain Trade,* p. 93; Guy A. Lee, "The Historical Significance of the Chicago Grain Elevator System," *Agricultural History* 11 (January 1937), 16–32.

18 Clark, *Grain Trade,* pp. 93–94; Morton Rothstein, "Antebellum Wheat and Cotton Exports: A Contrast in Marketing Organization and Economic Development," *Agricultural History* 40 (April 1966): 94–96. For a detailed study of the workings of the elevator industry, see Guy A. Lee, "History of the Chicago Grain Elevator Industry" (Ph.D. diss., Harvard University, 1938), esp. pp. 61–79. For grain prices, see Morton Rothstein, "America in the International Rivalry for the British Wheat Market, 1860–1914," *Mississippi Valley Historical Review* 47 (December 1960): 411.

19 Odle, "American Grain Trade of the Great Lakes," 9: 54–56, 109; Clark, *Grain Trade,* pp. 119–21. The availability of eastern credit was considered to be one of the primary causes of the diversion of trade from the river to the lakes (Clark, "Antebellum Grain Trade of New Orleans," p. 137).

20 See Larson, *Wheat Market and Farmer in Minnesota,* pp. 17–35, 81–82; Clark, *Grain Trade,* pp. 257–58; Solon J. Buck, *The Granger Movement* (Cambridge, Mass., 1913), pp. 16–18; Lee, "History of the Chicago Grain Elevator Industry," p. 131; and the *Prairie Farmer,* August 2, 1860, September 3, 1864.

21 Lee, "History of the Chicago Grain Elevator Industry," pp. 19–21, 131; B. F. Goldstein, *Marketing: A Farmer's Problem* (New York, 1928), p. 115; Larson, *Wheat Market and Farmer in Minnesota,* p. 81.

22 The competitive spirit of the terminal markets is described in Bayrd Still, "Patterns of Mid-Nineteenth Century Urbanization in the Middle West," *Mississippi Valley Historical Review* 28 (September 1941): 198–99, and in Clark, *Grain Trade,* pp. 102–3.

23 Clark, *Grain Trade,* chap. 5; George R. Taylor and Irene D. Neu, *The American Railroad Network, 1861–1890* (Cambridge, Mass., 1956), p. 57; Thomas D. Odle, "The American Grain Trade of the Great Lakes, 1825–1873" (Ph.D. diss., University of Michigan, 1951), pp. 89–96. The trunk line railroads captured a much higher percentage of westbound freight (Fishlow, *American Railroads and the Transformation of the Antebellum Economy,* pp. 263–69).

24 Lee, "History of the Chicago Grain Elevator Industry," pp. 113–24. Eastern control of the railroads is apparent from the lists of directors for the western roads given in Poor's *Manual* for this period.

25 On the difficult question of diversion, see Clark, *Grain Trade,* pp. 156–63, and chaps. 10–12, and Fishlow, *American Railroads and the Transformation of the Antebellum Economy,* pp. 275–98. The diversion of trade from the Ohio Valley had been very substantial before 1861. New Orleans' total receipts of western grain and grain products declined markedly during the fifties, but the trade out of St. Louis held up very well until the outbreak of war.

26 Clark, *Grain Trade,* chaps. 10, 12, 13.

27 The year 1856–57 was a case in point. Fishlow, *American Railroads and the Transformation of the Antebellum Economy,* p. 291.

28 Frederick Merk, *Economic History of Wisconsin During the Civil War Decade,* Publications of the State Historical Society of Wisconsin, Studies 1 (Madison, 1916), p. 365.

29 John Gordon MacNaughton, "Democratic Hostility to the Navigation and Commerce of the Great Lakes as a Neglected Factor in the Rise of the Republican Party" (Ph.D. diss., University of Buffalo, 1961), passim; Mentor L. Williams, "The Chicago River and Harbor Convention, 1847," *Mississippi Valley Historical Review* 35 (March 1949): 607–26; Thomas D. Odle, "The Commercial Interests of the Great Lakes and the Campaign Issues of 1860," *Michigan History* 50 (March 1956): 1–23.

30 For trade during the war, see Hunter, *Steamboats on the Western Rivers,* chap. 14, and Emerson D. Fite, "The Agricultural Development of the West during the Civil War," *Quarterly Journal of Economics* 20 (February 1906): 269. For political antagonism, see Frank L. Klement, *The Copperheads in the Middle West* (Chicago, 1960), pp. 6, 9–11, et passim.

31 Hunter, *Steamboats on the Western Rivers,* chap. 14; Belcher, *Economic Rivalry between St. Louis and Chicago,* pp. 139–45, 159–75.

32 Oscar O. Winther, *The Transportation Frontier: Trans-Mississippi West, 1865–1890* (New York, 1964), pp. 75–81; Hunter, *Steamboats on the Western Rivers,* pp. 566, 583.

33 For improvements in St. Louis and New Orleans, see Hunter, *Steamboats on the Western Rivers,* pp. 572–73. For the role of the Illinois Central Railroad, see J. M. Douglas to W. H. Osborn, July 1, 1868, and Osborn to Douglas, July 29, 1868, J. M. Doug-

las In-Letters, February 1866–December 1870; Douglas to L. J. Higby, August 26, 1868, Douglas In-Letters, vol. 5; and James Tucker to John Newell, October 19, 28, 1871, Newell In-Letters, vol. 2, all in the Illinois Central Archives, Newberry Library, Chicago. Tucker refers to the lack of credit facilities and the general apathy of the southern market as problems to be overcome. For the merchants' promises, see Hunter, *Steamboats on the Western Rivers,* pp. 567–84. St. Louis did enjoy a substantial revival after the war, but much of it was due to new business in the Missouri Valley rather than to the recovery of former business (Winther, *Transportation Frontier,* p. 75).

34 Taylor and Neu, *American Railroad Network,* pp. 67–76; Thomas Weber, *The Northern Railroads in the Civil War* (New York, 1952), pp. 14–15, 229; George G. Tunnell, "The Diversion of the Flour and Grain Traffic from the Great Lakes to the Railroads," *Journal of Political Economy* 5 (June 1897): 340–75, 413–20; Casey and Douglas, *Pioneer Railroad,* pp. 121–28; Derleth, *Milwaukee Road,* pp. 65, 87, 113; Corliss, *Main Line of Mid-America,* pp. 141, 149–54; Overton, *Burlington Route,* pp. 78, 92–94, 110–11, 116–32; Hayes, *Iron Road to Empire,* pp. 52–53. On the bridging of the Mississippi, see G. K. Warren, *Report on Bridging the Mississippi River between Saint Paul, Minn., and St. Louis, Mo.,* appendix X3 of the *Annual Report of the Chief of Engineers for 1878* (Washington, 1878), pp. 961–1028. For the reaction of river interests, see Benedict K. Zobrist, "Steamboat Men Versus Railroad Men: The First Bridging of the Mississippi River," *Missouri Historical Review* 59 (January 1965): 159–72. On the rationalization of trade, see Morton Rothstein, "International Market for Agricultural Commodities, 1850–1873," in D. T. Gilchrist and W. D. Lewis, eds., *Economic Change in the Civil War Era* (Greenville, Del., 1965), pp. 62–72.

35 For railroad mileage, see *Poor's Manual* (1875–76), pp. xxviii–xxix; Illinois, Railroad and Warehouse Commission, *Second Annual Report* (Springfield, 1873), pp. 19–20. For railroad rates, see U.S., Interstate Commerce Commission, *Railways in the United States in 1902. Part II: A Forty-Year Review of Changes in Freight Tariffs,* by J. M. Smith (Washington, D.C., 1903), pp. 94–95, 104; U.S., Department of Agriculture, Division of Statistics, *Changes in the Rates of Charge for Railroad and Other Transportation Services,* by H. T. Newcomb, rev. by Edward G. Ward, Jr. (Washington, D.C., 1901), pp. 21–22; Charles R.

Detrick, "The Effects of the Granger Laws," *Journal of Political Economy* 11 (March 1903) : 247, 249 n. 2; Julius Grodinsky, *The Iowa Pool, A Study in Railroad Competition, 1870–84* (Chicago, 1950), p. 4.

36 Fox and Wisconsin Rivers Improvement Commission, *Water Communication Between the Mississippi and the Lakes. Memorial to the Congress of the United States, and Supplement, on the Improvement of the Navigation of the Wisconsin and Fox Rivers Submitted by the Canal Conventions Held at Prairie du Chien, in the State of Wisconsin, Nov. 10, 1868, and at Portage City, Oct. 20, 1869, and the Proceedings of the Conventions* (Madison, 1870), p. 62; Commercial Convention, Detroit, *Proceedings of the Commercial Convention, Held in Detroit, July 11th, 12th, 13th, and 14th, 1865* (Detroit, 1865); National Ship-Canal Convention, *Proceedings of the National Ship-Canal Convention, Held at The City of Chicago, June 2 and 3, 1863* (Chicago, 1863), pp. 5–6.

37 D. Philip Locklin, "The Literature of Railway Rate Theory," *Quarterly Journal of Economics* 47 (February 1933) : 167; Alfred D. Chandler, Jr., *Henry Varnum Poor* (Cambridge, Mass., 1956), p. 24.

38 For the debate on rates, see E. B. Grant, *Boston Railways: Their Condition and Prospects* (Boston, 1856), pp. 87–89; Locklin, "Literature of Railway Rate Theory," pp. 170–71; Chandler, *Poor*, p. 150; Edward Chase Kirkland, *Men, Cities and Transportation: A Study in New England History, 1820–1900*, 2 vols. (Cambridge, Mass., 1948), 1: 344; and P. P. F. Degrand, *An Address on the Advantages of Low Fares and Low Rates of Freight* (Boston, 1845). The advocates of low rates seem to have prevailed.

39 Dionysius Lardner, *Railway Economy; A Treatise on the New Art of Transport, Its Management, Prospects, and Relations, Commercial, Financial, and Social, with an Exposition of the Practical Results of the Railways in Operation in the United Kingdom, on the Continent, and in America* (New York, 1950), p. 192. See also the testimony of J. D. Brooks of the Michigan Central and Solomon Drullard of the New York Central in N.Y., Legislature, Assembly, Select Committee on the Pro Rata Freight Bill, *Pro Rata Question. Opening Remarks of John Thompson, Esq., on Behalf of the Railroads, against a Pro Rata Law; and the Testimony of J. W. Brooks, Esq., before the Select Committee of the Assembly; also the Testimony of Solomon Drullard, Esq.,*

General Freight Agent New York Central Railroad (Albany, 1860), pp. 6, 17; the testimony of various railroad officials in Ohio, General Assembly, Senate, *Report of Special Committee on Rail Roads and Telegraphs Made to Senate of Ohio, February 1, 1867* (Columbus, 1867), pp. 31–32, 76, 161; and U.S. Congress, Senate, *Report of the Select Committee on Transportation Routes to the Seaboard*, 2 vols., 43d Cong., 1st sess., 1874, S. Rept. no. 307, 1: 128; 2: 45, 260 (hereafter cited as the *Windom Report*).

40 For the views of various railroad officials, see Chandler, *Poor,* pp. 31–32, and Frank Nelson Elliott, "The Causes and the Growth of Railroad Regulation in Wisconsin, 1848–1876" (Ph.D. diss., University of Wisconsin, 1956), pp. 252–55.

41 *Windom Report,* 1: 130–31; Massachusetts, Board of Railroad Commissioners, *Annual Report for the Year 1869* (Boston, 1870), p. 75; Albert Fink, *An Investigation into the Cost of Transportation on American Railroads with Deductions for Its Cheapening* (Louisville, 1874), p. 3; and testimony of E. W. Woodward in Ohio, Senate, *Report of Committee on Rail Roads and Telegraphs,* p. 50.

42 Charles Ellet, *Essay on the Laws of Trade, in Reference to the Works of Internal Improvement in the United States* (Richmond, Va., 1839), p. 15. For Ellet's influence, see Joseph Dorfman, *The Economic Mind in American Civilization, 1606–1865,* 2 vols. (New York, 1946), 2: 624–25.

43 Railroad officials were willing to concede that rates should bear some relation to cost, and they were always ready to explain certain changes in rates, such as the annual increase after the lakes and rivers had frozen, in terms of changing costs. But despite the truth of many of their arguments, the more candid among them agreed that the sole determining factor in fixing rates was what the traffic would bear. See the testimony of E. W. Woodward in Ohio, Senate, *Report of Committee on Rail Roads and Telegraphs,* p. 50, and that of J. D. Potts, E. D. Worcester, and H. D. Cook in the *Windom Report,* 2: 39, 247. See also Thomas C. Cochran, *Railroad Leaders—1845–1890: The Business Mind in Action* (Cambridge, Mass., 1953), p. 153.

44 For the freight agents' authority to alter rates, see the statement of J. W. Brooks in N.Y., Assembly, *Pro Rata Question,* p. 13; Cochran, *Railroad Leaders,* pp. 149, 153, 159; Chandler, *Poor,* p. 34; Harrison Standish Smalley, *Railroad Rate Control In Its Legal Aspects,* American Economic Association Publications, 3d

ser. 7, no. 2 (New York, 1905), pp. 332–33; and H. G. Brownson, *History of the Illinois Central to 1870,* University of Illinois Studies in the Social Sciences 4 (Urbana, 1915), pp. 65–66. For dealings with individual shippers, see the testimony of W. D. Griswald in Ohio, Senate, *Report of Committee on Rail Roads and Telegraphs,* p. 41; Charles Athiel Harper, "Some Economic and Social Influences of the Coming of the Railroads in Central Illinois Prior to 1860" (M.A. thesis, University of Illinois, 1923), p. 35; and William F. Gephart, *Transportation and Industrial Development in the Middle West,* Faculty of Political Science, Columbia University Studies in History, Economics and Public Law 34, no. 1 (New York, 1909), p. 176. For rate wars, see Arthur T. Hadley, *Railroad Transportation: Its History and Its Laws* (New York, 1885), pp. 93–94.

45 Larson, *Wheat Market and Farmer in Minnesota,* pp. 87–90; A. B. Stickney, *The Railroad Problem* (St. Paul, 1891), pp. 21–23; Merk, *Economic History of Wisconsin,* chap. 14.

46 Stickney, *Railroad Problem,* p. 24.

47 Illinois, Railroad and Warehouse Commission, *First Annual Report* (Springfield, 1872), p. 19; *Windom Report,* 2: 40, 682; William Larrabee, *The Railroad Question; A Historical and Practical Treatise on Railroads, and Remedies for Their Abuses* (Chicago, 1893), p. 84; Jonathan Periam, *The Groundswell: A History of the Origin, Aims, and Progress of the Farmers' Movement . . .* (St. Louis, 1874), pp. 453–54; *Chicago Tribune,* March 24, 1873.

48 Larson, *Wheat Market and Farmer in Minnesota,* pp. 89–90; *Rochester* (Minn.) *Federal Union,* June 18, 1870.

49 For the traffic manager's job, see Lardner, *Railway Economy,* chap. 13; N.Y., Legislature, Senate, Select Committee on the Pro Rata Freight Bill, *Testimony Taken before the Senate Select Committee to Whom Was Referred the Assembly Bill on Pro Rata, Together with Argument Made by Counsel in Behalf of the Railroads of This State against So Ruinous a Measure to the Railroads, and the Great Interests of the State, as the Pro Rata Assembly Bill* (Albany, 1860), p. 8; Cochran, *Railroad Leaders,* pp. 153, 155. For rate wars, see Hadley, *Railroad Transportation,* p. 71; Emory R. Johnson, *American Railway Transportation,* rev. ed. (New York, 1908), pp. 218–19. For rate discrimination, see U.S. Treasury Department, Bureau of Statistics, *First Annual Report on the Internal Commerce of the United States . . . for the Year 1876,* by Joseph Nimmo, Jr. (Washington, D.C., 1877),

p. 93. Cochran quotes J. I. Blair of the Delaware, Lackawanna & Western Railroad: "Our duty is to discriminate where we have competition and get our share and meet the trade, and whenever we can and there is no competition make it up—this we must do at every station be it large or small" (*Railroad Leaders,* pp. 154–55).

50 Stickney, *Railway Problem,* pp. 50–52; *Railroad Gazette,* April 15, 1871, p. 30.

51 George W. Sieber, "Railroads and Lumber Marketing, 1858–78: The Relationship between an Iowa Sawmill Firm and the Chicago and Northwestern Railroad," *Annals of Iowa,* 3d ser. 39 (summer 1967): 33–37; Robert F. Fries, *Empire in Pine: The Story of Lumbering in Wisconsin* (Madison, Wis., 1951), p. 93; *Railroad Gazette,* April 15, 1871, p. 30.

52 Stickney, *Railway Problem,* pp. 5–7, 50–51, 61–62; Charles F. Adams, Jr., *Railroads: Their Origin and Problems* (New York, 1878), pp. 118–19; *Prairie Farmer,* March 8, 1873; *Ottawa* (Ill.) *Free Trader,* January 15, 1870.

53 Stickney, *Railway Problem,* pp. 20, 29–30.

54 Smalley, *Railroad Rate Control in Its Legal Aspects,* pp. 332–33; Stickney, *Railway Problem,* pp. 61–62. On the land policies of two railroads, see Paul Wallace Gates, *The Illinois Central Railroad and Its Colonization Work* (Cambridge, Mass., 1934) and Richard C. Overton, *Burlington West: A Colonization History of the Burlington Railroad* (Cambridge, Mass., 1941). Managers often insisted that local business was the mainstay of their enterprise (Johnson and Supple, *Boston Capitalists and Western Railroads,* p. 110; Jervis, *Railroad Property,* pp. 291–98).

55 Harris to A. Anderson, March 14, 1873, Harris Out-Letters, vol. 30, Burlington Archives, Newberry Library, Chicago.

56 Harris to T. J. Carter, March 24, 1873, Burlington Archives.

57 Grodinsky, *Iowa Pool,* pp. 4–7; Chandler, *Poor,* pp. 150–51.

Chapter 2   RAILROAD RATE LAW

1 U.S., Treasury Department, Bureau of Statistics, *First Annual Report of the Internal Commerce of the United States . . . for the Year 1876,* by Joseph Nimmo, Jr. (Washington, D.C., 1877), p. 161. The revolutionary aspects of railroading are discussed in Walter Chadwick Noyes, *American Railroad Rates* (Boston, 1905), pp. 4–7, and Bruce Wyman, *The Special Law Governing*

Public Service Corporations and All Others Engaged in Public Employment, 2 vols. (New York, 1911), 1: 149–50. U.S., Interstate Commerce Commission, *First Annual Report of the Interstate Commerce Commission, December 1, 1887* (Washington, D.C., 1887), p. 4, deals briefly with the inability of the railroad to conform to common law principles.

2 Joseph A. Durrenberger, *Turnpikes: A Study of the Toll Road Movement in the Middle Atlantic States and Maryland* (Valdosta, Ga., 1931), p. 77. Railroad competition, however, did force canals to alter their rate structures in favor of long-haul freights (Harry N. Scheiber, "The Rate-Making Power of the State in the Canal Era: A Case Study," *Political Science Quarterly* 77, September 1962: 397–413).

3 Joseph K. Angell, *A Treatise on the Law of Carriers of Goods and Passengers, by Land and by Water* (Boston, 1849), pp. 111, 122–24; Wyman, *Special Law Governing Public Service Corporations,* 2: 1232–33.

4 For American colonial economic policies, see Henry W. Farnum, *Chapters in the History of Social Legislation in the United States to 1860* (Washington, D.C., 1938), chaps. 7–8. On state policies to 1860, see Oscar and Mary Handlin, *Commonwealth, a Study of the Role of Government in the American Economy: Massachusetts, 1774–1861* (New York, 1947); Louis Hartz, *Economic Policy and Democratic Thought: Pennsylvania, 1776–1860* (Cambridge, Mass., 1948); Milton S. Heath, *Constructive Liberalism: The Role of the State in Economic Development in Georgia to 1860* (Cambridge, Mass., 1954); and James N. Primm, *Economic Policy in the Development of a Western State: Missouri, 1820–1860* (Cambridge, Mass., 1954).

5 Raymond E. Hayes, "Business Regulation in Early Pennsylvania," *Temple University Law Quarterly* 10 (February 1936): 178; Frank I. Herriott, "Regulation of Trade and Morals by Iowa Town Councils prior to 1858," *Annals of Iowa,* 3d ser. 5 (July 1901): 126–30; Bayrd Still, "Patterns of Mid-Nineteenth Century Urbanization in the Middle West," *Mississippi Valley Historical Review* 28 (September 1941): 193–94; Edward A. Adler, "Business Jurisprudence," *Select Essays on Constitutional Law,* 5 vols. in 4 (Chicago, 1938), 2: 447–55; Breck P. McAllister, "Lord Hale and Business Affected with a Public Interest," *Select Essays on Constitutional Law,* 2: 467–69; Clyde B. Aitchison, "The Roots of the Act to Regulate Commerce," in U.S., Interstate

Commerce Commission, *Exercises Commemorating the Fifty Years' Service of the Interstate Commerce Commission* (Washington, D.C., 1937), pp. 43–44.

6 Mobile v. Yuille, 3 Ala. 137, 140–43 (1841). The reluctance of the state courts to interfere with the legislative regulation of business in this period is made abundantly clear in Leonard W. Levy, *The Law of the Commonwealth and Chief Justice Shaw* (Cambridge, Mass., 1957), pp. 136–37, 229–65, 311–12. Other cases concerning legislative or administrative regulation of rates and prices are Ogden v. Saunders, 25 U.S. (12 Wheat.) 213 (1827); Olcott v. Banfill, 4 N.H. 537 (1829); Chosen Freeholders of Hudson Co. v. The State, 4 Zabriskie 718 (N.J. Ct. Err. & App. 1853); State v. Perry, 5 Jones Law 252 (N.C. Sup. Ct. 1858); Commonwealth v. Duane, 98 Mass. 1 (1867); and Parker v. Metropolitan R.R., 109 Mass. 506 (1872). State legislatures were beginning to curtail the authority of municipal governments over local prices. See Guilotte v. New Orleans, 12 La. Ann. 432 (1857); and Dunham v. Trustees of Rochester, 5 Cow. 462 (N.Y. Sup. Ct. 1826). But the only case found that suggested any constitutional limitation on the legislative police power prior to 1871 is Webb v. Baird, 6 Ind. 13 (1854). In this case the court denied the right of the state to compel a lawyer to provide his services without charge under certain circumstances.

7 Joseph Henry Beale, Jr. and Bruce Wyman, *The Law of Railroad Rate Regulation with Special Reference to American Legislation,* 1st ed. (Boston, 1907), pp. 20–24; Wyman, *Special Law Governing Public Service Corporations,* 1: 6–14.

8 Munn v. Illinois, 94 U.S. 113, 133 (1877).

9 Wyman, *Special Law Governing Public Service Corporations,* 2: 1224–33; Alton D. Adams, "Reasonable Rates," *Journal of Political Economy* 12 (December 1903): 80–81. The courts did not set reasonable rates, but ruled on specific rates in specific cases. Thus they acted only in regard to unreasonableness. Nevertheless, it was common, even though less precise, to refer to the reasonableness of a rate as a matter for judicial consideration.

10 Edward L. Pierce, *A Treatise on American Railroad Law* (New York, 1857), pp. 3, 12; Isaac F. Redfield, *Law of Railways,* 5th ed., 2 vols. (Boston, 1873), 1: 94; Durrenberger, *Turnpikes,* pp. 77, 81–110; Edwin Merrick Dodd, Jr., "The First Half Century of Statutory Regulation of Business Corporations in Massachusetts," in *Harvard Legal Essays Written in Honor of*

and Presented to Joseph Henry Beale and Samuel Williston (Cambridge, Mass., 1934), pp. 99–107; Ivan L. Pollock, *History of Economic Legislation in Iowa* (Iowa City, 1918), pp. 12–14.

11 Wyman, *Special Law Governing Public Service Corporations,* 2: 1134–35, 1155–56, 1161; Isaac F. Redfield, *Leading American Railway Cases,* 2d ed., 2 vols. (Boston, 1872) has nothing with regard to rates or fares, right of regulation, or extortionate or discriminatory charges.

12 Joseph K. Angell and Thomas Durfee, *Treatise on the Law of Highways* (Boston, 1857), pp. 10–11; Bonaparte v. Camden & A.R.R., 3 Fed. Cas. 821 (No. 1617) (C.C.D.N.J. 1830); Isaac F. Redfield, *A Practical Treatise Upon the Law of Railways,* 1st ed. (Boston, 1858), pp. 234–35, 356; Wyman, *Special Law Governing Public Service Corporations,* 1: 149–50.

13 Beekman v. Saratoga & S.R.R., 3 Paige 45, 75 (N.Y. Ch. 1831).

14 Redfield, *Practical Treatise Upon the Law of Railways,* p. 356; Bloodgood v. Mohawk & H.R.R., 14 Wend. 51 (N.Y. Sup. Ct. 1835); Worcester v. Western R.R. Corp., 4 Met. 564 (Mass. Sup. Ct. 1843); Concord R.R. v. Greely, 17 N.H. 47 (1845); Whiting v. Sheboygan & Fond du Lac R.R., 25 Wis. 167 (1870); People v. Salem, 20 Mich. 452 (1870); Olcott v. The Supervisors, 83 U.S. (16 Wall.) 678 (1873); Baltimore & O.R.R. v. Maryland, 88 U.S. (21 Wall.) 456 (1874).

15 "Were gentlemen willing to grant an unlimited discretion to all railroad companies of charging such tolls as they may think proper? . . . It seemed to him that a wise legislator would . . . limit the exercise of that power. Such, at any rate, had been the universal practice" (statement of Richard Stillwell in Ohio, Constitutional Convention, *Report of the Debates and Proceedings of the Convention for the Revision of the Constitution of the State of Ohio, 1850–51,* 2 vols., Columbus, 1851, 1: 347). National Railway Convention, *Proceedings of the National Railway Convention, at the Musical Fund Hall, Philadelphia, Pa., July 4th and 5th, 1866* (Philadelphia, 1866), p. 6; Lardner, *Railway Economy,* p. 424.

16 Edward C. Kirkland, *Men, Cities and Transportation: A Study in New England History, 1820–1900,* 2 vols. (Cambridge, Mass., 1948), 1: 344–45; Noyes, *American Railroad Rates,* pp. 215–16.

17 Balthasar H. Meyer, *Railway Charters,* American Economic Association Publications, 3d ser., 1 (New York, 1900), p. 235; Dodd, "First Half Century of Statutory Regulations of Business

Corporations in Massachusetts," p. 116; Noyes, *American Railroad Rates,* pp. 5–6, 214.

18 William F. Gephart, *Transportation and Industrial Development in the Middle West,* Faculty of Political Science, Columbia University Studies in History, Economics and Public Law 34, no. 1 (New York, 1909), pp. 158–59. Frank Walker Stevens, *The Beginnings of the New York Central Railroad* (New York, 1926), pp. 278–85; *Merchants' Magazine and Commercial Review* 20 (1849): 651–52.

19 Noyes, *American Railroad Rates,* pp. 214–16; Balthasar H. Meyer, *Railway Legislation in the United States* (New York, 1903), pp. 57–61; Charles F. Adams, Jr., "Railroad Legislation," *Merchants' Magazine and Commercial Review* 57 (1867): 340–41; Kirkland, *Men, Cities and Transportation,* 1: 344–45; Edward C. Kirkland, *History of American Economic Life,* rev. ed. (New York, 1947), p. 292.

20 Charles Francis Adams, Jr., "Railroad Inflation," *North American Review* 108 (January 1869): 136; Leonard D. White, "Origin of Utility Commissions in Massachusetts," *Journal of Political Economy* 29 (March 1921): 189.

21 Adams, "Railroad Legislation," pp. 340–41, 343; Adams, "Railroad Inflation," pp. 136–37; Meyer, *Railway Legislation,* pp. 67–68; Kirkland, *Men, Cities and Transportation,* 1: 118; Noyes, *American Railroad Rates,* pp. 215–16; Hartz, *Economic Policy and Democratic Thought,* p. 259; "Rail-Roads and Canals," *New York Review* no. 12 (April 1840): 303–5.

22 Meyer, *Railway Legislation,* p. 67; Benjamin F. Wright, *The Contract Clause of the Constitution* (Cambridge, Mass., 1938), p. 85; Rasmus S. Saby, *Railroad Legislation in Minnesota, 1849 to 1875* (St. Paul, 1912), p. 178 n. 796; Pierce, *American Railroad Law,* pp. 37–38; Adams, "Railroad Legislation," p. 341.

23 Massachusetts, Board of Railroad Commissioners, *Annual Report for the Year 1869* (Boston, 1870), p. 58; Charles Carroll Bonney, *Rules of Law for the Carriage and Delivery of Persons and Property by Railway with the Leading Railway Statutes and Decisions of Illinois, Indiana, Michigan, Ohio, Pennsylvania, New York and the United States* (Chicago, 1864), passim; U.S., Congress, Senate, *Report of the Select Committee on Interstate Commerce,* 2 vols., 49th Cong., 1st sess., 1886, S. Rept. no. 46, 1: 34–35 (hereafter cited as the *Cullom Report*); U.S., Treasury Dept., *First Annual Report on the Commerce of the United States,*

pp. 171–79; *Merchants' Magazine and Commercial Review,* 20 (1849): 651–52; Adams, "Railroad Legislation," p. 341; Noyes, *American Railroad Rates,* pp. 215–16; Meyer, *Railway Legislation,* pp. 82, 92–94.

24 N.Y., Legislature, Assembly, *Report of a Majority of the Select Committee on Petitions for Regulating Freights on Railroads in the State* (Albany, 1860), p. 9.

25 The 1839 law which established the Rhode Island commission is a possible exception. It required that tolls be made "rateably in proportion to the distance" (John K. Towles, "Early Railroad Monopoly and Discrimination in Rhode Island," *Yale Review* 18, November 1909: 309). Kirkland, *Men, Cities and Transportation,* 1: 354–55. More typical is a New Hampshire statute of 1853: "All tolls shall be the same for all persons and for a like description of freight" (Kirkland, *Men, Cities and Transportation,* 2: 280).

26 Pierce, *American Railroad Law,* pp. 148–49; Chicago B. & Q.R.R. v. Parks, 18 Ill. 460, 464 (1864).

27 Fitchberg R.R. v. Gage, 78 Mass. 393 (1859); Shipper v. Pennsylvania R.R., 47 Pa. 338 (1864).

28 Kirkland, *Men, Cities and Transportation,* 1: 355; Towles, "Early Railroad Monopoly and Discrimination in Rhode Island," pp. 308–17; Rowland G. Hazard, "Relation of Railroad Corporations to the Public," *Merchants' Magazine and Commercial Review* 21 (1849): 623–24.

29 *Merchants' Magazine and Commercial Review* 21 (1849): 622–27; Rowland G. Hazard, *Remarks . . . before the Senate, on the Railroad Bill, in Reply to Mr. Ames* (Providence, R.I., 1854), passim; Towles, "Early Railroad Monopoly and Discrimination in Rhode Island," pp. 310–11.

30 Hazard, "Relation of Railroad Corporations to the Public," pp. 625–27; Towles, "Early Railroad Monopoly and Discrimination in Rhode Island," pp. 316–18.

31 Towles, "Early Railroad Monopoly and Discrimination in Rhode Island," pp. 316–17.

32 Ibid., p. 308.

33 N.Y., Legislature, Senate, Select Committee on the Pro Rata Freight Bill, *Testimony Taken Before the Senate Select Committee to Whom Was Referred the Assembly Bill on Pro Rata . . .* (Albany, 1860), p. 37.

34 N.Y., Assembly, *Report of the Select Committee on Regulating Freights on Railroads,* p. 3.

35 Poor's *Manual* (1881), pp. xxxi–xxxvii; N.Y., Senate, *Testimony on Pro Rata,* p. 63.

36 The railroads that paralleled the Erie Canal were originally required by their charters to pay state tolls on all freights that otherwise would have been shipped by canal. This disability had been removed by 1851 in order to permit the New York Central to compete with the newly completed New York and Erie Railroad (Stevens, *Beginnings of the New York Central Railroad,* pp. 273–74).

37 Poor's *Manual* (1881), pp. xxv–xxvii, xxxi–xxxvii; Henry O'Rielly, ed., *Proceedings of the New York State Conventions for "Rescuing the Canals from the Ruin with Which They Are Threatened"* . . . (New York, 1859), pp. 105–11, passim; N.Y., Senate, *Testimony on Pro Rata,* p. 63; Lucius Robinson, *Speech of Hon. Lucius Robinson of Chemung on the Pro Rata Bill, in Assembly, Feb. 27, 1860* (Albany, 1860), pp. 8–13; N.Y., Assembly, *Report of the Select Committee on Regulating Freights on Railroads,* pp. 9–10; *Opposition to Restrictions upon Trade. Remonstrance of the Business Men of New York* [Albany, 1860], p. 1; N.Y., Legislature, Assembly, Select Committee on the Pro Rata Freight Bill, *Pro Rata Question. Opening Remarks of John Thompson, Esq., on Behalf of the Railroads, Against a Pro Rata Law* . . . (Albany, 1860), p. 4.

38 Frederick Merk, "Eastern Antecedents of the Grangers," *Agricultural History* 23 (January 1949): 7–8; Lee Benson, *Merchants, Farmers, and Railroads: Railroad Regulation and New York Politics, 1850–1887* (Cambridge, Mass., 1955), pp. 9–16.

39 Quoted in Hartz, *Economic Policy and Democratic Thought,* p. 273 n. 180. See also N.Y., Assembly, *Report of the Select Committee on Regulating Freights on Railroads,* p. 21.

40 N.Y., Assembly, *Report of the Select Committee on Regulating Freights on Railroads,* pp. 21–23.

41 Hartz, *Economic Policy and Democratic Thought,* p. 296; *Cullom Report,* 1: 124; Allan Nevins, *John D. Rockefeller,* 2 vols. (New York, 1940), 1: 264; Pennsylvania, *Constitution of 1874,* art. 17.

42 *Hannibal* (Mo.) *Messenger,* December 17, 1859.

43 N.Y., Assembly, *Report of the Select Committee on Regulating Freights on Railroads,* p. 23; Ohio, General Assembly, Senate,

Report of Special Committee on Rail Roads and Telegraphs Made to Senate of Ohio. February 1, 1867 (Columbus, 1867), pp. 1–8; Gephart, *Transportation and Industrial Development in the Middle West,* pp. 184–89; Bonney, *Rules of Law for the Carriage and Delivery of Persons and Property by Railway,* p. 139; Nevins, *Rockefeller,* 1: 264.

44 Ohio, Senate, *Report of Committee on Rail Roads and Telegraphs,* passim; Gephart, *Transportation and Industrial Development in the Middle West,* pp. 186–91; Ohio, Department of Railroads and Telegraphs, *Annual Report of the Commissioner of Railroads and Telegraphs to the Governor of the State of Ohio, for the Year 1867* (Columbus, 1868), pp. 10–11.

45 N.Y., Assembly, *Report of the Select Committee on Regulating Freights on Railroads,* p. 23.

46 Philadelphia, W. & B.R.R. v. Bowers, 4 Houst. 506 (Del. Ct. Err. & App. 1873).

47 *Laws of Michigan,* 1869, 2 vols., 1: 182.

48 *Chicago Tribune,* January 19, 1869.

49 Adams, "Railroad Legislation," p. 348; Kirkland, *Men, Cities and Transportation,* 2: 231–38, 280–81; White, "Origin of Utility Commissions in Massachusetts," p. 189.

50 Massachusetts, Board of Railroad Commissioners, *Annual Report for the Year 1870* (Boston, 1871), p. 58.

51 Ibid., p. 110; Kirkland, *Men, Cities and Transportation,* 2: 283.

52 Charles Francis Adams, Jr., "Boston," *North American Review* 106 (1868): 1–25, 557–91.

53 *Nation* 12 (April 6, 1871): 233.

54 U.S., Congress, Senate, *Report of the Select Committee on Transportation Routes to the Seaboard,* 2 vols., 43d Cong., 1st sess., 1874, S. Rept. no. 307, 2: 97–109; N.Y., Legislature, Assembly, Special Committee on Railroads, *Report of Special Committee on Railroads . . . ,* 5 vols. (New York, 1879); Benson, *Merchants, Farmers, and Railroads,* passim.

55 Merk, "Eastern Antecedents of the Grangers," p. 8.

56 Massachusetts, Board of Railroad Commissioners, *Annual Report for 1870,* p. 58.

57 Hartz, *Economic Policy and Democratic Thought,* p. 11; Merk, "Eastern Antecedents of the Grangers," pp. 1–7.

58 Merk, "Eastern Antecedents of the Grangers," p. 8; N.Y., Assembly, *Pro Rata Question,* pp. 6–19; Ohio, Senate, *Report of Committee on Rail Roads and Telegraphs;* Towles, "Early Rail-

road Monopoly and Discrimination in Rhode Island," pp. 316–17; *Opposition to Restrictions upon Trade. Remonstrance of the Business Men of New York,* p. 1; Gephart, *Transportation and Industrial Development in the Middle West,* p. 188; Nevins, *Rockefeller,* 1: 259; *Chicago Tribune,* January 19, 1869; Kirkland, *Men, Cities and Transportation,* 2: 252.

59 *Nation* 12 (April 6, 1871): 233.

60 Kirkland, *Men, Cities and Transportation,* 2: 292–93.

61 Robinson, *Speech of Lucius Robinson,* p. 18, refers to regulation as "a backward step." *Nation* 6 (May 21, 1868): 408, calls state control "old fashioned." Thomas M. Cooley, "Limits to State Control of Private Business," *Princeton Review,* 4th ser. 1 (March, 1878): 233–71, traces nineteenth-century progress from control to freedom.

Chapter 3 THE STATES AND THEIR RAILROADS: PROMOTION VERSUS CONTROL

1 Dionysius Lardner, *Railway Economy* (New York, 1850), p. 419; Charles F. Adams, Jr., "Railroad Legislation," *Merchants' Magazine and Commercial Review* 57 (1867): 340, 343; Poor's *Manual* (1871–72), p. xxv; Carter Goodrich, *Government Promotion of American Canals and Railroads* (New York, 1960), chap. 2.

2 Sharpless v. Mayor of Philadelphia, 21 Pa. 147, 169–71 (1853); Brown v. Beatty, 34 Miss. 227, 240 (1857); Oscar and Mary F. Handlin, *Commonwealth, A Study of the Role of Government in the American Economy: Massachusetts, 1774–1861* (New York, 1947), p. 184; Isaac F. Redfield, *Law of Railways,* 5th ed., 2 vols. (Boston, 1873), 1: 94; Louis Hartz, *Economic Policy and Democratic Thought: Pennsylvania, 1776–1860* (Cambridge, Mass., 1948), p. 51; William F. Gephart, *Transportation and Industrial Development in the Middle West,* Faculty of Political Science, Columbia University Studies in History, Economics and Public Law 34, no. 1 (New York, 1909), pp. 158–59; Walter Chadwick Noyes, *American Railroad Rates* (Boston, 1905), p. 6.

3 The desire to separate the two functions of the railroad, as highways and as carriers, was not a passing fancy of the pioneer years. Proposals of this sort continued to appear and became quite prevalent during the Granger movement. *Illinois State Journal,* May 28, 1867; *Chicago Tribune,* January 14, 1871; *Prairie Farmer,*

April 30, 1870; Illinois, Constitutional Convention, *Debates and Proceedings of the Constitutional Convention of the State of Illinois, Convened at the City of Springfield, Tuesday, December 13, 1869,* 2 vols. (Springfield, 1870), 2: 1646, 1715; Iowa, State Agricultural Society, *Annual Report of the Secretary for 1872* (Des Moines, 1873), p. 211; John M. Palmer, *Personal Recollections of John M. Palmer: The Story of an Earnest Life* (Cincinnati, 1901), p. 390; Solon J. Buck, *The Granger Movement* (Cambridge, Mass., 1913), p. 130.

4 Massachusetts, Board of Railroad Commissioners, *Annual Report for the Year 1869* (Boston, 1870), pp. 13–14; Lucius Robinson, *Speech of Hon. Lucius Robinson of Chemung on the Pro Rata Bill in Assembly, Feb. 27, 1860* (Albany, 1860), p. 15; Edward Hungerford, *The Story of the Baltimore and Ohio Railroad,* 2 vols. (New York, 1928), 1: 27; Adams, "Railroad Legislalation," pp. 341–45; *Merchants' Magazine and Commercial Review* 20 (1849): 651.

5 Carter Goodrich, "The Revulsion Against Internal Improvements," *Journal of Economic History* 10 (November 1950): 145–69; Hartz, *Economic Policy and Democratic Thought,* pp. 82, 161.

6 Hartz, *Economic Policy and Democratic Thought,* pp. 79, 121, 161, 315–19.

7 J. Smith Homans and J. Smith Homans, Jr., *A Cyclopedia of Commerce and Commercial Navigation,* 2d ed. (New York, 1859), p. 374.

8 Handlin, *Commonwealth,* pp. 113, 130, 142–43, 161–64, 171–72, 194; Shaw Livermore, *Early American Land Companies: Their Influence on Corporate Development* (New York, 1939), pp. 214, 244.

9 Edwin Merrick Dodd, Jr., "The First Half Century of Statutory Regulation of Business Corporations in Massachusetts," in *Harvard Legal Essays Written in Honor of and Presented to Joseph Henry Beale and Samuel Williston* (Cambridge, Mass., 1934), p. 66; Joseph K. Angell and Samuel Ames, *Treatise on the Law of Private Corporations Aggregate,* 1st ed. (Boston, 1832), p. 25; Dartmouth College v. Woodward, 17 U.S. (4 Wheat.) 518, 668 (1819); Angell and Ames, *Law of Private Corporations,* 1st ed., p. 410.

10 Angell and Ames, *Law of Private Corporations,* 1st ed., p. 23; 6th ed., p. 29. Handlin, *Commonwealth,* p. 170.

11 Wales v. Stetson, 2 Mass. 143, 146 (1806); Dartmouth College v. Woodward, 17 U.S. (4 Wheat.) 518, 666–713 (1819).

12 Dartmouth College v. Woodward, 17 U.S. (4 Wheat.) 518, 668–69, 711 (1819).

13 Providence Bank v. Billings, 29 U.S. (4 Pet.) 514, 562 (1830); Edward L. Pierce, *A Treatise on American Railroad Law* (New York, 1857), pp. 40–41; Redfield, *Law of Railways,* p. 232; Isaac F. Redfield, commentary on Philadelphia, W. & B.R.R. v. Bowers, 4 Houst. 506 (Del. Ct. Err. & App. 1873), in *American Law Register,* n.s., 13 (1874): 186–90; Thomas M. Cooley, *A Treatise on the Constitutional Limitations Which Rest Upon the Legislative Power of the States of the American Union* (Boston, 1868), pp. 574–77.

14 Providence Bank v. Billings, 29 U.S. (4 Pet.) 514 (1830); Benjamin F. Wright, *The Growth of American Constitutional Law* (New York, 1942), pp. 63–64; Angell and Ames, *Law of Private Corporations Aggregate,* 1st ed., pp. 7–8; Hartz, *Economic Policy and Democratic Thought,* pp. 71–72.

15 The best known examples were the Boston & Lowell Railroad Co. of Massachusetts and the Camden & Amboy Railroad Co. of New Jersey.

16 U.S., Congress, House, *Public Aids to Domestic Transportation,* 79th Cong., 1st sess., 1945, H. Doc. no. 159, p. 165.

17 John K. Towles, "Early Railroad Monopoly and Discrimination in Rhode Island," *Yale Review* 18 (November 1909): 316–17.

18 General Railroad Association, *Journal of the Proceedings of the General Railroad Association at Their Meeting Holden in New York, Nov. 23, 1854* (Newark, N.J., 1855), p. 32; Adams, "Railroad Legislation," pp. 343–49; Ohio, Department of Railroads and Telegraphs, *Annual Report of the Commissioner of Railroads and Telegraphs to the Governor of the State of Ohio, for the year 1867* (Columbus, 1868), p. 11.

19 Theodore C. Pease, *The Frontier State* (Chicago, 1922), pp. 210–12.

20 Private ownership of the canal had been considered but rejected (Edwin Ruthven Perry, "Regulation of Railroads by the State of Illinois," prize essay, Northwestern University, 1900, pp. 21–22).

21 Pease, *Frontier State,* pp. 210–12; William K. Ackerman, *Early Illinois Railroads* (Chicago, 1884), p. 22; G. S. Callender, "The Early Transportation and Banking Enterprises of the States in

Relation to the Growth of Corporations," *Quarterly Journal of Economics* 17 (November 1902): 153; John H. Krenkel, *Illinois Internal Improvements, 1818–1848* (Cedar Rapids, Iowa, 1958), chap. 3.

22 Alexander Davidson and Bernard Stuvé, *A Complete History of Illinois from 1673 to 1873* (Springfield, Ill., 1874), p. 448.

23 Ibid., pp. 436–38, 443, 447; H. J. Stratton, "The Northern Cross Railroad," *Journal of the Illinois State Historical Society* 28 (July 1935): 10, 44–49; Pease, *Frontier State,* pp. 212–18; F. A. Cleveland and F. W. Powell, *Railway Promotion and Capitalization in the United States* (New York, 1909), pp. 100–101, 104–5.

24 *Sangamo* (Ill.) *Journal,* March 25, 1842; Stratton, "Northern Cross Railroad," p. 44.

25 Davidson and Stuvé, *Complete History of Illinois,* p. 448.

26 *Hunt's Merchants' Magazine* 27 (December 1852): 659.

27 Pease, *Frontier State,* pp. 231–35; Leland Hamilton Jenks, *The Migration of British Capital to 1875* (New York, 1927), pp. 99–104.

28 Public construction of the Illinois Central Railroad was suggested as late as 1851, but the tide of public opinion was running against the idea (Paul Wallace Gates, *The Illinois Central Railroad and Its Colonization Work,* Cambridge, Mass., 1934, pp. 46–47).

29 Illinois, *Constitution of 1848,* art. 10, sec. 6; art. 3, sec. 38.

30 Rasmus S. Saby, *Railroad Legislation in Minnesota 1849 to 1875* (St. Paul, 1912), p. 178 n. 796; Arthur Charles Cole, ed., *The Constitutional Debates of 1847* (Springfield, Ill., 1919), pp. iii–iv; Bessie Louise Pierce, *A History of Chicago,* 3 vols. (New York, 1937–57), 1: 72; Milo M. Quaife, ed., *The Convention of 1846* (Madison, Wis., 1919), pp. 549–50.

31 U.S., Congress, Senate, *Report of the Select Committee on Transportation Routes to the Seaboard,* 2 vols., 43d Cong., 1st sess., 1874, S. Rept. no. 307, 2: 140. In the Iowa constitutional convention debates of 1857 there was a protracted discussion of this question. Many of the delegates were convinced that no capitalist would invest a dollar in the state if a reservation clause was included. The same position was taken by a large number of delegates to the Minnesota conventions of 1857. Iowa adopted a reservation clause, but Minnesota did not. Iowa, Constitutional Convention, *Debates of the Constitutional Convention of the State of Iowa, Assembled at Iowa City, Monday, January 19, 1857,* 2 vols. (Davenport, 1857), 1: 108–72, 408–11; Minnesota

(Ter.), Democratic Constitutional Convention, *Debates and Proceedings of the Minnesota Constitutional Convention Including the Organic Act of the Territory* . . . (St. Paul, 1857), pp. 121–64, 213–29; Minnesota (Ter.), Republican Constitutional Convention, *Debates and Proceedings of the Constitutional Convention for the Territory of Minnesota, to Form a State Constitution Preparatory to Its Admission into the Union as a State* (St. Paul, 1858), pp. 325–33.

32 "The influence of railroads upon the present and future welfare of the state . . . is universally admitted to be most enormous, and carries with it the ultimate destiny of our state" (Illinois, General Assembly, House, *Report of the Committee on Internal Improvements, in Relation to Railroads in Illinois, Jan. 24, 1848,* 1849, Ill. H. Repts., p. 22).

33 Italics mine.

34 Illinois, General Assembly, House, *Majority Report of the Committee on Incorporation, on the Subject of Railroads, Jan. 22, 1849,* 1849, Ill. H. Repts., pp. 21–24.

35 Davidson and Stuvé, *Complete History of Illinois,* p. 564; Ackerman, *Early Illinois Railroads,* p. 56; Arthur C. Cole, *The Era of the Civil War, 1848–1870* (Springfield, Ill., 1919), p. 35; Joseph Hinckley Gordon, *Illinois Railway Legislation and Commission Control since 1870,* introduction by M. B. Hammond (Urbana, Ill., 1904), p. 12.

36 Earnest E. Calkins, *Genesis of a Railroad,* Illinois State Historical Society Transactions for 1935, no. 42 (Springfield, 1935), pp. 55–59; Richard C. Overton, *Burlington West: A Colonization History of the Burlington Railroad* (Cambridge, Mass., 1941), pp. 35–38.

37 William K. Ackerman, a president of the Illinois Central, maintained that the I.C. charter of 1851 would never have been accepted without a clause guaranteeing complete freedom as to rates (William K. Ackerman, *Historical Sketch of the Illinois Central Railroad, Together with a Brief Biographical Record of Its Incorporators and Some of Its Early Officers,* Chicago, 1890, p. 80). Chicago, Burlington, and Quincy Railroad Company, *Documentary History,* 3 vols. (Chicago, 1928), 1: 37; H. G. Brownson, *History of the Illinois Central to 1870* (Urbana, Ill., 1915); Gates, *Illinois Central Railroad and Its Colonization Work,* chap. 3; Calkins, *Genesis of a Railroad,* p. 63.

38 Colton, quoted in Overton, *Burlington West,* p. 509.

39 Ibid.

40 Illinois, General Assembly, House, *Journal,* 1853, pp. 47–48.

41 Hammond, in Gordon, *Illinois Railway Legislation,* pp. 5, 11–13; Cole, *Era of the Civil War,* p. 47.

42 The Illinois legislature for a time resisted all efforts to build railroad connections to St. Louis. Alton was made the terminal of the early roads in that part of the state. George R. Taylor and Irene D. Neu, *The American Railroad Network, 1861–1890* (Cambridge, Mass., 1956), p. 40.

43 Ibid., pp. 6, 15–34, 40, 58–63. Uncoordinated railroad systems were not a problem west of Chicago. Except for one Illinois road with its terminus in St. Louis, all the railroads of Illinois, Iowa, Wisconsin, and Minnesota were built to standard gauge.

44 Taylor and Neu, *American Railroad Network,* p. 6; Thomas C. Cochran, *Railroad Leaders—1845–1890: The Business Mind in Action* (Cambridge, Mass., 1953), pp. 34–35; Arthur M. Johnson and Barry E. Supple, *Boston Capitalists and Western Railroads* (Cambridge, Mass., 1967), pp. 107–9, 152–54, 340–42.

45 Edward C. Kirkland, *Men, Cities and Transportation: A Study in New England History, 1820–1900,* 2 vols. (Cambridge, Mass., 1948), 1: 223–66; Johnson and Supple, *Boston Capitalists and Western Railroads,* pp. 88–99, 107–26, 156–80.

46 Cochran, *Railroad Leaders,* pp. 26–28, 40.

47 Ibid., p. 40; John Moody, *The Railroad Builders: A Chronicle of the Welding of the States* (New Haven, 1919), pp. 35–36.

48 Taylor and Neu, *American Railroad Network,* pp. 15–34, 57, 67–76. For the popular reaction to absentee ownership of the Michigan Central, see Charles Hirschfeld, *The Great Railroad Conspiracy: The Social History of a Railroad War* (East Lansing, 1953).

49 Towles, "Early Railroad Monopoly and Discrimination in Rhode Island," pp. 316–17.

Chapter 4 ILLINOIS: THE TRIUMPH OF JUDICIAL REVIEW

1 *Chicago Times,* January 7, 1867; Juliet G. Sager, "Stephen A. Hurlbut, 1815–1882," *Journal of the Illinois State Historical Society* 28 (July 1935): 53–80; Richard V. Carpenter, ed., *Historical Encyclopedia of Illinois and History of Boone County,* 2 vols. (Chicago, 1909), 1: 240–41.

2 *Portrait and Biographical Record of Winnebago and Boone*

Counties, Illinois (Chicago, 1892), pp. 516–17; Carpenter, ed., *Historical Encyclopedia of Illinois,* 1: 178–79; *The Past and Present of Boone County, Illinois* (Chicago, 1877), pp. 267–71.

3 *The United States Biographical Dictionary and Portrait Gallery of Eminent and Self-Made Men. Illinois Volume* (New York and Chicago, 1876), pp. 625–26; Carpenter, ed., *Historical Encyclopedia of Illinois,* 1: 233.

4 As a result of discrimination against Rockford, farmers in the surrounding area were marketing their crops and buying their provisions in Freeport and Beloit (*Rock River* [Ill.] *Democrat,* May 18, 1858).

5 The bill could not be found in the State Archives of Illinois at Springfield.

6 Illinois, General Assembly, House, *Journal,* 1861, pp. 402, 583.

7 Illinois, Constitutional Convention, *Journal of the Constitutional Convention of the State of Illinois, Convened at Springfield, January 7, 1862* (Springfield, 1862), pp. 55, 148; *Illinois State Journal,* March 28, 1862.

8 *Illinois State Journal,* April 1, 1862.

9 Arthur C. Cole, *The Era of the Civil War, 1848–1870* (Springfield, Ill., 1919), p. 270; Alexander Davidson and Bernard Stuvé, *A Complete History of Illinois, from 1673 to 1873* (Springfield, Ill., 1874), p. 876.

10 Emerson D. Fite, "The Agricultural Development of the West during the Civil War," *Quarterly Journal of Economics* 20 (February 1906): 269; Emerson D. Fite, *Social and Industrial Conditions in the North During the Civil War* (New York, 1910), pp. 48, 110–15; Guy A. Lee, "History of the Chicago Grain Elevator Industry" (Ph.D. diss., Harvard University, 1938), pp. 136–37.

11 Fite, *Social and Industrial Conditions in the North During the Civil War,* pp. 47–52, 178; Cole, *Era of the Civil War,* pp. 354–56; Chicago, Board of Trade, *The Necessity of a Ship-Canal Between the East and the West. Report of the Proceedings of the Board of Trade, the Mercantile Association, and the Businessmen of Chicago* (Chicago, 1863), p. 27, et passim; Chicago, Committee on Statistics, *The Necessity of a Ship-Canal Between the East and the West. Report of the Committee on Statistics . . .* (Chicago, 1863); National Ship-Canal Convention, *Proceedings of the National Ship-Canal Convention. Held at the City of Chicago, June 2 and 3, 1863* (Chicago, 1863); W. H. Osborn to H. V.

Poor, Osborn to J. Sturgis, Osborn to W. Tracy, Osborn to J. Caird, all dated February 18, 1863; Osborn to Gov. Yates, March 11, 1863, Osborn Out-Letters, vol. 5, all in the Illinois Central Archives, Newberry Library, Chicago, Illinois. Frank L. Klement, "Middle Western Copperheadism and the Genesis of the Granger Movement," *Mississippi Valley Historical Review* 38 (March 1952): 681, et passim.

12 In the absence of full newspaper reports on the debates, it is impossible to determine the lines of cleavage on the railroad issue during this session. Illinois, General Assembly, Senate, *Journal,* 1863, pp. 70–71, 89, 162, 210–11; Illinois, General Assembly, House, *Journal,* 1863, pp. 117, 499, 669, 704; *Chicago Tribune,* January 14, February 6, 1863.

13 Cole, *Era of the Civil War,* pp. 373–82; Davidson and Stuvé, *Complete History of Illinois,* pp. 910–11; Fite, *Social and Industrial Conditions in the North during the Civil War,* pp. 15–22, 42–45, 78–79, 115–17.

14 *New York Journal of Commerce,* September 17, 1864.

15 *Chicago Tribune,* February 9, 1865.

16 Cole, *Era of the Civil War,* pp. 357–58; *Prairie Farmer,* December 24, 1864, January 7, September 23, 1865; Illinois, General Assembly, Senate, *Journal,* 1865, pp. 66, 86, 211, 305, 306, 350, 397, 436; Illinois, General Assembly, House, *Journal,* 1865, pp. 87, 197, 236, 296, 332, 384, 459, 461, 462, 497, 515, 594; Illinois General Assembly Records, "Miscellaneous Petitions, 1863–67," Illinois State Archives, Springfield, Illinois.

17 Ill., House, *Journal,* 1865, pp. 133, 159, 164, 506, 778–79, 833–34; Ill., Senate, *Journal,* 1865, p. 560; *Chicago Tri-Weekly Tribune,* January 13, February 9, 1865.

18 *Chicago Tri-Weekly Tribune,* January 28, 1865; Illinois, *Private Laws,* 1865, 2 vols., 2: 146, 190; *Chicago Tribune,* February 10, 1865. The movement to place regulatory provisions and reservation clauses in new charters and in amendments to old charters grew in strength during the late sixties. Illinois, General Assembly, House, *Journal,* 1867, 2 vols., 1: 47, 107; Illinois, *Private Laws,* 1867, 3 vols., 2: 538–43, 624, 682–85, 693, 729; Illinois, *Private Laws,* 1869, 4 vols., 3: 144.

19 *Illinois State Journal,* November 30, 1865, January 9, February 13, March, 1, 1866; *Prairie Farmer,* November 4, December 16, 23, 1865, March 3, 1866; *Chicago Evening Journal,* November 23, 27, 1865; *Chicago Tribune,* November 23, December 11, 1865; Cole, *Era of the Civil War,* p. 359.

20 *Chicago Tribune,* December 15, 1865.
21 *Belvidere* (Ill.) *Standard,* January 30, February 6, 1866; *Illinois State Journal,* December 18, 1865; *Chicago Tribune,* December 11, 24, 1865, January 4, 1866; Chicago, Joint Committee of the Board of Trade and Mercantile Association, *Produce and Transportation. The Railway and Warehouse Monopolies. Report of a Joint Committee of the Board of Trade and Mercantile Association. The Railway Companies Advised to Reduce Their Rates, and a Belief Expressed that They Will. A Review of the Grain Inspection Trouble* (Chicago, 1866), pp. 3–11; Bessie Louise Pierce, *A History of Chicago,* 3 vols. (New York, 1937–57), 2: 64–66; Lee, "History of the Chicago Grain Elevator Industry," pp. 135–36, 142–45, 155; Cole, *Era of the Civil War,* pp. 357–58, 383–85.
22 *Illinois State Journal,* December 17, 28, 1866, January 3, 1867; *Prairie Farmer,* January 5, 1867; *Chicago Tribune,* December 27, 28, 1866, January 11, 18, 1867; *Chicago Times,* January 18, 28, 1867; Cole, *Era of the Civil War,* p. 358.
23 U.S., Department of Agriculture, Division of Statistics, *Changes in the Rate of Charge for Railroad and Other Transportation Services,* by H. T. Newcomb, rev. by Edward G. Ward, Jr. (Washington, D.C., 1901), pp. 21–22.
24 *Chicago Republican,* January 21, 1867; *Belvidere* (Ill.) *Standard,* February 9, 1869; *Chicago Times,* February 2, 1867.
25 *Chicago Times,* January 7, February 19, 1867; *Chicago Tribune,* January 16, 17, 19, 1867.
26 *Chicago Tribune,* January 24, 29, 1867.
27 *Chicago Times,* January 27, 1867; *Chicago Tribune,* January 25, 1867.
28 *Chicago Times,* January 24, 25, 27, 28, February 1, 19, 21, 26, 1867; *Chicago Tribune,* February 9, 22, 1867; *Illinois State Journal,* January 30, February 6, 1867.
29 *Chicago Times,* January 31, February 7, 13, March 2, 1867; *Chicago Tribune,* February 6, 18, 19, 22, 1867.
30 *Chicago Times,* January 18, 1867. The *Tribune* also agreed that there was a sell-out (February 6, 1867).
31 *Chicago Times,* January 18, 1867; Lewis H. Haney, *A Congressional History of Railways in the United States,* 2 vols. (Madison, Wis., 1910), 2: 240.
32 *Prairie Farmer,* November 30, 1867; *Merchants' Magazine and Commercial Review* 59 (1868): 108–27, 161–80, 335–38, 404–6; *Belvidere* (Ill.) *Standard,* January 5, 1869; *Illinois State Journal,*

March 28, 1868. For Gov. Oglesby's message, see Illinois, *Reports*, 2 vols. (Springfield, 1869), 1: 1–2, 28. On the absence of agitation for control in 1868–69, see the *Chicago Tribune*, January 12, 1869. John M. Palmer, *Personal Recollections of John M. Palmer: The Story of an Earnest Life* (Cincinnati, 1901), pp. 281–88.

33 Illinois, General Assembly, House, *Journal*, 1869, 3 vols., 1: 206–7.

34 Davidson and Stuvé, *Complete History of Illinois*, p. 933. On Palmer's political independence, see Shelby Moore Cullom, *Fifty Years of Public Service, Personal Recollections* (Chicago, 1911), p. 191.

35 *Illinois State Journal*, January 6, 1869; *Chicago Times*, January 7, 13, 16, 20, 28, 1869; *Chicago Tribune*, January 21, 22, 26, 1869; J. N. Denison to J. F. Joy, January 19, 1869, Denison to S. P. Burt, January 22, 1869, Denison Out-Letters, vol. 5; Harris to Denison, February 2, 1869, Harris Out-Letters, vol. 14, all in the Burlington Archives, Newberry Library, Chicago, Illinois. Illinois, General Assembly, Senate, *Journal*, 1869, 2 vols., 1: 45, 210; Ill., House, *Journal*, 1869, 1: 284, 300, 342, 348, 350; Cole, *Era of the Civil War*, p. 360.

36 Illinois, *Reports*, 1869, 1: 401–7.

37 Ill., Senate, *Journal*, 1869, 1: 404, 566, 856; *Belvidere* (Ill.) *Standard*, March 16, 1869; *Chicago Tribune*, February 11, 1869; Illinois General Assembly Records, 1869, Senate Bill 495, Illinois State Archives.

38 *Chicago Tribune*, January 21, 22, 26, February 23, 24, March 3, 12, 1869; Ill., House, *Journal*, 1869, 1: 447, 798, 799, 849; Illinois General Assembly Records, "Petitions on the subject of regulating rates of tariff on railroads, 1869," Illinois State Archives; *Chicago Times*, February 24, 25, March 11, 1869; Illinois, *Public Laws*, 1869, pp. 309–12.

A regional breakdown of the final vote on the two Fuller bills shows that opposition to regulation was centered in the have-not areas south of a line between Burlington, Iowa, and Terre Haute, Indiana. Although this was the stronghold of the Democratic party in Illinois, there is no evidence of a party line on the railroad issue. Ill., Senate, *Journal*, 1869, 1: 210, 2: 97; Ill., House, *Journal*, 1869, 1: 350, 3: 223.

39 For the text of the Fuller Resolution, see Illinois, General Assembly, Senate, *Journal*, 1867, pp. 93–94, 171–72, 174–75.

40 *Chicago Tribune,* January 28, December 15, 1865.
41 Harris to Denison, March 17, 1869, Harris Out-Letters, vol. 15, Burlington Archives.
42 *Chicago Tribune,* March 13, 1869.
43 John Moses, *Illinois, Historical and Statistical,* 2 vols. (Chicago, 1892), 2: 785–86.
44 Davidson and Stuvé, *Complete History of Illinois,* pp. 912–13, 938–39; Cole, *Era of the Civil War,* p. 406; Moses, *Illinois, Historical and Statistical,* 2: 785–87.
45 *Chicago Times,* February 1, 1867; Ernest L. Bogart and Charles M. Thompson, *The Industrial State, 1870–1893* (Springfield, Ill., 1920), pp. 3–4.
46 Illinois, Constitutional Convention, *Debates and Proceedings of the Constitutional Convention of the State of Illinois, Convened at the City of Springfield, Tuesday, December 13, 1869,* 2 vols. (Springfield, 1870), 2: 1710.
47 Ibid., 1639.
48 Ibid., 1: 289, 344, 365, 451, 510, 589, 590, 627, 654, 679, 702, 736, 757, 782.
49 Ibid., 84, 148, 192, 212, 298, 532, 577, 834–35, 846; 2: 1237, 1477, 1643–44, 1655, 1659, 1711.
50 Ibid., 1: 317. For a similar statement by William P. Peirce of Grundy County, see ibid., 2: 1645–46.
51 Ibid., 2: 1641–43. This argument had been implicit in the debates over the proposed legislation of 1867 and 1869 but had never been stated so clearly. See Ill., Senate, *Journal,* 1867, pp. 93–94; Ill., House, *Journal,* 1869, 1: 258; *Chicago Tribune,* January 11, 12, 16, 17, 24, 25, 1867. At the same time others were taking the less tenable position that railroad companies were public corporations and therefore outside the protection of the *Dartmouth College* ruling. See the *Chicago Tribune,* January 21, 22, 1869. See also Ill., Constitutional Convention, *Debates and Proceedings,* 1: 147; 2: 1656.
52 Ill., Constitutional Convention, *Debates and Proceedings,* 1: 84, 262, 487; 2: 1320, 1627, 1652–54, 1655–57.
53 Illinois, *Constitution of 1870,* art. 13; Harold D. Woodman, "Chicago Businessmen and the 'Granger Laws,'" *Agricultural History* 36 (January 1962): 21–22.
54 Benjamin F. Wright, *The Contract Clause of the Constitution* (Cambridge, Mass., 1938), chap. 8. On the right of the legislature to deprive itself of power over rates, see above, p. 29.

55 Rowland G. Hazard, "The Relation of Railroad Corporations to the Public," *Merchants' Magazine and Commercial Review* 21 (1849): 622–27; Edward C. Kirkland, *Men, Cities and Transportation: A Study in New England History, 1820–1900,* 2 vols. (Cambridge, Mass., 1948), 2: 292–93. *Nation* 1 (September 14, 1865): 328–29; 16 (May 15, 1873): 328–29; 17 (October 16, 1873): 252. Charles F. Adams, Jr., "The Railroad System," *North American Review* 104 (April 1867): 496–97; Charles F. Adams, Jr., "Railroad Inflation," *North American Review* 108 (January 1869): 136–39; Charles F. Adams, Jr., "Railway Problems in 1869," *North American Review* 110 (January 1870): 149–50; Leonard Bacon, "Railways and the State," *New Englander* 30 (October 1871): 713–16, 737; Vermont, Railroad Commissioner, *Annual Report,* 1858 (Montpelier, Vt., 1859), p. 6.

56 P. 549.

57 Thomas M. Cooley, *A Treatise on the Constitutional Limitations Which Rest upon the Legislative Power of the States of the American Union* (Boston, 1868), p. 280.

58 *Legal Gazette* 5 (December 1873): 403–9; Isaac J. Redfield, Regulation of Interstate Traffic on Railways by Congress," *American Law Register,* n.s., 13 (January 1874): 9.

59 *Nation* 10 (May 26, 1870): 331; Charles Francis Adams, Jr., "The Government and the Railroad Corporations," *North American Review* 112 (January 1871): 51; *Commercial and Financial Chronicle,* May 28, 1870.

60 Ill., Constitutional Convention, *Debates and Proceedings,* 2: 1894–95. The total Illinois vote for president in 1868 was about 450,000. The vote for congressmen in the off-year election of 1870 was about 300,000. Moses, *Illinois, Historical and Statistical,* 2: 1212.

61 In ten counties in the northwestern part of the state the vote was 18,309 for, 554 against; in ten counties of the western bulge near Quincy, the vote was 13,792 for, 7,323 against; in the eleven southernmost counties, the vote was 3,065 for, 2,230 against. Ill., Constitutional Convention, *Debates and Proceedings,* 2: 1894–95.

62 *Chicago Tribune,* August 24, September 9, 1869; January 6, 18, July 4, 1870. *Prairie Farmer,* June 5, 1869; *Illinois State Journal,* March 26, April 12, June 30, 1869; *Cairo* (Ill.) *Evening Bulletin,* April 13, 1869; Chicago, Board of Trade, *Eleventh Annual Report* (Chicago, 1869), p. 10; Chicago, Board of Trade, *Twelfth Annual Report* (Chicago, 1870), pp. 5, 14–15; Chicago, Board of Trade, *Thirteenth Annual Report* (Chicago, 1871), p. 15; *Illinois*

State Journal, September 23, 1869; Wyatt Winton Belcher, *Economic Rivalry between St. Louis and Chicago, 1850–1880* (New York, 1947), pp. 159–75; Lee, "History of the Chicago Grain Elevator Industry," pp. 169–72; Frederick Merk, *Economic History of Wisconsin during the Civil War Decade,* Publications of the State Historical Society, Studies 1 (Madison, 1916), p. 324; C. H. Taylor, ed., *History of the Board of Trade of the City of Chicago,* 3 vols. (Chicago, 1917), 1: 385, 404–5; National Board of Trade, *Proceedings of the Second Annual Meeting* (Boston, 1870), pp. 71–74, 79; Jonathan Periam, *The Groundswell: A History of the Origin, Aims, and Progress of the Farmers' Movement* . . . (St. Louis, 1874), p. 228.

63 *Prairie Farmer,* April 30, 1870; Periam, *Groundswell,* pp. 223–30; Solon J. Buck, *The Granger Movement* (Cambridge, Mass., 1913), p. 128; John Lee Coulter, "Organization among the Farmers of the United States," *Yale Review* 18 (November 1909): 280; *Illinois State Journal,* March 8, 1869.

64 Illinois, General Assembly, Senate, *Journal,* 1871, 2 vols., 2: 19–20.

65 The Senate was composed of 22 lawyers, 10 farmers, 5 merchants, 2 physicians, 2 bankers, and 9 "agents and mechanics." Thirty-two were Republican; eighteen, Democratic. In the house there were 62 farmers, 61 lawyers, 21 merchants, 6 bankers, 5 manufacturers, 4 physicians, 4 agents, 2 ministers, 2 engineers, and 10 "others." One hundred two were Republican; seventy-five, Democratic. Moses, *Illinois, Historical and Statistical,* 2: 798; Rummel's *Illinois Hand-Book and Legislative Manual for 1871* (Springfield, 1871), pp. 175–82. On the Farmers' club, see *Prairie Farmer,* February 18, 25, 1871; *Chicago Tribune,* March 11, 1871.

66 *Chicago Tribune,* January 20, 26, 1871.

67 Ibid., January 19, 26, 1871.

68 Ibid., January 19, February 4, 10, 17, March 2, 1871.

69 Ill., Senate, *Journal,* 1871, pp. 204, 290; *Chicago Tribune,* January 23, 27, 1871; *Chicago Times,* January 20, 1871; Harris to J. W. Drummond, January 25, 1871, Harris Out-Letters, vol. 22, Burlington Archives.

70 *Chicago Tribune,* February 18, 26, March 8, 18, 1871.

71 Ibid., March 29, 30, 31, April 1, 1871.

72 Illinois, *Public Laws,* 1871–72, pp. 635–41.

73 *Belvidere* (Ill.) *Standard,* March 14, 1871; *Chicago Times,* January 20, 24, 26, 1871; *Chicago Tribune,* April 3, 1871. For a

contrasting view, see J. H. Raymond, "The People and the Railroads," *Lakeside Monthly* 7 (February 1872): 142–43. See also the *Prairie Farmer*, April 22, 1871, and the *Railroad Gazette* 2 (January 14, 21, 1871): 370–71, 394.

74 John K. Towles, "Early Railroad Monopoly and Discrimination in Rhode Island," *Yale Review* 18 (November 1909): 302–7.

75 Ill., *Public Laws*, 1871–72, pp. 762–73; Woodman, "Chicago Businessmen and the 'Granger Laws,'" p. 23.

76 Moses, *Illinois, Historical and Statistical*, 2: 1061–62; Illinois, Railroad and Warehouse Commission, *Second Annual Report* (Springfield, 1873), pp. 21–22, 44.

77 Ill., Railroad and Warehouse Commission, *Second Annual Report*, pp. 44–69, 71–97.

78 Ibid., pp. 99–114.

79 Illinois, Railroad and Warehouse Commission, *Third Annual Report* (Springfield, 1874), p. 151.

80 Ibid., p. 156.

81 Ibid., pp. 149–59.

82 Quoted in A. E. Paine, *The Granger Movement in Illinois* (Urbana, Ill., 1904), p. 34 n. 1.

83 *Chicago Tribune*, February 25, 26, 1873; *Prairie Farmer*, March 1, 1873.

84 Periam, *Groundswell*, pp. 233–48; "Proceedings of the Farmers' Convention Held at Bloomington, Ill., January 15th and 16th, 1873," in Illinois, Department of Agriculture, *Transactions*, 1873 (Springfield, 1874), pp. 224–96. On the many farmers' conventions, see the *Chicago Tribune*, January 10, 13, February 21, 1873, and Gov. Beveridge's remarks to the Springfield convention of 1873 in Periam, *Groundswell*, p. 282.

85 Willard C. Flagg, "The Farmers' Movement in the Western States," *Journal of Social Science* 6 (July 1874): 108.

86 *Chicago Tribune*, March 24, 1873; *Prairie Farmer*, March 8, 1873; testimony of Flagg, in U.S., Congress, Senate, *Report of the Select Committee on Transportation Routes to the Seaboard*, 2 vols., 43d Cong., 1st sess., 1874, S. Rept. no. 307, 2: 682. For farmers' petitions on "extortions by railways," see Illinois, General Assembly, House, *Journal*, 1873, pp. 272, 289, 312, 322, 323, 334, 386, 442. On the complaints of the Chicago merchants, see the *Chicago Tribune*, January 13, 1873, and George G. Tunell, "The Diversion of the Flour and Grain Traffic from the Great

Lakes to the Railroads," *Journal of Political Economy* 5 (June 1897): 342–47.

87 *Chicago Tribune,* March 2, 19, April 3, 1873. For reports of the farmers' conventions, see the *Prairie Farmer,* December 21, 1872, February 8, March 29, April 12, 19, 1873. See also Ill., House, *Journal,* 1873, p. 396.

88 The debates and proceedings of the legislature and its various committees are fully reported in the *Chicago Tribune,* January–April 1873. See also Solon J. Buck, "Independent Parties in the Western States, 1873–1876," in *Essays in American History Dedicated to Frederick Jackson Turner* (New York, 1910), pp. 141–43; Periam, *Groundswell,* pp. 280–87; statement of S. M. Smith, in [James Dabney McCabe], *History of the Grange Movement; or, The Farmers' War Against Monopolies* (Chicago, 1874), pp. 348, 370–71; *Prairie Farmer,* May 10, 1873.

89 Illinois, *Public Laws,* 1873, pp. 136–40.

90 Benjamin R. Twiss, *Lawyers and the Constitution: How Laissez Faire Came to the Supreme Court* (Princeton, 1942), p. 19. The writings of Charles Francis Adams, Jr. did much to popularize the commission as an agency of investigation and study. See his "Boston," *North American Review* 106 (January 1868): 15–19, and "The Government and the Railroad Corporations," *North American Review* 112 (January 1871): 58.

91 Robert E. Cushman, *The Independent Regulatory Commission* (New York, 1941), pp. 22–26, and Ivan L. Pollock, *History of Economic Legislation in Iowa* (Iowa City, 1918), pp. 12–20. On the Illinois Canal Commission, see James William Putnam, *The Illinois and Michigan Canal* (Chicago, 1918), pp. 67–69, 85–86. On the Illinois Public Works Commission, see Davidson and Stuvé, *Complete History of Illinois,* p. 437. See also Frederick C. Clark, *State Railroad Commissions and How They May Be Made Effective,* American Economic Association Publications 6, no. 6 (New York, 1891), pp. 23–25; Leonard D. White, "Origin of Utility Commissions in Massachusetts," *Journal of Political Economy* 29 (March 1921): 189; and Kirkland, *Men, Cities and Transportation,* 1: 281; 2: 230–40.

92 Gustave Koerner proposed such a system in 1871 (*Chicago Tribune,* February 24, 1871). On the European experience, see Ill., Railroad and Warehouse Commission, *Second Annual Report,* p. 13.

93 William K. Ackerman, *Historical Sketch of the Illinois Central Railroad* (Chicago, 1890), p. 145. The railroads were careful not to apply any pressure on the members of the railroad committees in 1873, because they were afraid of arousing even greater hostility (D. L. Phillips to Newell, March 17, 1873, George Trumbull to Newell, March 17, 1873, Newell In-Letters, vol. 9, Illinois Central Archives).

Chapter 5 IOWA: THE REVOLT OF THE RIVER TOWNS

1 Peter A. Dey, "Railroad Legislation in Iowa," *Iowa Historical Record* 9 (October 1893): 540–41; Ivan L. Pollock, *History of Economic Legislation in Iowa* (Iowa City, 1918), pp. 40–41; Earl S. Beard, "Local Aid to Railroads in Iowa," *Iowa Journal of History* 50 (January 1952): 1–17; Iowa, *Constitution of 1857,* Art. 8; Iowa, Constitutional Convention, *Debates of the Constitutional Convention of the State of Iowa, Assembled at Iowa City, Monday, January 19, 1857,* 2 vols. (Davenport, 1857), 1: 108–14, 144–61, 167, 171; *Dubuque Weekly Herald,* March 21, 1866. See the reports of railroad conventions in the *Iowa State Weekly Register* for the first quarter of 1866 and Benjamin F. Gue, *History of Iowa,* 4 vols. (New York, 1903), 3: 25–26, 58. For examples of antirestriction petitions, see Iowa, General Assembly, House, *Journal,* 1868, pp. 216, 364, 379. As late as 1865, Iowa had only 891 miles of railroad; in the same year Illinois had 3,157 miles.

2 Edgar R. Harlan, *A Narrative History of the People of Iowa,* 5 vols. (Chicago, 1931), 1: 299, 301; Robert E. Riegel, Trans-Mississippi Railroads during the Fifties," *Mississippi Valley Historical Review* 10 (September 1923): 153–55, 165, 171–72.

3 Wyatt W. Belcher, *The Economic Rivalry between St. Louis and Chicago, 1850–1880* (New York, 1947), pp. 102–13, 159–70; Bayrd Still, "Patterns of Mid-Nineteenth Century Urbanization in the Middle West," *Mississippi Valley Historical Review* 28 (September 1941): 198–99; Franklin T. Oldt, ed., *History of Dubuque County, Iowa* (Chicago, n.d.), pp. 133, 142; George W. Sieber, "Railroads and Lumber Marketing, 1858–78: The Relationship between an Iowa Sawmill Firm and the Chicago & Northwestern Railroad," *Annals of Iowa,* 3d ser., 39 (Summer 1967): 33–42.

4 Oldt, ed., *History of Dubuque County,* pp. 133, 142.

5 Iowa, General Assembly, Senate, *Journal,* 1860, pp. 167, 423; Iowa, General Assembly, House, *Journal,* 1860, pp. 297, 304; *Iowa State Daily Register,* February 14, 23, 24, 28, March 3, 14, 1860; Denison to J. F. Joy, March 8, 1865, J. N. Denison Out-Letters, vol. 1, Burlington Archives, Newberry Library, Chicago.

6 Iowa, State Agricultural Society, *Annual Report of the Secretary for 1862* (Des Moines, 1863), pp. 7, 126; Iowa, General Assembly, Senate, *Journal,* 1864, pp. 92, 114, 142, 484; Iowa, General Assembly, House, *Journal,* 1864, pp. 79, 85, 89, 102, 223–24, 511; U.S., Congress, House, *Report of the Northwestern Ship-Canal Convention,* 38 Cong., 2d sess., 1865, H. Misc. Doc. no. 23; Mississippi River Improvement Convention, *Proceedings of the Mississippi River Improvement Convention, Held at Dubuque, Iowa, February 14 and 15, 1866* (Dubuque, 1866); *Iowa State Weekly Register,* January 17, 1866; Harlan, *History of Iowa,* 2:21; Iowa, General Assembly, *Memorial of the Twelfth General Assembly of the State of Iowa to the United States Congress, Relative to Water Communication between the Atlantic and Mississippi,* in Iowa, *Legislative Documents,* 1868, 2; Iowa, State Agricultural Society, *Annual Report of the Secretary for 1869* (Des Moines, 1870), p. 27.

7 National Board of Trade, *Proceedings of the Second Annual Meeting* (Boston, 1870), p. 71; Iowa, General Assembly, Senate, *Journal,* 1873, pp. 29–30; Iowa, General Assembly, House, *Journal,* 1874, p. 420; Iowa, General Assembly, Senate, *Journal,* 1874, pp. 290, 313.

8 Benjamin F. Shambaugh, ed., *Messages and Proclamations of the Governors of Iowa,* 7 vols. (Iowa City, 1903–5), 3: 56–57; Iowa, General Assembly, House, *Journal,* 1866, pp. 235, 440–41; *Dubuque Weekly Herald,* March 14, 21, 1866; *Iowa State Weekly Register,* March 7, 14, 1866; *Iowa City Weekly State Press,* March 21, 1866.

9 *Iowa State Weekly Register,* March 7, 14, 21, 1866; Iowa, House, *Journal,* 1866, pp. 454–55, 763–64; *Dubuque Weekly Herald,* March 21, 28, 1866; Iowa, General Assembly, Senate, *Journal,* 1866, pp. 495, 540–41, 661. For a fuller development of the thesis that opposition to regulation came chiefly from the unserved western counties, see Earl S. Beard, "The Background of State Railroad Regulation in Iowa," *Iowa Journal of History* 51 (January 1953): 1–36.

10 Iowa, House, *Journal,* 1866, pp. 124–28.

11 *Iowa City Weekly State Press,* March 21, 1866.

12 Mississippi River Improvement Convention, *Proceedings,* pp. 10–27; *Iowa State Weekly Register,* January 17, 1866; letter of Samuel McNutt in D. C. Cloud, *Monopolies and the People,* 3d ed. (Davenport, Iowa, 1873), pp. 162–63; Milo Smith, "Answers to Inquiries in Relation to Commercial Movements to and from the State of Iowa" in U.S., Treasury Department, Bureau of Statistics, *First Annual Report on the Internal Commerce of the United States . . . for the Year 1876,* by Joseph Nimmo, Jr. (Washington, D.C., 1877), appendix no. 5, pp. 93–95; *Iowa State Weekly Register,* January–March 1866; *Dubuque Weekly Herald,* March 21, 1866.

13 Shambaugh, ed., *Messages and Proclamations,* 98–99, 118–21.

14 William H. Fleming, "Governor Samuel Merrill," *Annals of Iowa,* 3d ser., 5 (April 1902): 337–41; Harlan, *History of Iowa,* 2: 22, 25; Shambaugh, ed., *Messages and Proclamations,* 3: 398–99, 413–15.

15 Henry O'Connor, *Opinion of the Attorney General on the Powers of the Legislature to Regulate Tariffs on Railroads in the State of Iowa,* in Iowa, *Legislative Documents, 1868,* 2 vols. (Des Moines, 1868), vol. 2.

16 Iowa, General Assembly, Senate, *Journal,* 1868, pp. 227, 283, 435; Iowa, House, *Journal,* 1868, pp. 116, 216, 364, 379, 487, 490, 581. On the growing concern of the river-town commercial interests, see B. H. Booth to M. K. Jesup, December 24, 1867, Dubuque & Sioux City Railroad Co., New York Office, In-Letters, 1867–87, vol. 1, Illinois Central Archives, Newberry Library, Chicago; *Iowa State Weekly Register,* January 1, February 1868, passim; Harlan, *History of Iowa,* 2: 22. For the Doud amendments, see Iowa, *Laws of Iowa,* 1868, chap. 13, sec. 2; chap. 57, sec. 3; chap. 58, sec. 1; chap. 124, sec. 7.

17 Cloud, *Monopolies and the People,* pp. 165–66; Iola B. Quigley, "Some Studies in the Development of Railroads in Northeastern Iowa," *Annals of Iowa,* 3d ser., 20 (January 1936): 230–31; Gue, *History of Iowa,* 3: 25–26; Fleming, "Governor Samuel Merrill," pp. 347–48; Harlan, *Narrative History of the People of Iowa,* 1: 312–18.

18 In 1869 a carload of lumber could be shipped from Chicago to Independence, Iowa (75 miles west of Dubuque), for $11. It cost $10 to ship a similar load from Dubuque to Independence on

the Illinois Central. Wheat could be shipped from Ft. Dodge, Iowa, to Chicago (340 miles) for 40¢ a hundredweight. It cost 35¢ to send the same wheat from Ft. Dodge to Dubuque (150 miles). In neither case could the Dubuque merchants compete with their Chicago rivals. Statement of T. M. Monroe of Dubuque in National Board of Trade, *Proceedings of the Second Annual Meeting,* p. 70. See also the *Chicago Tribune,* December 10, 1869, and Belcher, *Economic Rivalry between St. Louis and Chicago,* p. 168. On the political influence of the railroads, see Larrabee, *Railroad Question,* p. 221.

19 Iowa, State Agricultural Society, *Annual Report of the Secretary for 1868* (Des Moines, 1869), pp. 7–8; Frank H. Dixon, *State Railroad Control with a History of Its Development in Iowa* (New York, 1896), p. 24; Milo Smith, "Commercial Movements to and from Iowa," p. 95.

20 Leonard Ralston has shown that the river towns were by no means unanimous in their support of rate regulation. Many of the businessmen along the river believed that more was to be gained by encouraging new construction. Support for restrictions was apt to be strongest immediately following the construction of a railroad bridge at each terminal. Leonard F. Ralston, "Railroads and the Government of Iowa, 1850–1872" (Ph.D. diss., State University of Iowa, 1960), pp. 418–25, 468–72.

21 Iowa, General Assembly, Senate, *Journal,* 1870, pp. 54, 117, 121, 129, 193, 203, 211, 219–21, 239, 246, 247, 251, 252, 454; Iowa, General Assembly, House, *Journal,* 1870, pp. 90, 114–15, 170, 180, 187, 196, 218, 224, 225, 272, 280, 300, 434–37; *Iowa State Daily Register,* January 28, March 18, 26, 1870; M. B. Mulkern to John M. Douglas, December 23, 1869, Booth to Jesup, December 27, 1869, Farley to Jesup, March 2, 1870, Dubuque & Sioux City Railroad Co., New York Office, In-Letters, 1867–87, vol. 1, Illinois Central Archives.

22 *Iowa City Weekly State Press,* February 23, 1870; *Iowa State Daily Register,* February 5, 1870. Richards claimed that it cost 60¢ to ship a barrel of flour from Downey, Iowa, to Davenport (42 miles), but only 35¢ to ship one from Downey to Chicago (260 miles).

23 *Iowa State Daily Register,* February 5, 1870. Sponsors of the Mills bill insisted that it would work no hardships on the railroads since it would not prevent them from raising their through rates to Chicago (ibid., March 24, 1870).

24 Iowa, House, *Journal,* 1870, pp. 218, 241, 400–401, 428, 442–43; *Iowa City Weekly State Press,* February 23, 1870; *Iowa State Daily Register,* March 12, 18, 26, 1870.

25 *Iowa State Daily Register,* March 26, 1870; Iowa, Senate, *Journal,* 1870, pp. 163–64, 224–26, 363, 378.

26 Mildred Throne, "Electing an Iowa Governor, 1871: Cyrus Clay Carpenter," *Iowa Journal of History* 48 (October 1950): 368–69; Shambaugh, ed., *Messages and Proclamations,* 4: 14–17, 20–23; Iowa, State Agricultural Society, *Annual Report of the Secretary for 1872* (Des Moines, 1873), pp. 201–14.

27 Iowa, General Assembly, House, *Journal,* 1872, pp. 80, 429, 473, 477, 481–83, 486–87; *Iowa City Weekly State Press,* March 20, 27, April 3, 10, 1872; *Iowa State Daily Register,* March 20, 21, 22, 1872.

28 Iowa, General Assembly, Senate, *Journal,* 1872, pp. 414–16; *Iowa State Daily Register,* March 29, 1872.

29 Iowa, Senate, *Journal,* 1872, pp. 466–67, 480, 482, 522, 612–14, 654–56; *Iowa State Daily Register,* April 4, 5, 6, 10, 18, 20, 1872; Gue, *History of Iowa,* 3: 58.

30 Mildred Throne, "The Grange in Iowa," *Iowa Journal of History* 47 (October 1949): 289–324. The convention of 1873 is described in Jonathan Periam, *The Groundswell: A History of the Origin, Aims, and Progress of the Farmer's Movement* (St. Louis, 1874), pp. 264–65. The report of the State Agricultural Society for 1872, issued early in 1873, gives an impression of general satisfaction with market conditions. The reports of local societies mention the transportation problem but none suggests rate regulation as a cure. The remedies proposed are more railroads and diversified industry.

31 *Iowa State Daily Register,* February 8, 9, 11, 12, 1873; Iowa, Senate, *Journal,* 1873, pp. 132–37; Iowa, General Assembly, House, *Journal,* 1873, pp. 112–19; *Iowa State Daily Register,* February 6, 1873; Iowa, *Iowa Code of 1873,* secs. 1297, 1304, 1305, 1306. See also the statement by Samuel McNutt, in Cloud, *Monopolies and the People,* pp. 168–69.

32 The Republican state ticket had won by a majority of 60,000 votes in 1872; in 1873 the Republican majority was cut to about 20,000. The new senate was composed of 34 Republicans, 16 opposition; the new house had 50 members from each party. Solon J. Buck, "Independent Parties in the Western States, 1873–1876," in *Essays in American History Dedicated to Frederick*

Jackson Turner (New York, 1910), pp. 149–57; Frederick E. Haynes, *Third Party Movements since the Civil War with Special Reference to Iowa* (Iowa City, 1916), pp. 67–73; Herbert Fairall, *Manual of Iowa Politics, State and National Conventions, Platforms, Candidates, and Official Vote of All Parties from 1838 to 1884* (Iowa City, 1884), pp. 83–84, 86–87, 91–92; [James Dabney McCabe], *History of the Grange Movement; or, The Farmer's War against Monopolies* (Chicago, 1874), pp. 513–14.

33 Shambaugh, ed., *Messages and Proclamations*, 4: 90–92, 112.

34 Iowa, General Assembly, House, *Journal*, 1874, pp. 247, 399–402; Iowa, General Assembly, Senate, *Journal*, 1874, pp. 39, 65, 211–18; *Iowa City Weekly State Press*, February 25, 1874; William P. Hepburn to James M. Walker, March 10, 1874, James M. Walker In-Letters, June 1873–August 1874, Burlington Archives; Solon J. Buck, *The Granger Movement* (Cambridge, Mass., 1913), pp. 170–71; Gue, *History of Iowa*, 3: 66.

35 Iowa, Senate, *Journal*, 1874, pp. 138, 197, 215–19, 277, 292, 294–95, 305; Gue, *History of Iowa*, 3: 66–71; Dey, "Railroad Legislation in Iowa," pp. 556–57; Iowa, *Laws of 1874*, chap. 68.

36 Dey, "Railroad Legislation in Iowa," pp. 556–57.

37 Larrabee, *Railroad Question*, p. 332.

38 U.S., Treasury Dept., *First Annual Report on the Commerce of the United States*, appendix no. 5, pp. 93–97.

39 Pollock, *History of Economic Legislation in Iowa*, pp. 47–48; Charles R. Aldrich, "Repeal of the Granger Law of Iowa," *Iowa Journal of History and Politics* 3 (April 1905): 256–70; Mildred Throne, "The Repeal of the Iowa Granger Law, 1878," *Iowa Journal of History* 51 (April 1953): 97–130. Miss Throne shows that the opposition to repeal came largely from the river towns.

Chapter 6 MINNESOTA: ROCHESTER VERSUS THE WINONA AND ST. PETER RAILROAD

1 Mildred L. Hartsough, "Transportation as a Factor in the Development of the Twin Cities," *Minnesota History* 7 (September 1926): 224; Robert E. Riegel, "Trans-Mississippi Railroads during the Fifties," *Mississippi Valley Historical Review* 10 (September 1923): 168.

2 Rasmus S. Saby, *Railroad Legislation in Minnesota, 1849 to 1875* (St. Paul, 1912), pp. 11–21, 29.

3 Ibid., pp. 7–8; Riegel, "Trans-Mississippi Railroads during the

Fifties," pp. 168–70; A. B. Stickney, *The Railway Problem, with Many Illustrative Diagrams* (St. Paul, 1891), pp. 8–10; Lester B. Shippee, "Social and Economic Effects of the Civil War with Special Reference to Minnesota," *Minnesota History Bulletin* 2 (May 1918): 400–401.

4 Republican and Democratic delegates proved unable to compromise a number of disputes involving elections and the organization of the proposed convention. The result was two conventions meeting under separate party banners, but a single constitution was eventually agreed upon by a conference committee. William W. Folwell, *A History of Minnesota,* 4 vols. (St. Paul, 1921–30), 1: 388–421.

5 Stickney, *Railway Problem,* pp. 8–9.

6 Minnesota (Ter.), Democratic Constitutional Convention, *Debates and Proceedings of the Minnesota Constitutional Convention Including the Organic Act of the Territory* . . . (St. Paul, 1857), pp. 121–48, 158–64; Minnesota (Ter.), Republican Constitutional Convention, *Debates and Proceedings of the Constitutional Convention for the Territory of Minnesota, to Form a State Constitution Preparatory to Its Admission into the Union as a State* (St. Paul, 1858), pp. 87, 325–33, 449, 475.

7 Minnesota, *Constitution of 1857,* art. 10.

8 Minn. (Ter.), Democratic Constitutional Convention, *Debates and Proceedings,* pp. 213–15, 219–21, 228–29; Minnesota, *Constitution of 1857,* art. 10.

9 Saby, *Railroad Legislation in Minnesota,* pp. 33–35; U.S., Department of Agriculture, Division of Statistics, *Changes in the Rates of Charge for Railroad and Other Transportation Services,* by H. T. Newcomb, rev. by Edward G. Ward, Jr. (Washington, D.C., 1901), p. 21; Minnesota, Railroad Commissioner, *Annual Report for 1871* (St. Paul, 1872), pp. 17–18.

10 Riegel, "Trans-Mississippi Railroads during the Fifties," p. 170; Saby, *Railroad Legislation in Minnesota,* pp. 49, 50–52, 57–60.

11 Poor's *Manual* (1875–76), pp. xxviii–xxix. For a survey of early construction, see Arthur J. Larson, "Building Minnesota's Railroad System," *Minnesota Alumni Weekly* 32 (April 1, 1933): 401–3; Frederick Merk, *Economic History of Wisconsin during the Civil War Decade,* publications of the State Historical Society, Studies 1 (Madison, 1916), pp. 349–59; Leland Hamilton Jenks, *The Migration of British Capital to 1875* (New York, 1927), p. 330.

12 Henrietta M. Larson, *The Wheat Market and the Farmer in Minnesota, 1858–1900,* Faculty of Political Science, Columbia University Studies in History, Economics and Public Law 122, no. 2 (New York, 1926), pp. 46–49; Merk, *Economic History of Wisconsin,* p. 323; *St. Paul Pioneer,* February 8, 1866.

13 *St. Paul Pioneer,* February 1, 8, 17, 1866; *Illinois State Journal,* January 22, 1866; Larson, *Wheat Market and Farmer in Minnesota,* pp. 48, 62–64; Merk, *Economic History of Wisconsin,* pp. 325–27, and plate facing p. 332; Lester B. Shippee, "Steamboating on the Upper Mississippi after the Civil War: A Mississippi Magnate," *Mississippi Valley Historical Review* 6 (March 1920): 470–502. See also Minnesota, Legislature, Senate, *Journal,* 1866, pp. 142, 154–55.

14 The house did consider a bill "to establish a uniform tariff for freight and passengers" (Minnesota, Legislature, House, *Journal,* 1867, pp. 98, 159, 228, 267; Minnesota, Legislature, Senate, *Journal,* 1867, p. 287). See also the *St. Paul Pioneer,* February 28, 1867.

15 Saby, *Railroad Legislation in Minnesota,* pp. 6–64; *St. Paul Pioneer,* January 31, 1871.

16 *St. Paul Pioneer,* February 27, 1867.

17 Minnesota, Railroad Commissioner, *Annual Report for 1873* (St. Paul, 1874), pp. 91–92; *St. Paul Pioneer,* March 2, 1867; Minnesota, Legislature, Senate, *Journal,* 1868, pp. 18, 203, 251–52; Minnesota, Legislature, House, *Journal,* 1869, p. 68; *St. Paul Pioneer,* January 17, 1868; Saby, *Railroad Legislation in Minnesota,* p. 64.

18 Larson, *Wheat Market and Farmer in Minnesota,* pp. 43–45, 57.

19 *St. Paul Pioneer,* January 13, February 20, 1870; Minnesota, *Executive Documents,* 1869 (St. Paul, 1870), p. 6; Minnesota, Legislature, Senate, *Journal,* 1870, pp. 65, 117, 249, 278, 283, 288, 330–33, 341; Minnesota, Legislature, House, *Journal,* 1870, pp. 214–15, 304, 326, 374, 380, 413; Folwell, *History of Minnesota,* 3: 33.

20 Saby, *Railroad Legislation in Minnesota,* pp. 87–89.

21 Larson, *Wheat Market and Farmer in Minnesota,* pp. 22, 32–35, 68, 72–73, 81.

22 Minnesota, Legislature, Special Joint Investigating Committee, *Report to the Legislature of the State of Minnesota. Thirteenth Session* (St. Paul, 1871), pp. 18–23.

23 Ibid., 18–20; *Rochester Federal Union,* June 18, July 2, 1870;

Minnesota, *Executive Documents,* 1877, 2 vols. (St. Paul, 1878), 2: 340–41. Larson accepts the explanation of the railroad companies and seems to feel that the farmers benefited by the discrimination. Larson, *Wheat Market and Farmer in Minnesota,* pp. 87–89, 93.

24 Minn., Railroad Commissioner, *Report for 1871,* pp. 17–18; Minn., Special Joint Investigating Committee, *Report to the Legislature. Thirteenth Session,* p. 21.

25 *Rochester Federal Union,* October 1, 1870; Saby, *Railroad Legislation in Minnesota,* pp. 89–90; *Proceedings of the Great Anti-Monopoly Convention, Held in the City of Rochester, Minnesota, Dec. 1, 1870, to Resist the Unjust Exactions and Aggressions of the Railroads of This State* (Rochester, [1870]), pp. 1–17, 28–29, 47–48, et passim.

26 Saby, *Railroad Legislation in Minnesota,* p. 93.

27 *St. Paul Daily Press,* January 5, 6, 1871; *St. Paul Pioneer,* January 6, 1871.

28 The membership of the convention committees is given in the *St. Paul Pioneer,* January 6, 1871. Sketches of most of the members may be found in Warren Upham and Mrs. Rose B. Dunlap, comps., *Minnesota Biographies, 1655–1912,* Minnesota Historical Society Collections 14 (St. Paul, 1912), pp. 12, 213, 269, 280, 336, 868.

29 Minnesota, *Executive Documents,* 1870, 2 vols. (St. Paul, 1871), 1: 32–55.

30 Minn., Special Joint Investigating Committee, *Report to the Legislature. Thirteenth Session;* Saby, *Railroad Legislation in Minnesota,* pp. 100–102, 104–6; Folwell, *History of Minnesota,* 3: 36; Minnesota, Legislature, Senate, *Journal,* 1871, pp. 67, 114–15, 176, 292–93; Minnesota, Legislature, House, *Journal,* 1871, pp. 310, 340; *St. Paul Pioneer,* February 22, 1871; Minnesota, *General Laws of 1871,* chap. 22; Stickney, *Railway Problem,* p. 90; Theodore Christianson, *Minnesota, the Land of Sky-Tinted Waters: A History of the State and Its People,* 5 vols. (Chicago and New York, 1935), 2: 19.

31 *St. Paul Daily Press,* February 24, 1871.

32 Minn., House, *Journal,* 1871, pp. 28, 82–83, 178, 190, 210–11, 321; Minn., Senate, *Journal,* 1871, pp. 254, 266–67, 269–70; *St. Paul Pioneer,* January 31, February 7, 21, 1871; Minnesota, *General Laws of 1871,* chap. 24; Saby, *Railroad Legislation in Minnesota,* pp. 106–8.

33 Compare the summary and table in Saby, *Railroad Legislation in Minnesota,* p. 106, with Minn., Railroad Commissioner, *Report for 1871,* pp. 17–18. See also the *Rochester Federal Union,* January 28, 1871.

34 Stickney, *Railway Problem,* p. 23. In 1874 Ignatius Donnelly claimed that the act of 1871 was passed for the benefit of Minnesota lumber interests. Lumber dealers were well represented in the antimonopoly conventions of 1870–71. Anti-Monopoly Party of Minnesota, *An Address to Their Constituents. A Review of the Legislation of 1874* (St. Paul, 1874), p. 10.

35 Saby, *Railroad Legislation in Minnesota,* pp. 114–16, 119–20; Minnesota, *Executive Documents,* 1871, 2 vols. (St. Paul, 1872), 1: 17–18; Saby, *Railroad Legislation in Minnesota,* p. 119; Minnesota, Legislature, Senate, *Journal,* 1872, pp. 95, 177, 223, 276; Minnesota, Legislature, House, *Journal,* 1872, pp. 622, 654, 657; *St. Paul Pioneer,* February 21, 1872; Minnesota, Legislature, Senate, *Journal,* 1873, pp. 24, 34, 40, 42, 86–87, 126, 136, 154, 187, 224–26; Minnesota, Legislature, House, *Journal,* 1873, pp. 131, 203, 234, 312, 366, 371, 416, 432, 473, 485, 532, 534.

36 Saby, *Railroad Legislation in Minnesota,* p. 110; Minnesota, Attorney General, *Report of the Attorney General,* in Minnesota, *Executive Documents,* 1873, 2 vols. (St. Paul, 1874), 2: 833.

37 Minn., Attorney General, *Report,* in Minn., *Executive Documents,* 1873, 2: 834; Blake v. Winona & St. P.R.R., 19 Minn. 362, 418–23 (1873).

38 Blake v. Winona & St. P.R.R., 19 Minn. 362, 418 (1873), State v. Winona & St. P.R.R., 19 Minn. 377, 434 (1873).

39 Minn., Railroad Commissioner, *Report for 1871,* p. 28; Lester B. Shippee, "The First Railroad between the Mississippi and Lake Superior," *Mississippi Valley Historical Review* 5 (September 1918): 141; Stickney, *Railway Problem,* pp. 40–43; Saby, *Railroad Legislation in Minnesota,* pp. 129–30.

40 Stickney, *Railway Problem,* pp. 43–44; Larson, *Wheat Market and Farmer in Minnesota,* pp. 77–78, 94; Shippee, "First Railroad between the Mississippi and Lake Superior," p. 142.

41 Solon J. Buck, "Independent Parties in the Western States, 1873–1876, "in *Essays in American History Dedicated to Frederick Jackson Turner* (New York, 1910), p. 150; Saby, *Railroad Legislation in Minnesota,* pp. 121–22, 125–27, 129, 133–34.

42 Minn., Railroad Commisssioner, *Report for 1873,* pp. 75, 101–19.

43 Minn., *Executive Documents,* 1873, pp. 18–19.

44 Folwell, *History of Minnesota,* 3: 50, 81–82.

45 That discrimination was the principal abuse is confirmed by the 1874 report of the new commissioner and by Gov. Davis's message of the following year. See Minnesota, Railroad Commissioner, *Annual Report for 1874* (St. Paul, 1874), p. 5, and Minnesota, *Executive Documents,* 1874, 2 vols. (St. Paul, 1875), 1: 30. See also the *St. Paul Pioneer,* February 7, March 3, 1874, and Hartsough, "Transportation as a Factor in the Development of the Twin Cities," pp. 226–27. The division of opinion in the legislature is discussed by Saby, *Railroad Legislation in Minnesota,* p. 141, and in the *St. Paul Pioneer,* February 19, 1874.

46 *St. Paul Pioneer,* January 20, 1874.

47 Minn., Railroad Commissioner, *Report for 1873,* pp. 120–21; *St. Paul Pioneer,* January 20, 1874; Minnesota, Legislature, Senate, *Journal,* 1874, pp. 553–65.

48 Opinions favorable to the railroads are found in Minnesota, Legislature, House, *Journal,* 1874, p. 185; *St. Paul Pioneer,* February 7, 19, 1874; and D. W. Craig, "Concerning Railroads," *The Busy West* 1 (April 1872): 13–14.

49 Saby, *Railroad Legislation in Minnesota,* p. 58. See also Harold F. Peterson, "Early Minnesota Railroads and the Quest for Settlers," *Minnesota History* 13 (March 1932): 25–44. Folwell, *History of Minnesota,* 3: map facing p. 74 shows important rivers, railroads, and the distribution of population as of 1875.

50 *St. Paul Daily Press,* January 9, 17, 18, February 11, 1874; *St. Paul Pioneer,* February 19, 24, 1874; Minn., House, *Journal,* 1874, pp. 57, 120, 179, 182, 185, 217.

51 John Hicks suspects that Donnelly was out to ruin the railroads. He had once been considered a safe railroad man and had gained the political support of the companies, but subsequently they dropped him, and Donnelly never forgave them. John D. Hicks, "The Political Career of Ignatius Donnelly," *Mississippi Valley Historical Review* 8 (June–September 1921): 83–94. For a more recent interpretation, see Martin Ridge, *Ignatius Donnelly, The Portrait of a Politician* (Chicago, 1962), pp. 124–36.

52 Minn., Senate, *Journal,* 1874, pp. 30, 291, 341–44; *St. Paul Pioneer,* February 25, 1874.

53 Minn., House, *Journal,* 1874, pp. 424, 463, 497–98, 549–50, 563; Minn., Senate, *Journal,* 1874, pp. 431–32, 440, 469, 474, 477–78, 481–82; *St. Paul Pioneer,* March 3, 4, 6, 1874.

54 Anti-Monopoly Party of Minnesota, *An Address to Their Constituents,* p. 1.

55 Minnesota, *General Laws of 1874,* chap. 26; Saby, *Railroad Legislation in Minnesota,* pp. 143–46.

56 Saby, *Railroad Legislation in Minnesota,* pp. 155, 164–72. The 1875 legislature passed a number of special acts in aid of construction, but they usually included reservation clauses (ibid., p. 173).

57 Hartsough, "Transportation as a Factor in the Development of the Twin Cities," pp. 221–25; Larson, *Wheat Market and Farmer in Minnesota,* pp. 17–22, 27.

Chapter 7   WISCONSIN: POLITICS AND THE POTTER LAW

1 Charles F. Adams, Jr., "The Granger Movement," *North American Review* 120 (April 1875): 416.

2 Wisconsin, *Constitution of 1848,* art. 8, sec. 10, art. 11, sec. 1. See also Milo M. Quaife, ed., *The Convention of 1846* (Madison, Wis., 1919) pp. 549–50; Milo M. Quaife, ed., *The Attainment of Statehood* (Madison, Wis., 1928), pp. 39, 416–20, 583–85; and Balthasar H. Meyer, *A History of Early Railroad Legislation in Wisconsin,* State Historical Society of Wisconsin Collections 14 (Madison, 1898), pp. 233–44.

3 Meyer, *History of Railroad Legislation in Wisconsin,* pp. 261–65, 272–74, 284–91. See also Governor Farwell's message, in Wisconsin, *Legislative Journals,* 1853, appendix, p. 6; messages of Governor Barstow, in Wisconsin, *Governor's Message and Accompanying Documents,* 1855, pp. 24–25 (hereafter cited as Wisconsin *Documents*); Wisconsin *Documents,* 1856, p. 16; Governor Bashford's message, in Wisconsin, Legislature, Senate, *Journal,* 1857, appendix, p. 17; and Balthasar H. Meyer, *Early General Railway Legislation in Wisconsin, 1853–1874,* Transactions of the Wisconsin Academy of Sciences, Arts, and Letters 12 (Madison, 1898), pp. 343–45.

4 Meyer, *Early Railway Legislation in Wisconsin,* pp. 353–62; Frederick Merk, *Economic History of Wisconsin during the Civil War Decade,* Publications of the State Historical Society, Studies 1 (Madison, 1916), chap. 9.

5 Poor's *Manual* (1875–76), pp. xxviii–xxix; Wisconsin, Railroad Commissioners, *First Annual Report* (Madison, 1875), p. 87; William F. Raney, *Wisconsin: A Story of Progress* (New York,

1940), p. 181; Merk, *Economic History of Wisconsin,* chap. 11, esp. pp. 240, 275–77.

6 John G. Thompson, *The Rise and Decline of the Wheat Growing Industry in Wisconsin,* University of Wisconsin, Bulletins, Economics and Political Science Series 5, no. 3 (Madison, 1908), p. 146; Wisconsin, Legislature, Senate, *Journal,* 1859, pp. 207, 366; Wisconsin, Legislature, Assembly, *Journal,* 1859, p. 128; Wisconsin, Legislature, Senate, *Journal,* 1861, pp. 38, 96, 235, 246, 304–8, 319, 491, 654, 683; Wisconsin, Legislature, Assembly, *Journal,* 1861, pp. 637, 883, 908; Wisconsin, Legislature, Senate, *Journal,* 1862, p. 108; Wisconsin, Legislature, Assembly, *Journal,* 1862, pp. 251, 390, 489, 519, 661, 846, 1010, 1015, 1168, 1172, 1181, 1185, 1186, 1193, 1220; Wisconsin State Agricultural Society, *Transactions,* 1862 (Madison, 1863), p. 100; *Wisconsin State Journal,* April 4, 1862; Meyer, *Early Railway Legislation in Wisconsin,* pp. 365–74; Wisconsin, Legislature, Assembly, *Journal,* 1863, p. 584; Wisconsin, Legislature, Senate, *Journal,* 1864, pp. 122, 178, 214, 272, 319, 437, 465, 514; Wisconsin, Legislature, Assembly, *Journal,* 1864, index of petitions, pp. 928–29; *Wisconsin State Journal,* March 9, 1864.

7 Wis., Assembly, *Journal,* 1864, pp. 717–24.

8 Ibid., pp. 394, 492, 546, 600, 606, 630, 644, 659, 682, 724–27, 857; *Wisconsin State Journal,* February 19, March 14, 24, April 5, 1864; Merk, *Economic History of Wisconsin,* pp. 336–37.

9 Wisconsin *Documents,* 1865, 1: xxii–xxiii.

10 Wisconsin, Senate Bills, no. 101, 1866, Wisconsin State Law Library, Madison.

11 *Wisconsin State Journal,* March 14, 15, 16, 1866.

12 Wisconsin, Legislature, Senate, *Journal,* 1866, pp. 525, 883–97, 969–72, 984–85, 1011–12.

13 *Wisconsin State Journal,* March 21, April 6, 1866; Wisconsin, Assembly Bills, no. 351, 1866; Wisconsin, Legislature, Assembly, *Journal,* 1866, pp. 478, 504, 594, 682–83, 700–701, 732–33.

14 Wis., Assembly, *Journal,* 1866, pp. 1125–26; Wis., Senate, *Journal,* 1866, pp. 754, 985–86, 1029.

15 Thompson, *Rise and Decline of Wheat Growing in Wisconsin,* pp. 58–59; Merk, *Economic History of Wisconsin,* pp. 324–30, 337, 360–62; Fox and Wisconsin Rivers Improvement Commission, *Water Communication Between the Mississippi and the Lakes. Memorial to the Congress of the United States, and Supplement, on the Improvement of the Navigation of the Wisconsin and Fox*

Rivers Submitted by the Canal Conventions Held at Prairie du Chien, in the State of Wisconsin, Nov. 10, 1868, and at Portage City, Oct. 20, 1869, and the Proceedings of the Conventions (Madison, 1870); Merk, *Economic History of Wisconsin,* pp. 278–87, Poor's *Manual* (1875–76), pp. xxviii–xxix.

16 Wisconsin *Documents,* 1866, p. xi.

17 Wisconsin, Legislature, Assembly, *Journal,* 1867, pp. 63, 264, 427–28, 488–89; Wisconsin, Legislature, Senate, *Journal,* 1867, pp. 642–49, 777–78; Milo M. Quaife, *Wisconsin, Its History and Its People, 1634–1924,* 4 vols. (Chicago, 1924), 1: 584–85.

18 Wisconsin, Assembly Bills, nos. 68(1868), 72 and 312 (1869), 368 and 369 (1872), 264 (1873), State Law Library, Madison; Wisconsin Senate Bills, nos. 248 (1870), 89 and 115 (1873), State Law Library, Madison; Wisconsin, Legislature, Assembly, *Journal,* 1869, pp. 66, 237, 399, 558–60; Wisconsin, Legislature, Senate, *Journal,* 1870, pp. 30, 235, 423, 536; Wisconsin, Legislature, Assembly, *Journal,* 1872, p. 306; Wisconsin, Legislature, Senate, *Journal,* 1873, pp. 39–40, 113, 125, 279, 322, 436, 487, 514, 533; Wisconsin, Legislature, Assembly, *Journal,* 1873, pp. 213, 808, 852; *Wisconsin State Journal,* March 29, April 11, 1867, March 8, 1870; Wisconsin *Documents,* 1873, 1: 28–29.

19 Thompson, *Rise and Decline of Wheat Growing in Wisconsin,* pp. 71–72; Merk, *Economic History of Wisconsin,* p. 307; Herman J. Deutch, "Disintegrating Forces in Wisconsin Politics of the Early Seventies, 11," *Wisconsin Magazine of History* 15 (March 1932): 288; Wisconsin State Agricultural Society, *Transactions,* 1869 (Madison, 1870), p. 143.

20 Frank Nelson Elliott, "The Causes and the Growth of Railroad Regulation in Wisconsin, 1848–1876" (Ph.D. diss., University of Wisconsin, 1956), p. 280; Robert J. Casey and W.A.S. Douglas, *Pioneer Railroad: The Story of the Chicago and North Western System* (New York, 1948), p. 134; Thompson, *Rise and Decline of Wheat Growing in Wisconsin,* p. 117.

21 *Eau Claire Free Press,* June 13, 1867, cited in August Derleth, *The Milwaukee Road* (New York, 1948), p. 102; Wisconsin, Legislature, Senate, *Journal,* 1871, pp. 379, 348, 388; Wisconsin, Legislature, Assembly, *Journal,* 1871, pp. 235, 265, 314.

22 Dale Treleven, "Commissions, Corners and Conveyance: The Origins of Anti-Monopolism in Milwaukee" (M.A. thesis, University of Wisconsin, 1968), chap. 1, esp. p. 22; Derleth, *Milwaukee Road,* pp. 71–72, 87, 111–12; Graham A. Cosmas, "The

Democracy in Search of Issues: The Wisconsin Reform Party, 1873–1877," *Wisconsin Magazine of History* 46 (Winter 1962–63): 95–96; Deutch, "Disintegrating Forces in Wisconsin Politics, II," p. 285.

23 Elliott, "Causes and Growth of Railroad Regulation in Wisconsin," stresses the many causes of friction between the railroads and the general public.

24 Deutch, "Disintegrating Forces in Wisconsin Politics, II," pp. 289–96; *Dictionary of American Biography*, s.v. "Washburn, Cadwallader Colden"; Quaife, *Wisconsin, Its History and Its People*, 1: 586; Wisconsin *Documents*, 1872, pp. 22–23; Cosmas, "Democracy in Search of Issues," pp. 94, 97–98, 101.

25 Cosmas, "Democracy in Search of Issues," pp. 93–99.

26 Ibid., p. 99; William L. Burton, "Wisconsin's First Railroad Commission: A Case Study in Apostasy," *Wisconsin Magazine of History* 45 (Spring 1962): 192; Treleven, "Commissions, Corners and Conveyance," pp. 92, 96–97.

27 Deutch, "Disintegrating Forces in Wisconsin Politics, II," pp. 294–95; Burton, "Wisconsin's First Railroad Commission," p. 192.

28 Herman J. Deutch, "Disintegrating Forces in Wisconsin Politics in the Early Seventies, III," *Wisconsin Magazine of History* 15 (June 1932): 392–93.

29 Wisconsin *Documents*, 1874, 1: 18–23.

30 Wisconsin, Legislature, Senate, *Journal*, 1874, pp. 165–66.

31 Deutch, "Disintegrating Forces in Wisconsin Politics, II," p. 293; A. B. Stickney, *The Railway Problem, with Many Illustrative Diagrams* (St. Paul, 1891), pp. 41–44.

32 Treleven, "Commissions, Corners and Conveyance," chap. 1.

33 Ibid., pp. 7–11, 35–40, 72–77, 81.

34 Ibid., p. 70.

35 Ibid., pp. 9–10, 54–56.

36 Ibid., pp. 112–13; Wisconsin, Assembly Bills, no. 466, 1874, State Law Library, Madison.

37 Treleven, "Commissions, Corners and Conveyance," pp. 97–113; Wisconsin, Assembly Bills, no. 333, 1874; *Wisconsin State Journal*, March 3, 1874; *Milwaukee Daily Sentinel*, March 6, 1874.

38 Treleven, "Commissions, Corners and Conveyance," pp. 10–11, 97–114; Wisconsin, Legislature, Assembly, *Journal*, 1874, pp. 559–60.

39 *Wisconsin State Journal*, February 28, March 3, 5, 1874; *Mil-*

waukee Daily Sentinel, March 6, 1874; Robert T. Daland, "Enactment of the Potter Law," *Wisconsin Magazine of History* 33 (September 1949) : 53; Deutch, "Disintegrating Forces in Wisconsin Politics, III," p. 394.

40 Wisconsin, Senate Bills, no. 132, 1874, State Law Library, Madison; Treleven, "Commissions, Corners and Conveyance," pp. 118–19, and appendix.

41 Deutch, "Disintegrating Forces in Wisconsin Politics, III," pp. 393–94.

42 Treleven, "Commissions, Corners and Conveyance," pp. 113–16; Cosmas, "Democracy in Search of Issues," pp. 103–4; Daland, "Enactment of the Potter Law," p. 53.

43 Treleven, "Commissions, Corners and Conveyance," p. 117; Wis., Assembly, *Journal,* 1874, pp. 223, 367, 475, 501, 502, 548, 559, 560, 632–36; Wisconsin, Legislature, Senate, *Journal,* 1874, pp. 197, 376–77, 382, 386, 423, 467, 518, 670, 673, 686; *Nation* 19 (October 8, 1874) : 235; Wisconsin, *Laws of 1874,* pp. 599–606, 758–60; Elliott, "Causes and Growth of Railroad Regulation in Wisconsin," pp. 296–97.

44 Treleven, "Commissions, Corners and Conveyance," pp. 113–14, 120–21, 127–30; Burton, "Wisconsin's First Railroad Commission," p. 194.

45 Derleth, *Milwaukee Road,* p. 79; Stickney, *Railway Problem,* pp. 43–44; Wisconsin State Agricultural Society, *Transactions,* 1872–73 (Madison, 1873), pp. 84–85, 440; Thompson, *Rise and Decline of Wheat Growing in Wisconsin,* pp. 71–72; William L. Burton, "The First Wisconsin Railroad Commission: Reform or Political Expediency?" (M.A. thesis, University of Wisconsin, 1952), chap. 3. There were only three members of the Grange in the Wisconsin legislature of 1874. Two were Republicans; one was a Democrat. All voted consistently for antimonopoly measures. Treleven, "Commissions, Corners and Conveyance," pp. 94, 159 n. 20.

46 Letter of Edward F. Adams to the *Nation* 19 (October 8, 1874) : 235.

47 Deutch, "Disintegrating Forces in Wisconsin Politics, III," pp. 396–406; Treleven, "Commissions, Corners and Conveyance," pp. 132–34; Elliott, "Causes and Growth of Railroad Regulation in Wisconsin," pp. 306–9, 310–15; Attorney General v. Railroad Companies, 35 Wis. 425 (1874); Cosmas, "Democracy in Search of Issues," pp. 105–8.

Chapter 8 THE GRANGERS AND THE GRANGER LAWS

1 The best study of the Granger movement in all its aspects is
Solon J. Buck, *The Granger Movement* (Cambridge, Mass.,
1913). For the origins and purposes of the Patrons of Husbandry,
see Buck, *Granger Movement*, chap. 2, and Oliver H.
Kelley, *The Origin and Progress of the Order of the Patrons of Husbandry in the United States; A History from 1866 to 1873* (Philadelphia, 1875).

2 Buck, *Granger Movement*, pp. 72–73, and chap. 3; Rasmus Saby,
Railroad Legislation in Minnesota, 1849 to 1875 (St. Paul, 1912),
pp. 123–27; Charles W. Pierson, "The Rise of the Granger
Movement," *Popular Science Monthly* 32 (December 1887):
204–6; Charles W. Pierson, "The Outcome of the Granger
Movement," *Popular Science Monthly* 32 (January 1888): 372;
"Proceedings of the Farmers' Convention Held at Bloomington,
Ill., January 15th and 16th, 1873," in Illinois, Department of
Agriculture, *Transactions*, 1873 (Springfield, 1874), p. 289.

3 U.S., Congress, Senate, *Report of the Select Committee on Transportation Routes to the Seaboard*, 2 vols., 43d Cong., 1st sess.,
1874, S. Rept. no. 307, 2: 656–59, 665–66 (hereafter cited as the
Windom Report); "Proceedings of the Farmers' Convention Held
at Bloomington," pp. 224–25, 232, 266; Iowa State Agricultural
Society, *Annual Report of the Secretary*, 1872 (Des Moines,
1873), pp. 10–11; Wisconsin State Agricultural Society, *Transactions*, 1862 (Madison, 1863), p. 100; Wisconsin State Agricultural Society, *Transactions*, 1872–73 (Madison, 1873), pp. 76,
84–85, 440; Wisconsin State Agricultural Society, *Transactions*,
1873–74 (Madison, 1874), pp. 173–76, 183–85, 198; National
Grange, *Proceedings of the Seventh Session* (New York, 1874),
p. 13; *St. Paul Pioneer*, October 10, 1873; Ignatius Donnelly,
Facts for the Granges (St. Paul, 1873), pp. 1–11; Kelley, *Origins
and Progress of the Patrons of Husbandry*, p. 265; [James Dabney McCabe], *History of the Grange Movement; or, The
Farmer's War Against Monopolies* (Chicago, 1874), pp. 379–
82, 513; Stephe R. Smith, *Grains for the Grangers, Discussing
All Points Bearing upon the Farmers' Movement for the Emancipation of White Slaves from the Slave-Power of Monopoly*
(Chicago, 1873), pp. 121–27; Charles F. Adams, Jr., "The
Granger Movement," *North American Review* 70 (April 1875):
401–2, 406–12; William Bross, "The Transportation Question,"

Lakeside Monthly 9 (May 1873): 387–89; Buck, *Granger Movement,* chap. 7; Lewis H. Haney, *A Congressional History of Railways in the United States,* 2 vols. (Madison, Wis., 1910), 2: 257; Henrietta M. Larson, *The Wheat Market and the Farmer in Minnesota, 1858–1900,* Faculty of Political Science, Columbia University Studies in History, Economics and Public Law 122, no. 2 (New York, 1926), pp. 98–102; Mildred Throne, "The Grange in Iowa, 1868–1875," *Iowa Journal of History* 47 (October 1949): 295–96, 312–13; Benton W. Wilcox, "A Historical Definition of Northwestern Radicalism," *Mississippi Valley Historical Review* 26 (December 1939): 394; Jonathan B. Turner, "Railroad Corporations; or, The Natural Versus the Artificial Man," in Illinois, Department of Agriculture, *Transactions,* 1873 (Springfield, 1874), pp. 137–58.

4 Adams, "Granger Movement," p. 398; Donnelly, *Facts for the Granges,* pp. 11–15; National Grange, *Proceedings of the Seventh Session,* pp. 78–79; "Proceedings of the Farmers' Convention Held at Bloomington," pp. 294–95; Jonathan Periam, *The Groundswell: A History of the Origin, Aims, and Progress of the Farmers' Movement . . .* (St. Louis, 1874), pp. 358–60, 453–54; *Windom Report,* 2: 647–48, 652–53, 682; W. A. Anderson, "The Granger Movement in the Middle West with Special Reference to Iowa," *Iowa Journal of History and Politics* 22 (January 1924): 24–25. On the large number of business and professional men who joined the granges, see D. Wyatt Aiken, *The Grange: Its Origins, Progress and Educational Purposes* (Washington, D.C., 1883), pp. 19–20; Theodore Christianson, *Minnesota, the Land of the Sky-Tinted Waters: A History of the State and Its People,* 5 vols. (Chicago and New York, 1935), 2: 14.

5 William D. Barns, "Oliver Hudson Kelley and the Genesis of the Grange: A Reappraisal," *Agricultural History* 41 (July 1967): 239–40.

6 Ibid., pp. 229–42; Horace Samuel Merrill, *Bourbon Democracy in the Middle West, 1865–1896* (Baton Rouge, La., 1953), pp. 94–96; Frank Klement, "Midwestern Copperheadism and the Genesis of the Granger Movement," *Mississippi Valley Historical Review* 38 (March 1952): 679–94.

7 Solon J. Buck, "Independent Parties in the Western States, 1873–1876," in *Essays in American History Dedicated to Frederick Jackson Turner* (New York, 1910), pp. 137–38; Frederick Emory Haynes, *Third Party Movements since the Civil War with Spe-*

cial Reference to Iowa (Iowa City, 1916), pp. 67–68; Mildred Throne, "The Anti-Monopoly Party in Iowa, 1873–1874," *Iowa Journal of History* 52 (October 1954): 289–326; Herman J. Deutch, "Disintegrating Forces in Wisconsin Politics of the Early Seventies," *Wisconsin Magazine of History* 15 (December 1931; March, June 1932): 168–81, 282–96, 391–411; Graham Cosmas, "The Democracy in Search of Issues: The Wisconsin Reform Party, 1873–1877," *Wisconsin Magazine of History* 46 (Winter 1962–63): 93–108; Martin Ridge, *Ignatius Donnelly: The Portrait of a Politician* (Chicago, 1962), pp. 153–56, 160–63.

8 *Nation* 16 (April 10, 1873): 249, 397–98; 19 (July 16, 1874): 37; 19 (August 20, 1874): 122. Charles F. Adams, Jr., "Granger Movement," pp. 394–424; W. M. Grosvenor, "The Communist and the Railway," *International Review* 4 (September 1877): 585–99.

9 Ignatius Donnelly led many of the Minnesota Grangers into the Anti-Monopoly party, but the party, with the exception of Donnelly, supported commission control (Ridge, *Ignatius Donnelly*, pp. 153, 160–61).

10 Throne, "Anti-Monopoly Party in Iowa," pp. 311–12; William L. Burton, "Wisconsin's First Railroad Commission: A Case Study in Apostasy," *Wisconsin Magazine of History* 45 (Spring 1962): 192–93; Saby, *Railroad Legislation in Minnesota*, pp. 133–34; Buck, "Independent Parties in the Western States," p. 151.

11 Isaiah L. Sharfman, *The Interstate Commerce Commission: A Study in Administrative Law and Procedure*, 4 vols. in 5 (New York, 1931–37), 1: 16; John E. Benton, "The State Commissions and the Interstate Commerce Commission," in Interstate Commerce Commission, *Exercises Commemorating the Fifty Years' Service of the Interstate Commerce Commission* (Washington, D.C., 1937), p. 33.

Chapter 9 PUBLIC POLICY AND PRIVATE RIGHTS

1 Ruggles v. Illinois, 108 U.S. 526 (1883); Illinois Cent. R.R. v. Illinois, 108 U.S. 541 (1883). The most complete account of this litigation is in Charles Fairman, "The So-called Granger Cases, Lord Hale and Justice Bradley," *Stanford Law Review* 5 (1953): 587–679. There is little more to be said on the subject, but see C. Peter Magrath, *Morrison R. Waite: The Triumph of Character* (New York, 1963), pp. 173–203.

2 94 U.S. 113–87 (1877).
3 The Illinois law of 1873 was under review in three cases, but none of them involved questions of constitutionality. Chicago & A.R.R. v. Wiswall, 90 U.S. (23 Wall.) 507 (1875); Chicago B. & Q.R.R. v. The People, 77 Ill. 443 (1875); Illinois Cent. R.R. v. Illinois, 95 Ill. 313 (1880) and 108 U.S. 541 (1883).
4 Chicago & A.R.R. v. People *ex rel.* Koerner, 67 Ill. 11 (1873); State v. Winona & St. P.R.R., 19 Minn. 377 (1873); Blake v. Winona & St. P.R.R., 19 Minn. 362 (1873); Munn v. The People, 69 Ill. 80 (1874).
5 Peik v. Chicago & N.W. Ry., 94 U.S. 164 (1877) (the correct spelling is Piek, but due to a court reporter's error, it is known as Peik); Lawrence v. Chicago & N.W. Ry., 94 U.S. 164 (1877); Winona & St. P.R.R. v. Blake, 94 U.S. 180 (1877); Chicago, M. & St. P. Ry. v. Ackley, 94 U.S. 179 (1877); Munn v. Illinois, 94 U.S. 113 (1877); Stone v. Wisconsin, 94 U.S. 181 (1877); Chicago, B. & Q.R.R. v. Iowa, 94 U.S. 155 (1877). The eighth Granger case was Southern Minn. R.R. v. Coleman, 94 U.S. 181 (1877). It originated as Coleman v. McElrath, but was not reported. For background, see *In re* McElrath, 16 Fed. Cas. 72 (No. 8780) (D. Minn. 1873).
6 For histories of the companies, see Robert J. Casey and W. A. S. Douglas, *Pioneer Railroad* (New York, 1948); August Derleth, *The Milwaukee Road* (New York, 1948); and Richard C. Overton, *Burlington Route* (New York, 1965). For the railroads' opinion of the Granger laws, see Charles R. Detrick, "The Effects of the Granger Acts," *Journal of Political Economy* 11 (March 1903): 238–39; Harris to W. P. Hepburn, March 20, 1874, Harris Out-Letters, vol. 33; Harris to O. H. Browning, July 24, 1874, Harris Out-Letters, vol. 34; Walker to Hepburn, March 2, 1874; and Walker to John N. Denison, March 20, 1874, J. M. Walker Out-Letters, vol. 4, all in the Burlington Archives, Newberry Library, Chicago, Illinois.
7 For extensive quotations from these opinions, see "The Wisconsin Railroad Acts," *American Law Review* 9 (1874): 50–73.
8 Quoted in Derleth, *Milwaukee Road,* p. 105.
9 Piek v. Chicago & N.W. Ry., 19 Fed. Cas. 625 (No. 11138) (C.C.W.D. Wis. 1874); Lawrence v. Chicago & N.W. Ry., 19 Fed. Cas. 625 (No. 11138) (C.C.W.D. Wis. 1874).
10 Chicago, B. & Q.R.R. v. Attorney General, 5 Fed. Cas. 594 (No. 2666) (C.C.D. Iowa 1875). For additional information on

this subject, see George H. Miller, "Chicago, Burlington and Quincy Railroad Company v. Iowa," *Iowa Journal of History* 54 (October 1956): 289–312.

11 John Crerar to M. K. Jesup, May 11, 1868, Dubuque & Sioux City R.R., New York Office, 1867–87, In-Letters, vol. 1, Illinois Central Archives, Newberry Library, Chicago, Illinois; Walker to Sidney Bartlett, April 18, 1874; Walker to David Rorer, September 9, 1874; Walker to Orville H. Browning, September 9, 1874, Walker Out-Letters, vol. 5, Burlington Archives; Charles F. Adams, Jr., "The Granger Movement," *North American Review* 120 (April 1875): 395, 412; Alfons J. Beitzinger, *Edward G. Ryan: Lion of the Law* (Madison, Wis., 1960), pp. 108–11.

12 Quoted in John W. Cary, *Piek v. Chicago & North Western Railway: Argument* [1875], p. 38.

13 The relevant cases are summarized in Charles F. Adams, Jr., "Legislative Control over Railway Charters," *American Law Review* 1 (April 1867): 451–76. See also Isaac Redfield, commentary on Philadelphia, W. & B.R.R. v. Bowers, 4 Houst. 506 (Del. Ct. Err. & App. 1873), in *American Law Register,* n.s., 13 (1874): 186–90.

14 People v. Hawley, 3 Mich. 330 (1854); People v. Gallagher, 4 Mich. 244 (1856); Lincoln v. Smith, 27 Vt. 328 (1854); State v. Paul, 5 R.I. 185 (1858); State v. Kuran, 5 R.I. 497 (1858); Metropolitan Board of Excise v. Barrie, 34 N.Y. 657 (1866). Beebe v. The State, 6 Ind. 501 (1855), may be an exception, but the issue is not quite parallel.

15 Wynehamer v. The People, 13 N.Y. 378 (1856).

16 The term *private business* was still used in its original sense in the late nineteenth century (Thomas C. Cochran, *Railroad Leaders,* Cambridge, Mass., 1953, p. 189). Louis Hartz, *Economic Policy and Democratic Thought: Pennsylvania, 1776–1860* (Cambridge, Mass., 1948), pp. 20, 69–79, 121, 174–75, 310; Oscar and Mary F. Handlin, *Commonwealth, A Study of the Role of Government in the American Economy: Massachusetts, 1774–1861* (New York, 1947), pp. 231–32; Julius Goebel, in Shaw Livermore, *Early American Land Companies* (New York, 1939), pp. xxv–xxvi; "Rail-Roads and Canals," *New York Review* no. 12 (April 1840): 302; Alexander Davidson and Bernard Stuvé, *Complete History of Illinois from 1673 to 1873* (Springfield, Ill., 1874), p. 438; Balthasar H. Meyer, *A History of Early Railroad Legislation in Wisconsin,* State Historical Society of Wisconsin Collections 14 (Madison, 1898), pp. 242–44.

17 Joseph K. Angell and Samuel Ames, *Treatise on the Law of Private Corporations Aggregate,* 1st ed. (Boston, 1832), pp. 7–8.

18 Ibid., 6th ed. (Boston, 1858), p. 29.

19 Opinion of the Justices, 58 Me. 590, 593 (1870).

20 Ibid., p. 610.

21 Allen v. Inhabitants of Jay, 60 Me. 124, 136 (1872).

22 Clark v. City of Des Moines, 19 Iowa 199 (1865); Chamberlain v. City of Burlington, 19 Iowa 395 (1865); Lowell v. Boston, 111 Mass. 454 (1873); Loan Association v. Topeka, 87 U.S. (20 Wall.) 655 (1875). Compare these with the attitude of the court in Thomas v. Leland, 24 Wend. 65 (N.Y. Sup. Ct. 1840). Clyde E. Jacobs discusses the development of the public purpose doctrine in *Law Writers and the Courts: The Influence of Thomas M. Cooley, Christopher G. Tiedeman, and John F. Dillon Upon American Constitutional Law* (Berkeley and Los Angeles, 1954), pp. 187–246.

23 Sharpless v. Mayor of Philadelphia, 21 Pa. 147, 170 (1853). For a summary of a number of similar cases, see Rogers v. Burlington, 70 U.S. (3 Wall.) 654 (1865).

24 Hansen v. Vernon, 27 Iowa 28, 53 (1869).

25 The People v. Salem, 20 Mich. 452, 486 (1870).

26 Whiting v. Sheboygan & Fond du Lac R.R., 25 Wis. 167 (1870).

27 Olcott v. The Supervisors, 83 U.S. (16 Wall.) 678 (1873). On the Supreme Court's handling of this problem, see Charles Fairman, *Mr. Justice Miller and the Supreme Court, 1862–1890* (Cambridge, Mass., 1939), pp. 207–36.

28 Piek v. Chicago & N.W. Ry., 19 Fed. Cas. 625 (No. 11138) (C.C.W.D. Wis. 1874); Chicago, B. & Q.R.R. v. Attorney General, 5 Fed. Cas. 594 (No. 2666) (C.C.D. Iowa, 1875); Walker to Charles E. Perkins, May 22, 1875, Walker Out-Letters, Burlington Archives; Frank Nelson Elliott, "The Causes and the Growth of Railroad Regulation in Wisconsin" (Ph.D. diss., University of Wisconsin, 1956), p. 305.

29 Attorney General v. Railroad Companies, 35 Wis. 425 (1874). For a full discussion of Ryan's opinion, see Robert S. Hunt, *Law and Locomotives: The Impact of the Railroad on Wisconsin Law in the Nineteenth Century* (Madison, Wis., 1958), pp. 98–131. The Illinois case was Munn v. The People, 69 Ill. 80 (1874).

30 The case from the Minnesota courts was Winona & St. P.R.R. v. Blake, 94 U.S. 180 (1877); those from Wisconsin were Chicago, M. & St. P. Ry. v. Ackley, 94 U.S. 179 (1877), and Stone

v. Wisconsin, 94 U.S. 181 (1877); that from Illinois was Munn v. Illinois, 94 U.S. 113 (1877). The cases on appeal from federal courts were Piek v. Chicago & N.W. Ry., 94 U.S. 164 (1877); Lawrence v. Chicago & N.W. Ry., 94 U.S. 164 (1877); Chicago, B. & Q.R.R. v. Iowa, 94 U.S. 155 (1877); and Southern Minn. R.R. v. Coleman, 94 U.S. 180 (1877).

31 Fairman, "The So-called Granger Cases," pp. 631–32; David A. Wells, "How Will the United States Supreme Court Decide the Granger Railroad Cases?" *Nation* 19 (October 29, 1874): 282–84.

32 Charters and statutes allowing railroad companies a specified return on their investment before rate restrictions went into effect would be a case in point. See above p. 30.

33 Munn v. Illinois, 94 U.S. 113, 134 (1877).

34 Charles Grove Haines, "Judicial Review of Legislation in the United States and the Doctrine of Vested Rights and of Implied Limitations on Legislatures," *Texas Law Review* 3 (December 1924): 1–2.

35 Howard J. Graham, "Procedure to Substance—Extra Judicial Rise of Due Process, 1830–1860," *California Law Review* 40 (Fall 1952–53): 480–500; Henry Carter Adams, *Public Debts: An Essay on the Science of Finance* (New York, 1887), pp. 376–77, et passim; Haines, "Judicial Review of Legislation," 2 (April, June 1924): 286–88, 398, 404–5.

36 Thomas M. Cooley, *A Treatise on the Constitutional Limitations Which Rest upon the Legislative Power of the States of the American Union* (Boston, 1868); Benjamin R. Twiss, *Lawyers and the Constitution* (Princeton, 1942), p. 34.

37 Charles Warren, *The Supreme Court in United States History,* 3 vols. (Boston, 1922), 3: 288–89; Jacobus ten Broek, *The Antislavery Origins of the Fourteenth Amendment* (Berkeley and Los Angeles, 1951), pp. 25–26, et passim; Twiss, *Lawyers and the Constitution,* passim.

38 Slaughterhouse Cases, 83 U.S. (16 Wall.) 36 (1873).

39 Bartemeyer v. Iowa, 85 U.S. (18 Wall.) 129 (1873). Railroad company lawyers noted the importance of the decision at the time (Howard J. Graham, "Justice Field and the Fourteenth Amendment," *Yale Law Journal* 52 [September 1943]: 862 n. 51).

40 Wells, "How Will the United States Supreme Court Decide the Granger Railroad Cases?" pp. 282–84; "The Wisconsin Railroad Acts," *American Law Review* 9 (October 1874): 50–53; "The Potter Act at Washington," *American Law Review* 9 (January 1875): 212–35.

41 Fairman discusses the qualifications of various counsel in "The So-called Granger Cases," pp. 634–49.

42 Magrath, *Waite*, p. 178.

43 William P. Clough, *Winona & St. Peter v. Blake: Brief for Defendant in Error* [1875], pp. 70–71. See also James K. Edsall, *Munn v. Illinois: Argument for Defendants in Error* (Springfield, Ill., 1875).

44 F. T. Frelinghuysen, *Chicago, Burlington & Quincy R.R. Co. v. Iowa: Argument* [1875], p. 16.

45 Cary, *Argument,* p. 10.

46 O. H. Browning, *Chicago, Burlington & Quincy R.R. Co. v. Iowa: Argument* (Chicago, 1875), p. 61.

47 John N. Jewett, *Munn v. Illinois: Further Argument* (1875), pp. 19–20. For similar assertions of property rights see W. C. Goudy, *Munn v. Illinois: Brief and Argument* (Chicago, 1874), p. 33; John N. Jewett, *Munn v. Illinois: Argument* (Chicago, 1874), p. 23; Jewett, *Further Argument,* pp. 15–16; C. B. Lawrence, *Piek v. Chicago & North Western Ry. Co.: Argument* (Chicago, 1875), pp. 28–30; B. C. Cook, *Piek v. Chicago & North Western Ry. Co.: Argument* (Chicago, 1875), pp. 14–15, 22–25; Cary, *Argument,* pp. 9–19; and E. W. Stoughton, *Piek v. Chicago & North Western Ry. Co.: Statement and Points for Appellants* (New York, 1875), pp. 15–20, 59–60.

48 Stoughton, *Statement,* pp. 17, 24–25.

49 Browning, *Argument,* p. 52.

50 Cary, *Argument,* p. 83.

51 Lawrence, *Argument,* p. 41.

52 Goudy, *Brief and Argument,* p. 46.

53 Cary, *Argument,* p. 37.

54 Jewett, *Argument,* p. 37.

55 Jewett, *Further Argument,* p. 26.

56 Frelinghuysen, *Argument,* p. 19. See also Lawrence, *Argument,* pp. 30–31; Cook, *Argument,* pp. 14–15; and Stoughton, *Statement,* pp. 15–17.

57 Lawrence, *Argument,* p. 50. See also Stoughton, *Statement,* p. 42, and F. T. Frelinghuysen, *Additional Argument* (Washington, 1876), pp. 3, 50–51.

58 Browning, *Argument,* p. 65. For additional arguments concerning the meaning of due process, see Cook, *Argument,* pp. 33–34; Goudy, *Brief and Argument,* pp. 29–34; Jewett, *Argument,* pp. 11, 31–37; Jewett, *Further Argument,* pp. 18–19; and Lawrence, *Argument,* pp. 19–23.

59 For their argument that rates should bear some relation to costs, counsel relied on Albert Fink, *Cost of Railroad Transportation, Railroad Accounts, and Government Regulation of Railroad Tariffs* (Louisville, Ky., 1875).

60 Edwin W. Sigmund, "The Granger Cases: 1877 or 1876?" *American Historical Review* 58 (April 1953): 571-74; Munn v. Illinois, 94 U.S. 113, 136 (1877); Carl B. Swisher, *Stephen J. Field, Craftsman of the Law* (Washington, 1930), p. 372; Felix Frankfurter, *The Commerce Clause under Marshall, Taney and Waite* (Chapel Hill, 1937), pp. 88-89.

61 Munn v. Illinois, 94 U.S. 113, 125, 134 (1877). See also Peik v. Chicago & N.W. Ry., 94 U.S. 164, 178 (1877); Chicago M. & St. P. Ry. v. Ackley, 94 U.S. 179 (1877).

62 Munn v. Illinois, 94 U.S. 113, 135 (1877); Chicago B. & Q.R.R. v. Iowa, 94 U.S. 155, 163 (1877); Peik v. Chicago & N.W. Ry., 94 U.S. 164, 177-78 (1877).

63 Chicago B. & Q.R.R. v. Iowa, 94 U.S. 155, 161-63 (1877); Peik v. Chicago & N.W. Ry., 94 U.S. 164, 176 (1877); Winona & St. P.R.R. v. Blake, 94 U.S. 180 (1877); Stone v. Wisconsin, 94 U.S. 181, 182-83 (1877).

64 Chicago B. & Q.R.R. v. Iowa, 94 U.S. 155, 162-63 (1877).

65 Munn v. Illinois, 94 U.S. 113, 126, 127 (1877).

66 Ibid., p. 132.

67 Chicago, B. & Q.R.R. v. Iowa, 94 U.S. 155, 161 (1877).

68 Matthew Hale, "De Portibus Maris," in Francis Hargrave, ed., *A Collection of Tracts Relative to the Law of England from Manuscripts* (Dublin, 1787), p. 78. Hale's opinion is also cited in Munn v. Illinois, 94 U.S. 113, 127 (1877).

69 Aldnutt v. Inglis, 104 Eng. Rep. 206 (K. B. 1810). Ellenborough's opinion is also cited in Munn v. Illinois, 94 U.S. 113, 127-28 (1877).

70 Fairman, "The So-called Granger Cases," pp. 670-79, et passim.

71 Ibid., p. 670. On Bradley, see also pp. 591-92, 652-61.

72 Munn v. Illinois, 94 U.S. 113, 127-28 (1877).

73 Fairman, "The So-called Granger Cases," pp. 587-90, 652-58; Munn v. Illinois, 94 U.S. 113, 127 (1877). On Hale's business categories, see Breck P. McAllister, "Lord Hale and Business Affected with the Public Interest," *Select Essays on Constitutional Law,* 5 vols. in 4 (Chicago, 1938), 2: 467-69, and Edward A. Adler, "Business Jurisprudence," in *Select Essays on Constitutional Law,* 2: 455; Magrath, *Waite,* p. 187. See also Bradley's

discussion of monopolies in the Sinking Fund Cases, 99 U.S. 700; 747 (1878).

74 Munn v. Illinois, 94 U.S. 113, 134 (1877); Magrath, *Waite,* p. 187.

75 Munn v. Illinois, 94 U.S. 113, 133 (1877).

76 For reactions to the decisions in the Granger cases, see Charles Warren, *The Supreme Court in United States History,* 3: 303–12.

77 Fairman, *Mr. Justice Miller,* p. 67.

78 Magrath, *Waite,* pp. 188, 205–9; Frankfurter, *Commerce Clause,* pp. 81–82; Munn v. Illinois, 94 U.S. 113, 138–54 (1877).

79 Munn v. Illinois, 94 U.S. 113, 136 (1877).

80 Ibid., pp. 184–86.

81 Ibid., p. 184.

82 Chicago, M. & St. P. Ry. v. Minnesota, 134 U.S. 418 (1890).

83 Smyth v. Ames, 169 U.S. 466 (1898). Later modifications of the Court's ruling are discussed by Fairman, "The So-called Granger Cases," pp. 657–70; John R. Commons, *Legal Foundations of Capitalism* (New York, 1924); Twiss, *Lawyers and the Constitution;* and Arnold M. Paul, *Conservative Crisis and the Rule of Law* (Ithaca, N.Y., 1960).

Chapter 10 SUMMARY

1 Charles E. Perkins of the Burlington admitted in 1875 that there was no doubt about the power of the state to regulate the rates of railroads if their charters did not protect them. "This power we have never heard denied" (Perkins Memorandum, [December 1875], Letterbook 2, p. 389, Perkins Papers, London, Canada).

2 Arthur M. Johnson and Barry E. Supple, *Boston Capitalists and Western Railroads* (Cambridge, Mass., 1967), p. 188; Albert Fishlow, *American Railroads and the Transformation of the Antebellum Economy* (Cambridge, Mass., 1965), pp. 189–96; Carter Goodrich, *Government Promotion of American Canals and Railroads, 1800–1890* (New York, 1960), chap. 7.

TABLE OF CASES

BIBLIOGRAPHICAL ESSAY

The principal sources for a study of law and legislation in the United States are the published documents of the state and federal governments.

UNITED STATES GOVERNMENT DOCUMENTS

For testimony essential to an understanding of the rail road problem, see U.S., Congress, Senate, *Report of the Select Committee on Transportation Routes to the Seaboard,* 2 vols., 43d Cong., 1st sess., 1874, S. Rept. no. 307 (the so-called *Windom Report*) and U.S., Congress, Senate, *Report of the Select Committee on Interstate Commerce,* 2 vols., 49th Cong., 1st sess., 1886, S. Rept. no. 46 (the so-called *Cullom Report*). Other important congressional documents include U.S., Congress, House, *Report of the Northwestern Ship-Canal Convention,* 38th Cong., 2d sess., 1865, H. Misc. Doc. no. 23 and U.S., Congress, House, *Public Aids to Domestic Transportation,* 79th Cong., 1st sess., 1945, H. Doc. no. 159.

For historical information on the period covered in this study, see U.S., Interstate Commerce Commission, *First Annual Report* (Washington, D.C., 1887); U.S., Interstate Commerce Commission, *Railways in the United States in 1902: Part II. A Forty-Year Review of Changes in Freight Tariffs,* by J. M. Smith (Washington, D.C., 1903); U.S., Interstate Commerce Commission, *Exercises Commemo-*

263

rating the Fifty Years' Service of the Interstate Commerce Commission (Washington, D.C., 1937); U.S., Department of Agriculture, *The Grange: Its Origin, Progress and Educational Purposes,* by D. Wyatt Aiken, Special Report no. 55 (Washington, D.C., 1883); U.S., Department of Agriculture, Division of Statistics, *Changes in the Rate of Charge for Railroad and Other Transportation Services,* by H. T. Newcomb, rev. by Edward G. Ward, Jr. (Washington, D.C., 1901); and G. K. Warren, *Report on Bridging the Mississippi River between St. Paul, Minn., and St. Louis, Mo.,* Appendix X3, in Chief of Engineers, *Annual Report for 1878* (Washington, D.C., 1878). For testimony on the western railroad problem, see U.S., Treasury Department, Bureau of Statistics, *First Annual Report on the Internal Commerce of the United States . . . for the Year 1876,* by Joseph Nimmo, Jr. (Washington, D.C., 1887).

The United States Supreme Court *Reports* were used extensively (see the Table of Cases), but for a full understanding of the issues involved in the Granger cases the Court's records and briefs were indispensable. These are compendiums of privately published briefs and arguments, official records from the state and lower federal courts, and miscellaneous exhibits used in connection with each suit. The particular collection used for this study is in the Michigan State Law Library, Lansing, Michigan. Lower federal court opinions are published in National Reporter System, *The Federal Cases Comprising Cases Argued and Determined in the Circuit and District Courts of the United States, 1789–1880* (St. Paul, 1894–97).

STATE GOVERNMENT DOCUMENTS

The published records of state constitutional conventions vary as to completeness but are most helpful in establishing popular attitudes on constitutional issues. The later ones include full transcripts of debates. The relevant volumes for Illinois are Arthur Charles Cole, ed., *The Constitutional Debates of 1847,* Collections of the Illinois State Historical Library 15 (Springfield, 1919); Illinois, Constitutional Convention, *Journal of the Constitutional Convention of the State of Illinois, Convened at Springfield, January 7, 1862* (Springfield, 1862); Illinois, Constitutional Convention, *Journal of the Constitutional Convention of the State of Illinois, Convened at Springfield, December 13, 1869* (Springfield, 1870); and Illinois, Constitutional Convention, *Debates and Proceedings of the Constitutional Convention of the State of Illinois Convened at the City of Spring-*

field, Tuesday, December 13, 1869, 2 vols. (Springfield, 1870). For Iowa, see Iowa, Constitutional Convention, *Debates of the Constitutional Convention; of the State of Iowa, Assembled at Iowa City, Monday, January 19, 1857,* 2 vols. (Davenport, 1857). For Minnesota, see Minnesota (Ter.), Democratic Constitutional Convention, *Debates and Proceedings of the Minnesota Constitutional Convention Including the Organic Act of the Territory* . . . (St. Paul, 1857) and Minnesota (Ter.), Republican Constitutional Convention, *Debates and Proceedings of the Constitutional Convention for the Territory of Minnesota, to Form a State Constitution Preparatory to Its Admission into the Union as a State* (St. Paul, 1858). For Wisconsin, see Milo M. Quaife, ed., *The Convention of 1846* (Madison, 1919) and *The Attainment of Statehood* (Madison, 1928).

The basic government documents for each state are as follows:

Illinois (all published at Springfield):

Reports to the General Assembly (1838–75)
Senate *Journal* (1849–73)
House *Journal* (1849–73)
Private Laws (1865–73)
Public Laws (1869–73)
Railroad and Warehouse Commission, *Annual Reports* (1871–73)
State Agricultural Society, *Transactions* (1856–70)
Supreme Court *Reports* (see the Table of Cases)

Iowa (all published at Des Moines unless otherwise indicated):

Messages and Proclamations of the Governors of Iowa, ed. Benjamin F. Shambaugh, 7 vols. (Iowa City, 1903–5)
Legislative Documents (1859–74)
Senate *Journal* (1856–74)
House *Journal* (1856–74)
Public Laws (1868, 1874)
The Code: Containing All the Statutes of the State of Iowa, of a General Nature, Passed at the Adjoined Session of the Fourteenth General Assembly (1873)
Board of Railroad Commissioners, *Annual Reports* (1878, 1884)
State Agricultural Society, *Annual Reports of the Secretary* (1860–74)
Supreme Court *Reports* (see the Table of Cases)

Minnesota (all published at St. Paul):

Executive Documents (1858–74, 1877)
Senate *Journal* (1857–74)
House *Journal* (1857–74)
General Laws (1871, 1874)
Special Joint Railroad Investigating Committee, *Report to the Legislature of the State of Minnesota. Thirteenth Session* (1871)
Railroad Commissioner, *Reports, with Reports of Railroad Corporations* (1871–73)
Railroad Commissioners, *Annual Report* (1874)
Supreme Court *Reports* (see the Table of Cases)

Wisconsin (all published at Madison):

Governor's Messages and Accompanying Documents (1853–75)
Senate *Journal* (1853–74)
Assembly *Journal* (1858–74)
Laws (1874)
Legislative Manual (1862–74)
Railroad Commissioners, *Annual Reports* (1874–75)
State Agricultural Society, *Transactions* (1851–75)
Supreme Court *Reports* (see the Table of Cases)

In dealing with the background of the Granger laws a number of other state government reports were consulted: Massachusetts, Board of Railroad Commissioners, *Annual Reports,* 1869–73 (Boston, 1870–74); Ohio, General Assembly, Senate, *Report of Special Committee on Rail Roads and Telegraphs Made to Senate of Ohio, February 1, 1867* (Columbus, 1867); Ohio, Department of Railroads and Telegraphs, *Annual Report of the Commissioner of Railroads and Telegraphs to the Governor of the State of Ohio, for the Year 1867* (Columbus, 1868); Vermont, Railroad Commissioner, *Annual Reports to the General Assembly,* 1858–69 (Montpelier, 1859–70).

A number of pamphlet reprints from government documents were used in connection with eastern prorata movements: R. G. Hazard, *Remarks before the* [Rhode Island] *Senate, on the Railroad Bill, in Reply to Mr. Ames* (Providence, 1854); N.Y., Legislature, Assembly, Select Committee on the Pro Rata Freight Bill, *Pro Rata Question. Opening Remarks of John Thompson, Esq., on Behalf of the Railroads, against a Pro Rata Law; and the Testimony of J. W.*

Brooks, Esq., before the Select Committee of the Assembly; Also the Testimony of Solomon Drullard, Esq., General Freight Agent New York Central Railroad (Albany, 1860); N.Y., Legislature, Senate, *Report of the Minority of the Select Committee on the Pro Rata Freight Bill, Together with a Remonstrance from the Chamber of Commerce to the Assembly, Feb. 8, 1860* (Albany, 1860); Lucius Robinson, *Speech of Hon. Lucius Robinson of Chemung on the Pro Rata Bill, in Assembly, Feb. 27, 1860* (Albany, 1860); N.Y., Legislature, Senate, *Report of a Minority of the Select Committee, on Petitions and Bills for Imposing Tolls on Certain Railroads* (Albany, 1860); N.Y., Legislature, Assembly, *Report of a Majority of the Select Committee on Petitions for Regulating Freights on Railroads in the State* (Albany, 1860); N.Y., Legislature, Assembly, Pro Rata Select Committee, *Proceedings before the Committee, and Proofs and Arugments Offered against the Pro Rata Measure, Fraught with So Much Injury to the People, to the Commerce and Business of the State, and to the Railroads Themselves* (Albany, 1860); N.Y., Legislature, Senate, Select Committee on the Pro Rata Freight Bill, *Testimony Taken Before the Senate Select Committee to Whom Was Referred the Assembly Bill on Pro Rata, Together with the Argument Made by Counsel in Behalf of the Rail Roads of the State, Against So Ruinous a Measure to the Railroads, and the Great Interests of the State, as the Pro Rata Assembly Bill* (Albany, 1860); and *Opposition to Restrictions upon Trade. Remonstrance of the Business Men of New York* [Albany, 1860].

NEWSPAPERS AND PERIODICALS

State legislative journals report all formal action on bills and may contain petitions and some committee reports, but the texts of the bills, amendments, and committee reports and the transcripts of debates must be found elsewhere. In some cases the original bills have been preserved in state archives, in other cases important committee reports have been published separately, but for much of the basic legislative action the daily newspapers of the state capitals and other major cities are the only source. Since state politics were reported very fully during the period of this study, it is possible to obtain extensive information in the press. Without this supplement, the legislative journals are of limited value. Newspapers are also the principal source of information on antimonopoly meetings and conventions. The following papers were used for their political reporting as well as for their editorial comment: *Chicago Times; Chicago Daily Tribune; Illinois State Journal; Iowa State Daily Register; Iowa City State Press; St. Paul Daily Pioneer; St. Paul Daily Press; Wisconsin State Journal;* and the *Milwaukee Daily Sentinel.* Other newspapers of special interest are: *Belvidere* (Ill.) *Standard; The Prairie Farmer; Rock River* (Ill.) *Democrat; Dubuque Weekly Herald;* and the *Rochester* (Minn.) *Federal Union.*

The railroad problem was a major topic of interest in the national and regional periodicals of the day. Special articles are cited by the author under Other Primary Sources, but the news and editorials of the following periodicals were most useful (dates indicate volumes covered): *Nation* (New York, 1865–75); *Hunt's Merchants' Magazine and Commercial Review* (New York, 1848–50, 1860–70); *Hunt's Merchants' Magazine,* 1850–60; *Commercial and Financial Chronicle* (New York, 1865–76); *American Railroad Journal* (New York, 1831–74); *Railroad Gazette* (New York and Chicago, 1871–74); *American Law Register* (1861–77); and the *American Law Review* (1866–77). Volumes of the *Nation* for 1874–75 contain a number of important letters to the editor concerning the origins of the Potter law.

MANUSCRIPTS

The most important manuscript collections used for this study were Illinois General Assembly Records, Illinois State Archives, Springfield; Wisconsin Assembly Bills and Wisconsin Senate Bills, both in the Wisconsin State Law Library, Madison; Chicago, Burlington, and Quincy Railroad Archives, Newberry Library, Chicago; Illinois Central Railroad Archives, Newberry Library, Chicago; and the Cunningham-Overton Collection of the Charles E. Perkins Papers in the custody of Professor Richard C. Overton, London, Canada. Indispensable guides to the railroad archives are Elisabeth Coleman Jackson and Carolyn Curtis, comps., *Guide to the Burlington Archives in the Newberry Library, 1851–1901* (Chicago, 1949) and Carolyn Curtis Mohr, comp., *Guide to the Illinois Central Archives in the Newberry Library, 1851–1906* (Chicago, 1951).

OTHER PRIMARY SOURCES

The attitudes of various interest groups are indicated in the reports of their organizations and conventions. See particularly,

Chicago, Board of Trade, *Annual Reports* (1858–70); National Board of Trade, *Proceedings of the Annual Meetings* (Boston, 1870–72; Chicago, 1873); Patrons of Husbandry, *Proceedings of the National Grange* (Washington, 1873; New York, 1874; Louisville, 1875); General Railroad Association, *Journal of the Proceedings of the General Railroad Association at Their Meeting Holden in New York, Nov. 23, 1854* (Newark, N.J., 1855); Henry O'Rielly, ed., *Proceedings of the New York State Conventions for "Rescuing the Canals from the Ruin with Which They Are Threatened"* . . . (New York, 1859); National Railway Convention, *Proceedings of the National Railway Convention, at the Musical Fund Hall, Philadelphia, Pa., July 4th & 5th, 1866* (Philadelphia, 1866); National Ship-Canal Convention, *Proceedings of the National Ship-Canal Convention, Held at the City of Chicago, June 2 and 3, 1863* (Chicago, 1863); Chicago, Committee on Statistics, *The Necessity of a Ship-Canal Between the East and the West. Report of the Committee on Statistics* . . . (Chicago, 1863); National Canal Convention, *Memorial to the President and Congress of the United States by the National Canal Convention Assembled at Chicago, June 2, 1863* (Chicago, 1863); Chicago, Board of Trade, *The Necessity of a Ship-Canal Between the East and the West. Report of the Proceedings of the Board of Trade, the Mercantile Association, and the Businessmen of Chicago* (Chicago, 1863); Joint Committee of the [Chicago] Board of Trade and Mercantile Association, *Produce and Transportation. The Railway and Warehouse Monopolies. The Railway Companies Advised to Reduce Their Rates, and a Belief Expressed That They Will. A Review of the Warehouse and Grain Inspection Trouble* (Chicago, 1866); Mississippi River Improvement Convention, *Proceedings of the Mississippi River Improvement Convention, Held at Dubuque, Iowa, February 14 and 15, 1866* (Dubuque, 1866); Mississippi River Improvement Convention, *Proceedings of the River Improvement Convention Held in St. Louis, February 12 & 13, 1867* (St. Louis, 1867); Fox and Wisconsin Rivers Improvement Commission, *Water Communication between the Mississippi and the Lakes. Memorial to the Congress of the United States, and Supplement, on the Improvement of the Navigation of the Wisconsin and Fox Rivers Submitted by the Canal Conventions Held at Prairie du Chien, in the State of Wisconsin, Nov. 10, 1868, and at Portage City, Oct. 20, 1869, and the Proceedings of the Conventions* (Madison, Wis., 1870); and Anti-Monopoly Convention, *Proceedings of the Great Anti-Monopoly Convention, Held in the City of Rochester, Minnesota,*

Dec. 1, 1870, to Resist the Unjust Exactions and Aggressions of the Railroads of This State (Rochester, [1870]).

Early attempts to deal with the economics of railroad transportation include P. P. F. Degrand, *An Address on the Advantages of Low Fares and Low Rates of Freight* (Boston, 1840); Charles Ellet, *An Essay on the Laws of Trade, in Reference to the Works of Internal Improvement in the United States* (Richmond, Va., 1839); Henry Fairbairn, *A Treatise on the Political Economy of Railroads; in Which the New Mode of Locomotion is Considered in Its Influence upon the Affairs of Nations* (London, 1836); Albert Fink, *An Investigation into the Cost of Transportation on American Railroads with Deductions for Its Cheapening* (Louisville, Ky., 1874); E. B. Grant, *Boston Railways. Their Condition and Prospects* (Boston, 1856); John B. Jervis, *Railroad Property, A Treatise on the Construction and Management of Railways* (New York, 1861); Dionysius Lardner, *Railway Economy; A Treatise on the New Art of Transport, Its Management, Prospects, and Relations, Commercial, Financial, and Social, with an Exposition of the Practical Results of the Railways in Operation in the United Kingdom, on the Continent, and in America* (New York, 1850); and Louis Peck Morehouse, *Concerning the Cost of Transportation on Railroads* (New York, 1874).

Charles Francis Adams, Jr., stands first among contemporary observers who tried to define the proper relationship between railroads and government. Adams, who was chairman of the Massachusetts Board of Railroad Commissioners (1872–79), wrote the following: "Railroad Legislation," *Merchants' Magazine and Commercial Review* 57 (November 1867): 339–55; "The Railroad System," *North American Review* 104 (April 1867): 476–511; "Boston," *North American Review* 106 (January, April 1868): 1–25, 557–91; "Railroad Inflation," *North American Review* 108 (January 1869): 130–64; "A Chapter of Erie," *North American Review* 109 (July 1869): 30–106; "Railway Problems in 1869," *North American Review* 110 (January 1870): 116–50; "The Government and the Railroad Corporations," *North American Review* 112 (January 1871): 31–61; "The Granger Movement," *North American Review* 120 (April 1875): 394–424; "The State and the Railroads," *Atlantic Monthly* 37, 38 (March, June, July 1876): 360–71, 691–99, 72–85; and *Railroads; Their Origin and Problems* (New York, 1878).

Other contemporary works dealing with the railroad problem are Leonard Bacon, "Railways and the State," *New Englander* 30 (October 1871): 713–38; William Bross, "The Transportation Question," *Lakeside Monthly* 9 (May 1873): 387–89; Henry C. Carey, *Principles of Social Science,* 3 vols. (Philadelphia, 1858–60); D. W. C[raig], "Concerning Railroads," *The Busy West* 1 (April 1872): 13–14; "The Great Railway Monopoly," *London Quarterly Review* (American ed.) 125 (October 1868): 149–71; W. M. Grosvenor, "The Communist and the Railway," *International Review* 4 (September 1877): 585–99 and "The Railroads and the Farms," *Atlantic* 32 (November 1873): 591–610; Rowland G. Hazard, "Relation of Railroad Corporations to the Public," *Merchants' Magazine and Commercial Review* 21 (December 1849): 622–27; J. Smith Homans and J. Smith Homans, Jr., *A Cyclopedia of Commerce and Commercial Navigation,* 2d ed. (New York, 1859); George Perkins Marsh, *Man and Nature; or, Physical Geography as Modified by Human Action* (New York, 1864); John Stuart Mill, *Principles of Political Economy,* 5th ed., 2 vols. (London, 1862); James Parton, *Manual for the Instruction of "Rings," Railroad and Political* (New York, 1866); Josiah Quincy, "Our Railroad System," *Merchants' Magazine and Commercial Review* 57 (December 1867): 432–42; "Railroads and Canals," *New York Review* no. 12 (April 1840): 301–22; J. H. Raymond, "The People and the Railroads," *Lakeside Monthly* 7 (February 1872): 141–47; and Francis Wayland, *The Elements of Political Economy* (Boston, 1840).

In a category by itself is Henry Varnum Poor, *Manual of the Railroads of the United States,* 57 vols. (New York, 1868–1924), esp. vols. 1–7, 14. It is the standard reference for statistical and financial information and a source of editorial commentary by a leading authority on railroad finance.

Books, pamphlets, and articles which give the farmer's view of transportation and marketing problems include Anti-Monopoly Party of Minnesota, *An Address of the Anti-Monopoly Party of Minnesota to Their Constituents. A Review of the Legislation of 1874* (St. Paul, 1874); D. C. Cloud, *Monopolies and the People,* 3d ed. (Davenport, Iowa, 1873); Ignatius Donnelly, *Facts for the Granges* (1873); Willard C. Flagg, "The Farmers' Movement in the Western States," *Journal of Social Science: Containing the Transactions of the American Association* no. 6 (July 1874): 100–115; Oliver Hudson Kelley, *Origin and Progress of the Order of the Patrons of Husbandry in the United States; A History from 1866 to 1873* (Philadelphia, 1875); [James Dabney McCabe], *History of the Grange Movement; or, The Farmer's War Against Monopolies* (Chicago, 1874); Jonathan Periam, *The Groundswell: A History of the Origin, Aims, and Progress of the Farmers' Movement* . . . (St. Louis, 1874); Stephe R. Smith, *Grains for the Grangers, Discussing All Points Bearing upon the Farmers' Movement for the Emancipation of White Slaves from the Slave-Power of Monopoly* (Chicago, 1873); and Wisconsin Granger, "The Grange and the Potter Law," *International Review* 3 (September 1876): 665–73.

The legal background of rate regulation is revealed in compilations and treatises published before 1874. Joseph Kinnicut Angell, *A Treatise on the Law of Carriers of Goods and Passengers, by Land and by Water* (Boston, 1849); Joseph Kinnicut Angell and Samuel Ames, *A Treatise on the Law of Private Corporations Aggregate*, 1st ed. (Boston, 1832), 6th ed. (Boston, 1858); Joseph K. Angell and Thomas Durfee, *Treatise on the Law of Highways* (Boston, 1857); Charles Carroll Bonney, *Rules of Law for the Carriage and Delivery of Persons and Property by Railway with the Leading Railway Statutes and Decisions of Illinois, Indiana, Michigan, Ohio, Pennsylvania, New York and the United States. Prepared for Railroad Companies and the Legal Profession* (Chicago, 1864); Thomas M. Cooley, *A Treatise on the Constitutional Limitations Which Rest upon the Legislative Power of the States of the American Union* (Boston, 1868); Frank Gilbert, *Railway Law in Illinois* (Chicago, 1873); Edward L. Pierce, *A Treatise on American Railroad Law* (New York, 1857); Isaac F. Redfield, ed., *Leading American Railway Cases*, 2d ed., 2 vols. (Boston, 1872) and *A Practical Treatise upon the Law of Railways*, 2d ed. (Boston, 1858), 5th ed., 2 vols. (Boston, 1873).

Of a somewhat different character are contemporary articles by eminent lawyers expressing their opinions on the validity of state regulation. See, for example, Charles Francis Adams, Jr., "Legislative Control over Railway Charters," *American Law Review* 1 (April 1867): 451–76; Thomas M. Cooley, "Limits to State Control of Private Business," *Princeton Review* 1 (March 1878): 233–71; James K. Edsall, "The Granger Cases and the Police Power," *American Bar Association Reports* 10 (1887): 288–316; James A. Garfield, "The Future of the Republic, Its Dangers and Its Hopes," *Legal Gazette* 5 (December 19, 1873): 408–9; Isaac Redfield, "Regulation of Interstate Traffic on Railways by Congress," *American Law Register*, n.s., 13 (January 1874): 1–13; and David A. Wells, "How Will the United States Supreme Court Decide the Granger Railroad Cases?" *Nation* 19 (October 29, 1874): 282–84.

The recollections of many of the participants in the struggles over adoption and repeal of the Granger laws appeared in the form of memoirs and histories. William K. Ackerman, *Historical Sketch of the Illinois Central Railroad, Together with a Brief Biographical Record of Its Incorporators and Some of Its Early Officers* (Chicago, 1890); Charles P. Aldrich, "Repeal of the Granger Law of Iowa," *Iowa Journal of History and Politics* 3 (April 1905): 256–70; Shelby Moore Cullom, *Fifty Years of Public Service, Personal Recollections* (Chicago, 1911); Peter A. Dey, "Railroad Legislation in Iowa," *Iowa Historical Record* 9 (October 1893): 540–66; Benjamin F. Gue, *History of Iowa*, 4 vols. (New York, 1903); William Larrabee, *The Railroad Question; A Historical and Practical Treatise on Railroads, and Remedies for Their Abuses* (Chicago, 1893); Gustave Koerner, *Memoirs of Gustave Koerner, 1809–1896*, ed. Thomas J. McCormack, 2 vols. (Cedar Rapids, Iowa, 1909); John M. Palmer, *Personal Recollections of John M. Palmer: The Story of an Earnest Life* (Cincinnati, 1901); Pioneer Law Makers' Association of Iowa, *Proceedings of the Reunions* (Des Moines, 1897–1907); John M. Stahl, *The Real Farmer* (Quincy, Ill., [ca. 1908]); Isaac Stephenson, *Recollections of a Long Life* (Chicago, 1915); and A. B. Stickney, *The Railway Problem, with Many Illustrative Diagrams* (St. Paul, 1891). Orville H. Browning, *The Diary of Orville Hickman Browning*, ed. Theodore C. Pease and J. G. Randall, 2 vols. (Springfield, Ill., 1925–33) is an important source for constitutional and legal developments in both Illinois and Iowa.

SECONDARY SOURCES

For general background, four volumes of the Rinehart Economic History of the United States provide a basic introduction to the subject: George R. Taylor, *The Transportation Revolution, 1815–1860* (New York, 1951); Paul W. Gates, *The Farmer's Age: Agriculture, 1815–1860* (New York, 1860); Fred A. Shannon, *The Farmers' Last Frontier: Agriculture, 1860–1897* (New York, 1945); and Edward C. Kirkland, *Industry Comes of Age: Business, Labor and Public Policy, 1860–1897* (New York, 1961). Two long essays on American economic development contain a great many valuable insights: Louis M. Hacker, *The Triumph of American Capitalism* (New York, 1940) and Thomas C. Cochran and William Miller, *The Age of Enterprise: A Social History of Industrial America* (New York, 1942).

Albert Fishlow, *American Railroads and the Transformation of the Antebellum Economy* (Cambridge, Mass., 1965) provides an excellent introduction on the impact of railroad transportation to 1860. Thomas Weber, *The Northern Railroads in the Civil War, 1861–1865* (New York, 1952) and George R. Taylor and Irene Neu, *The American Railroad Network, 1861–1890* (Cambridge, Mass., 1956) deal with significant changes in the later period. Older studies include John Luther Ringwalt, *Development of Transportation Systems in the United States* (Philadelphia, 1888) and Caroline E. MacGill et al., *History of Transportation in the United States before 1860* (Washington, D.C., 1917).

Thomas C. Cochran, *Railroad Leaders—1845–1890, The Business Mind in Action* (Cambridge, Mass., 1953) is a fine introduction to the role of the entrepreneur. Arthur M. Johnson and Barry E. Supple, *Boston Capitalists and Western Railroads* (Cambridge, Mass., 1967) and Alfred D. Chandler, Jr., *Henry Varnum Poor* (Cambridge, Mass., 1956) deal with important aspects of railroad promotion and finance. Also helpful are Henry Greenleaf Pearson, *An American Railroad Builder: John Murray Forbes* (Boston, 1911) and Leland Hamilton Jenks, *The Migration of British Capital to 1875* (New York, 1927). On railroad economics I have used D. Philip Locklin, *Economics of Transportation*, 3d ed. (Chicago, 1949) along with a number of older texts: Arthur Twining Hadley, *Railroad Transportation, Its History and Its Laws* (New York, 1885); Emory R. Johnson, *American Railway Transportation*, rev. ed. (New York, 1908); F. A. Cleveland and F. W. Powell, *Railway Promotion and Capitalization in the United States* (New York, 1909); and William Z. Ripley, *Railroads: Finance and Organization* (New York, 1915). More specialized studies of rate making include D. Philip Locklin, "The Literature on Railway Rate Theory," *Quarterly Journal of Economics* 47 (February 1933): 167–230; Walter Chadwick Noyes, *American Railroad Rates* (Boston, 1905); William Z. Ripley, *Railroads: Rates and Regulation*, new ed. (New York, 1913); Julius Grodinsky, *The Iowa Pool, A Study in Railroad Competition, 1870–84* (Chicago, 1950); Robert E. Riegel, "The Iowa Pool," *Iowa Journal of History and Politics* 22 (October 1924): 569–82; and Paul W. MacAvoy, *The Economic Effects of Regulation* (Cambridge, Mass., 1965). B. F. Goldstein, *Marketing: A Farmer's Problem* (New York, 1928) provided useful background on that subject.

Pertinent regional economic histories are Emerson D. Fite, *Social and Industrial Conditions in the North During the Civil War* (New

York, 1910) and "The Agricultural Development of the West during the Civil War," *Quarterly Journal of Economics* 20 (February 1906): 259–78; William F. Gephart, *Transportation and Industrial Development in the Middle West* (New York, 1909); Oscar O. Winther, *The Transportation Frontier: Trans-Mississippi West, 1865–1890* (New York, 1964); Robert E. Riegel, *The Story of Western Railroads* (New York, 1926) and "Trans-Mississippi Railroads during the Fifties," *Mississippi Valley Historical Review* 10 (September 1923): 153–72; Allan G. Bogue, *From Prairie to Corn Belt: Farming on the Illinois and Iowa Prairies in the Nineteenth Century* (Chicago, 1963); Lewis E. Atherton, *The Pioneer Merchant in Mid-America* (Columbia, Mo., 1939) and "The Services of the Frontier Merchant," *Mississippi Valley Historical Review* 24 (September 1937): 153–70.

The most complete study of the western grain trade to 1860 is John G. Clark, *The Grain Trade of the Old Northwest* (Urbana, Ill., 1966). The same author has also published "The Antebellum Grain Trade of New Orleans: Changing Patterns in the Relation of New Orleans with the Old Northwest," *Agricultural History* 38 (July 1964): 131–42. For the later period, see L. B. Schmidt, "The Internal Grain Trade of the United States, 1860–1890," *Iowa Journal of History and Politics* 19, 20 (April, July 1921; January 1922): 196–245, 414–55, 70–131. Herbert J. Wunderlich, "The Foreign Grain Trade of the United States, 1835–1860," *Iowa Journal of History and Politics* 33 (January 1935): 27–76, should be supplemented with Morton Rothstein's newer studies: "Antebellum Wheat and Cotton Exports: A Contrast in Marketing Organization and Economic Development," *Agricultural History* 40 (April 1966): 91–100; "America in the International Rivalry for the British Wheat Market, 1860–1914," *Mississippi Valley Historical Review* 47 (December 1960): 401–18; and "International Market for Agricultural Commodities, 1850–1873," in D. T. Gilchrist and W. D. Lewis, eds., *Economic Changes in the Civil War Era* (Greenville, Del., 1965), pp. 62–72.

Louis Hunter, *Steamboats on the Western Rivers* (Cambridge, Mass., 1949) is the most complete study of the river trade, but F. H. Dixon, *A Traffic History of the Mississippi River System* (Washington, D.C., 1909); William J. Petersen, *Steamboating on the Upper Mississippi: The Water Way to Iowa* (Iowa City, 1937); and Lester B. Shippee, "Steamboating on the Upper Mississippi after the Civil War: A Mississippi Magnate," *Mississippi Valley Historical Review*

6 (March 1920): 470–502 deal with the same subject from different points of view.

Thomas D. Odle, "The American Grain Trade of the Great Lakes, 1825–1873," *Inland Seas* 7 (1951): 237–45; 8 (1952): 23–28, 99–104, 177–92, 248–54; 9 (1953): 52–58, 105–9, 162–68, 256–62 provides a scholarly introduction on the trade of the Great Lakes. Special features of this trade are dealt with in George G. Tunell, "The Diversion of the Flour and Grain Traffic from the Great Lakes to the Railroads," *Journal of Political Economy* 5 (June 1897): 340–75, 413–20; Thomas D. Odle, "The Commercial Interests of the Great Lakes and the Campaign Issues of 1860," *Michigan History* 40 (March 1956): 1–23; Mentor L. Williams, "The Chicago River and Harbor Convention, 1847," *Mississippi Valley Historical Review* 35 (March 1949): 607–26; and John Gordon MacNaughton, "Democratic Hostility to the Navigation and Commerce of the Great Lakes as a Neglected Factor in the Rise of the Republican Party" (Ph.D. diss., University of Buffalo, 1961).

Rivalry between the river and the railroads is covered in Merle E. Reed, *New Orleans and the Railroads: The Struggle for Commercial Empire, 1830–1860* (Baton Rouge, 1966); Wyatt Winton Belcher, *The Economic Rivalry between St. Louis and Chicago, 1850–1880* (New York, 1947); G. W. Stephens, *Some Aspects of Early Intersectional Rivalry for the Commerce of the Upper Mississippi Valley*, Washington University Studies, Humanistic Series 10 (April 1923), pp. 277–300; John B. Appleton, *The Declining Significance of the Mississippi as a Commercial Highway in the Middle of the Nineteenth Century*, Geographical Society of Philadelphia Bulletin 28 (October 1930), pp. 267–84; R. B. Way, *The Commerce of the Lower Mississippi in the Period 1830–1860*, Mississippi Valley Historical Association Proceedings 10 (1918–19), pp. 57–68; and Benedict K. Zobrist, "Steamboat Men Versus Railroad Men: The First Bridging of the Mississippi River," *Missouri Historical Review* 59 (January 1965): 159–72.

Studies of economic development in Illinois include William V. Pooley, *The Settlement of Illinois from 1830 to 1850* (Madison, Wis., 1908); Richard Bardolph, "Illinois Agriculture in Transition, 1820–1870," *Journal of the Illinois State Historical Society* 41 (September, December 1948): 244–64, 415–37; Judson Fiske Lee, "Transportation—A Factor in the Development of Northern Illinois Previous to 1860," *Journal of the Illinois State Historical Society* 10 (April 1917): 17–85; Carl Ortwin Sauer, *Geography of the Upper Illinois*

Valley and History of Its Development, Illinois State Geological Survey Bulletin no. 27 (Urbana, Ill., 1916); Harlan H. Barrows, *Geography of the Middle Illinois Valley,* Illinois State Geological Survey Bulletin no. 15 (Urbana, Ill., 1910); John H. Krenkel, *Illinois Internal Improvements, 1818–1848* (Cedar Rapids, Iowa, 1958); James William Putnam, *The Illinois and Michigan Canal* (Chicago, 1918); William K. Ackerman, *Early Illinois Railroads* (Chicago, 1884); C. A. Harper, *The Railroad and the Prairie,* Illinois State Historical Society Transactions for 1923 (Springfield, 1923), pp. 102–10; Charles Athiel Harper, "Some Economic and Social Influences of the Coming of the Railroad in Central Eastern Illinois Prior to 1860" (M. A. thesis, University of Illinois, 1923); H. J. Stratton, "The Northern Cross Railroad," *Journal of the Illinois State Historical Society* 28 (July 1935): 5–52; Earnest E. Calkins, *Genesis of a Railroad,* Illinois State Historical Society Transactions for 1935, no. 42 (Springfield, 1935), pp. 39–72; Guy A. Lee, "History of the Chicago Grain Elevator Industry" (Ph.D. diss., Harvard University, 1938); Guy A. Lee, "The Historical Significance of the Chicago Grain Elevator System," *Agricultural History* 11 (January 1937): 16–32; C. H. Taylor, ed., *History of the Board of Trade of the City of Chicago,* 3 vols. (Chicago, 1917); and Bessie Louise Pierce, *History of Chicago,* 3 vols. (New York, 1937–57).

Economic growth in Iowa is treated in Cardinal Goodwin, "The American Occupation of Iowa, 1833 to 1860," *Iowa Journal of History and Politics* 17 (January 1919): 83–102; William J. Peterson, "Railroads Come to Iowa," *Palimpsest* 41 (April 1960); Iola B. Quigley, "Some Studies in the Development of Railroads in Northeast Iowa," *Annals of Iowa,* 3d ser., 20 (January 1936): 219–31; and George W. Sieber, "Railroads and Lumber Marketing, 1858–78: The Relationship between an Iowa Sawmill Firm and the Chicago and Northwestern Railroad," *Annals of Iowa,* 3d ser., 39 (Summer 1967): 33–46.

The early economic development of Minnesota is covered by Wilson P. Shortridge, *The Transition of a Typical Frontier with Illustrations from the Life of Henry Hastings Sibley* (Menasha, Wis., 1919); E. Van Dyke Robinson, *Early Economic Conditions and the Development of Agriculture in Minnesota* (Minneapolis, 1915); Lester B. Shippee, "Social and Economic Effects of the Civil War with Special Reference to Minnesota," *Minnesota History Bulletin* 2 (May 1918): 389–412; and "The First Railroad between the Mississippi and Lake Superior," *Mississippi Valley Historical Review* 5 (September 1918):

121–42; Daniel J. Elazar, "The Inauguration of Minnesota's Railroad System," *Journal of the West* 5 (April 1966): 225–50; Arthur J. Larson, "Building Minnesota's Railroad System," *Minnesota Alumni Weekly* 32 (April 1933): 401–3; Harold F. Peterson, "Early Minnesota Railroads and the Quest for Settlers," *Minnesota History* 13 (March 1932): 25–44; Mildred L. Hartsough, "Transportation as a Factor in the Development of the Twin Cities," *Minnesota History* 7 (September 1926): 218–33; and especially Henrietta M. Larson, *The Wheat Market and the Farmer in Minnesota, 1858–1900*, Faculty of Political Science, Columbia University Studies in History, Economics and Public Law 122, no. 2 (New York, 1926).

Frederick Merk, *Economic History of Wisconsin during the Civil War Decade*, Publications of the State Historical Society, Studies 1 (Madison, 1916) is a model of careful scholarship. Also useful for economic developments in Wisconsin are Joseph Schafer, *A History of Agriculture in Wisconsin* (Madison, 1922); John G. Thompson, *The Rise and Decline of the Wheat Growing Industry in Wisconsin*, University of Wisconsin Bulletins, Economics and Political Science Series 5, no. 3 (Madison, 1908), pp. 295–544; Orin Grant Libby, *Significance of the Lead and Shot Trade in Early Wisconsin History*, State Historical Society of Wisconsin Collections 13 (Madison, 1895), pp. 293–334; and Robert F. Fries, *Empire in the Pine: The Story of Lumbering in Wisconsin* (Madison, 1951).

Histories of the Granger railroads vary in quality and detail. August Derleth, *The Milwaukee Road: Its First Hundred Years* (New York, 1948); Robert J. Casey and W. A. S. Douglas, *Pioneer Railroad: The Story of the Chicago and North Western System* (New York, 1948); Carlton J. Corliss, *Main Line of Mid-America: The Story of the Illinois Central* (New York, 1950); and William Edward Hayes, *Iron Road to Empire: The History of 100 Years of the Progress and Achievements of the Rock Island Lines* (New York, 1953) are centennial histories written for the general public. H. G. Brownson, *History of the Illinois Central to 1870*, University of Illinois Studies in the Social Sciences 4 (Urbana, Ill., 1915); Paul Wallace Gates, *The Illinois Central Railroad and Its Colonization Work* (Cambridge, Mass., 1934); and Richard C. Overton, *Burlington West: A Colonization History of the Burlington Railroad* (Cambridge, Mass., 1941) are written for specialists in the field. Overton's *Burlington Route; A History of the Burlington Lines* (New York, 1965) is a scholarly centennial history.

The changing relationship between government and the economy during the nineteenth century continues to intrigue and to baffle historians. Four studies sponsored by the Social Science Research Council's Committee on Research in Economic History have added much needed information on the role of state government in the antebellum period: Oscar and Mary F. Handlin, *Commonwealth, A Study of the Role of Government in the American Economy: Massachusetts, 1774–1861* (New York, 1947); Louis Hartz, *Economic Policy and Democratic Thought: Pennsylvania 1776–1860* (Cambridge, Mass., 1948); Milton S. Heath, *Constructive Liberalism: The Role of the State in Economic Development in Georgia to 1860* (Cambridge, Mass., 1954); and James N. Primm, *Economic Policy in the Development of a Western State: Missouri, 1820–1860* (Cambridge, Mass., 1954). The concept of an active state that emerges from these studies, particularly for the period before the panic of 1837, confirms the findings of a number of earlier works: Henry Carter Adams, *Public Debts: An Essay on the Science of Finance* (New York, 1887); Henry W. Farnam, *Chapters in the History of Social Legislation in the United States to 1860* (Washington, D.C., 1938); Shaw Livermore, *Early American Land Companies: Their Influence on Corporate Development* (New York, 1939); G. S. Callender, "The Early Transportation and Banking Enterprises of the States in Relation to the Growth of Corporations," *Quarterly Journal of Economics* 17 (November 1902): 111–62; Edwin Merrick Dodd, Jr., "The First Half Century of Statutory Regulation of Business Corporations in Massachusetts," in *Harvard Legal Essays Written in Honor of and Presented to Joseph Henry Beale and Samuel Williston* (Cambridge, Mass., 1934), pp. 65–132; Edward Chase Kirkland, *Men, Cities and Transportation: A Study in New England History, 1820–1900* (Cambridge, Mass., 1948); Raymond E. Hayes, "Business Regulation in Early Pennsylvania," *Temple University Law Quarterly* 10 (February 1936): 155–78; and Joseph A. Durrenberger, *Turnpikes: A Study of the Toll Road Movement in the Middle Atlantic States and Maryland* (Valdosta, Ga., 1931).

More recent studies of state economic policy are Carter Goodrich, *Government Promotion of American Canals and Railroads, 1800–1890* (New York, 1954) and "The Revulsion against Internal Improvements," *Journal of Economic History* 10 (November 1950): 145–69; and Harry N. Scheiber, "The Rate Making Power of the State in the Canal Era: A Case Study," *Political Science Quarterly* 77 (September 1962): 397–413. The role of municipal government in the antebellum economy is treated in Bayrd Still, "Patterns of

Mid-Nineteenth Century Urbanization in the Middle West," *Mississippi Valley Historical Review* 28 (September 1941) : 187–206 and Frank I. Herriott, "Regulation of Trade and Morals by Iowa Town Councils Prior to 1858," *Annals of Iowa*, 3d ser., 5 (July 1901) : 126–34. Limitations on the liberty of the individual as a result of active state regulation are discussed in John P. Roche, "American Liberty: An Examination of the 'Tradition of Freedom,'" in Milton R. Konvitz and Clinton Rossiter, eds., *Aspects of Liberty* (Ithaca, N.Y., 1958).

Early state policy towards railroads is given special consideration in Balthasar Henry Meyer, *Railway Legislation in the United States* (New York, 1903) and *Railway Charters*, American Economic Association Publications, 3d ser., 1 (New York, 1900), pp. 231–44; Frederick Merk, "Eastern Antecedents of the Grangers," *Agricultural History* 23 (January 1949) : 1–8; John K. Towles, "Early Railroad Monopoly and Discrimination in Rhode Island, 1835–1855," *Yale Review* 18 (November 1909) : 299–319; Stephen Salsbury, *The State, the Investor, and the Railroad: The Boston and Albany, 1825–1867* (Cambridge, Mass., 1967) ; Harry R. Pierce, *Railroads of New York: A Study in Government Aid, 1826–1875* (Cambridge, Mass., 1953) ; Lee Benson, *Merchants, Farmers, and Railroads: Railroad Regulation and New York Politics, 1850–1887* (Cambridge, Mass., 1955) ; Maxwell Ferguson, *State Regulation of Railroads in the South* (New York, 1916) ; and Taylor and Neu's *The American Railroad Network*, previously cited.

The evolution of federal government policy towards railroads is detailed in Lewis H. Haney, *A Congressional History of Railways in the United States*, 2 vols. (Madison, Wis., 1910) ; I. L. Sharfman, *The Interstate Commerce Commission: A Study in Administrative Law and Procedure*, 4 vols. in 5 (New York, 1931–37) ; Gabriel Kolko, *Railroads and Regulation, 1877–1916* (Princeton, N.J., 1965) ; Clyde B. Aitchison, "The Roots of the Act to Regulate Commerce," in Interstate Commerce Commission, *Exercises Commemorating the Fifty Years' Service of the Interstate Commerce Commission* (Washington, D.C., 1937), pp. 37–51; and John E. Benton, "The State Commissions and the Interstate Commerce Commission," in Interstate Commerce Commission, *Exercises Commemorating the Fifty Years' Service of the Interstate Commerce Commission*, pp. 22–36.

The legal background of state railroad policy is covered in Edward A. Adler, "Business Jurisprudence," in *Select Essays on Constitutional Law*, 5 vols. in 4 (Chicago, 1938), 2: 436–59; Franklin D. Jones,

"Historical Development of the Law of Business Competition, I," *Yale Law Journal* 35 (June 1926): 905–38; Joseph Henry Beale, Jr. and Bruce Wyman, *The Law of Railroad Rate Regulation with Special Reference to American Legislation* (Boston, 1907); Bruce Wyman, *Railroad Rate Regulation with Special Reference to the Powers of the Interstate Commerce Commission under the Acts to Regulate Commerce* (New York, 1915) and *The Special Law Governing Public Service Corporations and All Others Engaged in Public Employment,* 2 vols. (New York, 1911); Harrison Standish Smalley, *Railroad Rate Control in Its Legal Aspects,* American Economic Association Publications, 3d ser., 7 (New York, 1905), pp. 327–473; Alton D. Adams, "Reasonable Rates," *Journal of Political Economy* 12 (December 1903): 79–97; Isaac Beverly, *Discrimination by Railroads and Other Public Utilities* (Raleigh, N. C., 1947); Robert E. Cushman, *The Independent Regulatory Commissions* (New York, 1941); Leonard D. White, "Origin of Utility Commissions in Massachusetts," *Journal of Political Economy* 29 (March 1921): 177–97; and Frederick C. Clark, *State Railroad Commissions and How They May Be Made Effective* (Baltimore, 1891). James Willard Hurst's *Law and the Conditions of Freedom in the Nineteenth Century United States* (Madison, Wis., 1956) provides an excellent introduction to nineteenth-century American legal history.

There is still a need for modern, detailed investigations of political history in the Granger states during the post-Civil War period. Only Wisconsin has received adequate treatment. Horace Samuel Merrill, *Bourbon Democracy of the Middle West, 1865–1896* (Baton Rouge, 1953), deals mainly with national issues but provides a useful introduction from the Democratic point of view. One of the best multivolume works on a single state is Clarence Alvord, ed., *The Centennial History of Illinois,* vol. 2, Theodore Calvin Pease, *The Frontier State, 1818–1848* (Chicago, 1922); vol. 3, Arthur C. Cole, *The Era of the Civil War, 1848–1870* (Springfield, 1919); and vol. 4, Ernest L. Bogart and Charles M. Thompson, *The Industrial State, 1870–1893* (Springfield, 1920). Alexander Davidson and Bernard Stuvé, *A Complete History of Illinois from 1673 to 1873* (Springfield, 1874) and John Moses, *Illinois Historical and Statistical,* 2 vols. (Chicago, 1892) are still useful. Edgar Rubey Harlan, *A Narrative History of the People of Iowa,* 5 vols. (Chicago, 1931) should be supplemented with Ivan L. Pollock, *History of Economic Legislation in Iowa* (Iowa City, 1918) and Herbert Fairall, *Manual of Iowa Politics, State and National. Conventions, Platforms, Candidates, and Official Vote of*

All Parties, from 1838 to 1884 (Iowa City, 1884). For the history of Minnesota there are two series: William Watts Folwell, *A History of Minnesota*, 4 vols. (St. Paul, 1921–30) and Theodore Christianson, *Minnesota, the Land of Sky-Tinted Waters: A History of the State and Its People*, 5 vols. (Chicago and New York, 1935). Two older works on Wisconsin, Henry Colin, ed., *Wisconsin in Three Centuries, 1634–1905*, 4 vols. (New York, 1906) and Milo M. Quaife, *Wisconsin, Its History and Its People, 1634–1924*, 4 vols. (Chicago, 1924) are complemented by a good one-volume text, William Francis Raney, *Wisconsin: A Story of Progress* (New York, 1940) and an interpretive essay by Larry Gara, *A Short History of Wisconsin* (Madison, 1962).

Few of the leaders of the early movement for state regulation of railroads achieved national stature, but the following books and articles were helpful for both biographical details and local political history: Juliet G. Sager, "Stephen A. Hurlbut, 1815–1882," *Journal of the Illinois State Historical Society* 28 (July 1935): 53–80; William H. Fleming, "Governor Samuel Merrill," *Annals of Iowa*, 3d ser., 5 (April 1902): 335–51; John D. Hicks, "The Political Career of Ignatius Donnelly," *Mississippi Valley Historical Review* 8 (June–September 1921): 80–132; Martin Ridge, *Ignatius Donnelly: The Portrait of a Politician* (Chicago, 1962); and Gaillard Hunt, *Israel, Elihu and Cadwallader Washburn: A Chapter in American Biography* (New York, 1925). Other biographical information is available in the many dictionaries, biographical encyclopedias, county histories, and publications of the various state historical societies put out during the last quarter of the nineteenth century.

The politics of railroad regulation in the various states has received uneven attention, most often in connection with the farmers' movement. It is the central consideration in Edwin Ruthven Perry, "Regulation of Railroads by the State of Illinois" (Seminary in Political Science thesis, Northwestern University, 1900); Fred Earle Newton, "Railway Legislation in Illinois from 1828 to 1870" (M.A. thesis, University of Illinois, 1901); Joseph Hinckley Gordon, *Illinois Railway Legislation and Commission Control since 1870*, University of Illinois Bulletin, 1, no. 12 (Urbana, 1904); and Harold D. Woodman, "Chicago Businessmen and the Granger Laws," *Agricultural History* 36 (January 1962): 16–24. The Iowa movement is dealt with in Frank H. Dixon, *State Railroad Control with a History of Its Development in Iowa* (New York, 1896); Frederick Emory Haynes, *Third Party Movements since the Civil War with Special*

Reference to Iowa (Iowa City, 1916); Earl S. Beard, "The Background of State Railroad Regulation in Iowa," *Iowa Journal of History* 51 (January 1953): 1–36; Mildred Throne, "The Repeal of the Iowa Granger Law, 1878," *Iowa Journal of History* 51 (April 1953): 97–130 and "The Anti-Monopoly Party in Iowa, 1873–1874," *Iowa Journal of History* 52 (October 1954): 289–326; and Leonard F. Ralston, "Railroads and the Government of Iowa, 1850–1872" (Ph.D. diss., State University of Iowa, 1960). Rasmus S. Saby, *Railroad Legislation in Minnesota, 1849 to 1875* (St. Paul, 1912) is a careful study of the beginnings of regulation in that state.

Railroad legislation in Wisconsin has been studied at great length. Balthasar H. Meyer, *A History of Early Railroad Legislation in Wisconsin,* State Historical Society of Wisconsin Collections 14 (Madison, 1898), pp. 206–300 covers the topic to 1853. The same author continued his study in *Early General Railway Legislation in Wisconsin, 1853–1874,* Transactions of the Wisconsin Academy of Science, Arts and Letters 12 (Madison, 1898), pp. 337–88. Frederick Merk covered the period of the 1860s and early 1870s in his previously cited *Economic History of Wisconsin during the Civil War Decade.* On the basis of new manuscript collections in the State Historical Society of Wisconsin, Herman J. Deutch gave a fresh interpretation to the period in "Disintegrating Forces in Wisconsin Politics of the Early Seventies," *Wisconsin Magazine of History* 15 (December 1931; March, June 1932): 168–81, 282–96, 391–411. These same manuscripts, together with new acquisitions, have been used to advantage by Robert T. Daland, "Enactment of the Potter Law," *Wisconsin Magazine of History* 33 (September 1949): 45–55; Frank Nelson Elliott, "The Causes and Growth of Railroad Regulation in Wisconsin, 1848–1876" (Ph.D. diss., University of Wisconsin, 1956); William L. Burton, "Wisconsin's First Railroad Commission: A Case Study in Apostasy," *Wisconsin Magazine of History* 45 (Spring 1962): 190–98 and "The First Wisconsin Railroad Commission: Reform or Political Expediency?" (M.A. thesis, University of Wisconsin, 1952); Graham Cosmas, "The Democracy in Search of Issues: The Wisconsin Reform Party, 1873–1877," *Wisconsin Magazine of History* 46 (Winter 1962–63): 93–108; and Dale Treleven, "Commissions, Corners and Conveyance: The Origins of Anti-Monopolism in Milwaukee" (M.A. thesis, University of Wisconsin, 1968).

Railroad politics in relation to the farmers' movement is treated in Solon J. Buck, *The Granger Movement* (Cambridge, Mass., 1913); *The Agrarian Crusade* (New Haven, 1921); and "Independent Parties in the Western States, 1873–1876," in *Essays in American History Dedicated to Frederick Jackson Turner* (New York, 1910). Charles W. Pierson covered the subject more briefly in "The Rise of the Granger Movement," *Popular Science Monthly* 32 (December 1887): 199–208 and in "The Outcome of the Granger Movement," *Popular Science Monthly* 32 (January 1888): 368–73. Carl Cleveland Taylor, *The Farmers' Movement, 1620–1920* (New York, 1953) places the Granger movement in a much larger context. Special aspects of the movement are covered in Frank L. Klement, "Midwestern Copperheadism and the Genesis of the Granger Movement," *Mississippi Valley Historical Review* 38 (March 1952): 679–94 and *The Copperheads in the Middle West* (Chicago, 1960). See also A. E. Paine, *The Granger Movement in Illinois* (Urbana, Ill., 1904); Stanley L. Jones, "Agrarian Radicalism in the Illinois Constitutional Convention of 1862," *Journal of the Illinois State Historical Society* 48 (Autumn 1955): 271–82; W. A. Anderson, "The Granger Movement in the Middle West with Special Reference to Iowa," *Iowa Journal of History and Politics* 22 (January 1924): 3–51; Mildred Throne, "The Grange in Iowa, 1868–1875," *Iowa Journal of History* 47 (October 1949): 289–324; Chester McArthur Destler, *American Radicalism, 1865–1901: Essays and Documents* (New London, Conn., 1946); and Benton W. Wilcox, "A Historical Definition of Northwestern Radicalism," *Mississippi Valley Historical Review* 26 (December 1939): 377–94. William D. Barnes reconsiders the motives behind the founding of the Patrons of Husbandry in "Oliver Hudson Kelley and the Genesis of the Grange: A Reappraisal," *Agricultural History* 41 (July 1967): 229–42. The impact of the Granger laws on company revenues is measured by Charles R. Detrick, "The Effects of the Granger Acts," *Journal of Political Economy* 11 (March 1903): 237–56.

The Granger cases are treated in some detail in all standard works on constitutional development. One of the fullest treatments is Charles Warren, *The Supreme Court in United States History*, 3 vols. (Boston, 1922). Special aspects of the cases are dealt with in Felix Frankfurter, *The Commerce Clause under Marshall, Taney and Waite* (Chapel Hill, 1937); Benjamin F. Wright, *The Contract Clause of the Constitution* (Cambridge, Mass., 1938); and Edwin W. Sigmund, "The Granger Cases: 1877 or 1876?" *American Historical Review* 58 (April 1953): 571–74. John R. Commons, *Legal Foundations of Capitalism* (New York, 1924) and Arnold M. Paul,

Conservative Crisis and the Rule of Law (Ithaca, N.Y., 1960) help place the Granger cases in larger perspective. The same is true of Leonard W. Levy's study of state jurisprudence, *The Law of the Commonwealth and Chief Justice Shaw* (Cambridge, Mass., 1957). The background of the Wisconsin Granger cases is dealt with in Robert S. Hunt, *Law and Locomotives: The Impact of the Railroad on Wisconsin Law in the Nineteenth Century* (Madison, Wis., 1958) and Alfons J. Beitzinger, *Edward G. Ryan: Lion of the Law* (Madison, Wis., 1960). The Iowa Granger case is covered in George H. Miller, "Chicago, Burlington and Quincy Railroad Company v. Iowa," *Iowa Journal of History* 54 (October 1956): 289–312.

The relevant biographies include C. Peter Magrath, *Morrison R. Waite: The Triumph of Character* (New York, 1963); Carl B. Swisher, *Stephen J. Field, Craftsman of the Law* (Washington, 1930); Howard J. Graham, "Justice Field and the Fourteenth Amendment," *Yale Law Journal* 52 (September 1943): 851–89; Charles Fairman, *Mr. Justice Miller and the Supreme Court, 1862–1890* (Cambridge, Mass., 1939). See also Charles Fairman, "What Makes a Great Justice? Mr. Justice Bradley and the Supreme Court, 1870–1892," *Boston University Law Review* 30 (January 1950): 49–102 and "The So-called Granger Cases, Lord Hale, and Justice Bradley," *Stanford Law Review* 5 (July 1953): 587–679.

The evolution of newer ideas of due process is covered in Edward S. Corwin, "The Doctrine of Due Process of Law before the Civil War," *Harvard Law Review* 24 (March, April 1911): 366–85, 460–79 and *Liberty against Government* (Baton Rouge, La., 1948); Charles Grove Haines, "Judicial Review of Legislation in the United States and the Doctrines of Vested Rights and of Implied Limitations on Legislatures," *Texas Law Review* 2, 3 (April, June, December 1924): 257–90, 387–421, 1–43; Lowell J. Howe, "The Meaning of 'Due Process of Law' Prior to the Adoption of the Fourteenth Amendment," *California Law Review* 18 (September 1930): 583–610; Benjamin R. Twiss, *Lawyers and the Constitution: How Laissez Faire Came to the Supreme Court* (Princeton, 1942); Jacobus ten Broek, *The Antislavery Origins of the Fourteenth Amendment* (Berkeley and Los Angeles, 1951); Robert G. McCloskey, *American Conservatism in the Age of Enterprise: A Study of William Graham Sumner, Stephen J. Field and Andrew Carnegie* (Cambridge, Mass., 1951); Howard J. Graham, "Procedure to Substance—Extra-Judicial Rise of Due Process, 1830–1860," *California Law Review* 40 (Fall

1952–53): 483–500; and Wallace Mendelson, "A Missing Link in the Evolution of Due Process," *Vanderbilt Law Review* 10 (December 1956): 125–37.

On the development of the public interest doctrine, see Breck P. McAllister, "Lord Hale and Business Affected with the Public Interest," in the previously cited *Select Essays on Constitutional Law,* 2: 467–94; Clyde E. Jacobs, *Law Writers and the Courts: The Influence of Thomas M. Cooley, Christopher G. Tiedeman, and John F. Dillon upon American Constitutional Law* (Berkeley and Los Angeles, 1954); and Alan Jones, "Thomas M. Cooley and 'Laissez-Faire Constitutionalism': A Reconsideration," *Journal of American History* 53 (March 1967): 751–71.

INDEX

287